Economics As a Science
of Human Behaviour

RECENT ECONOMIC THOUGHT SERIES

Editor:

Warren G. Samuels
Michigan State University
East Lansing, Michigan, U.S.A.

Other books in the series:

Feiwel, G.: SAMUELSON AND NEOCLASSICAL ECONOMICS
Wade, L.: POLITICAL ECONOMY: MODERN VIEWS
Zimbalist, A.: COMPARATIVE ECONOMIC SYSTEMS: RECENT VIEWS
Darity, W.: LABOR ECONOMICS: MODERN VIEWS
Jarsulic, M.: MONEY AND MACRO POLICY
Samuelson, L.: MICROECONOMIC THEORY
Bromley, D.: NATURAL RESOURCE ECONOMICS: POLICY PROBLEMS AND
    CONTEMPORARY ANALYSIS
Mirowski, P.: THE RECONSTRUCTION OF ECONOMIC THEORY
Field, A.: THE FUTURE OF ECONOMIC HISTORY
Lowry, S.: PRE-CLASSICAL ECONOMIC THOUGHT
Officer, L.: INTERNATIONAL ECONOMICS
Asimakopulos, A.: THEORIES OF INCOME DISTRIBUTION
Earl, P.: PSYCHOLOGICAL ECONOMICS; DEVELOPMENT, TENSIONS, PROSPECTS
Thweatt, W.: CLASSICAL POLITICAL ECONOMY
Peterson, W.: MARKET POWER AND THE ECONOMY
DeGregori, T.: DEVELOPMENT ECONOMICS
Nowotny, K.: PUBLIC UTILITY REGULATION
Horowitz, I.: DECISION THEORY
Mercuro, N.: LAW AND ECONOMICS
Hennings, K. and Samuels, W.: NEOCLASSICAL ECONOMIC THEORY, 1870 TO 1930
Samuels, W.: ECONOMICS AS DISCOURSE
Lutz, M.: SOCIAL ECONOMICS
Weimer, D.: POLICY ANALYSIS AND ECONOMICS
Bromley, D. and Segerson, K.: THE SOCIAL RESPONSE TO ENVIRONMENTAL RISK
Roberts, B. and Feiner, S.: RADICAL ECONOMICS

Economics As a Science
of Human Behaviour
Towards a New Social Science Paradigm

Bruno S. Frey
University of Zurich

Kluwer Academic Publishers
Boston / Dordrecht / London

Distributors for North America:
Kluwer Academic Publishers
101 Philip Drive
Assinippi Park
Norwell, Massachusetts 02061 USA

Distributors for all other countries:
Kluwer Academic Publishers Group
Distribution Centre
Post Office Box 322
3300 AH Dordrecht, THE NETHERLANDS

Library of Congress Cataloging-in-Publication Data

Frey, Bruno S.
    Economics as a science of human behaviour: towards a new social
science paradigm/Bruno S. Frey.
        p.   cm.—(Recent economic thought series)
    Includes bibliographical references and indexes.
    ISBN 0-7923-9192-6
    1. Economics. 2. Social sciences. I. Title. II. Series.
HB71.F72   1992
330—dc20   91-42195
                                                                CIP

Printed on acid-free paper.

Printed in the United States of America

Contents

vi

Preface

This book champions the view that *economics is a social science,* and that, moreover, it may serve as a *new paradigm for the social sciences.* Economics is taken to be part of those sciences which deal with actual problems of society by providing insights, improving our understanding and suggesting solutions. I am aware that the way problems are addressed here has little in common with economics as it is generally understood today; most economists make strong efforts to imitate the exact sciences. Economics tends to become a branch of applied mathematics; the majority of all publications in professional journals and books are full of axioms, lemmas and proofs, and they are much concerned with purely formal deductions. Often, when the results are translated into verbal language, or when they are applied empirically, disappointingly little of interest remains.

The book wants to show that another type of economics exists which is surprisingly little known. This type of economics has its own particular point of view. It centres on a concept of man, or a model of human behaviour, which differs from those normally used in other social sciences such as sociology, political science, law, or psychology. I do not, however, claim that economics is the only legitimate social science. On the

contrary, economics can provide useful insights only in collaboration with
the other social sciences—an aspect which has been disregarded by
mathematically oriented economics.

What insights can this economic way of thinking provide? This question
will be answered in the book by offering selected applications. The
value of a specific approach cannot be assessed by theoretical argument
only; its usefulness is revealed in conjunction with the analysis of
specific problems.

Part A discusses the economic approach, human behaviour being the
focal point. The relationship to the psychological view of man is extensively treated. Part B applies the economic approach to six different
areas which are outside the scope of topics dealt with in conventional
economics:

natural environment

politics

art

family

conflict

history

The characteristics of the approach used here becomes particularly
clear when it is applied to such areas which are not normally looked at
from the economic point of view. Part C deals with the limits of this
approach and discusses possible further developments. In particular,
ethical and psychological aspects are illuminated.

This book is suitable for both beginners and advanced students of
economics who are looking for an introduction into behaviourally oriented
economics, also known under such terms as "Non-Market Economics,"
"New Political Economy," or "New Institutionalism." The book is also
written for sociologists, political scientists, lawyers and psychologists who
want to know more about what is sometimes called "Economic Imperialism." Finally, the book may serve the general reader who wants to know
what insights modern applied economics may bring him or her. I have
tried to keep the text as easy to understand as possible, and where forced
to use professional terms, I have explained them. In chapter 4, which
deals with the influence of economic conditions on election outcomes, an
econometric (statistical) approach is used. I have attempted to show that

the "economic view of the world" is not speculative and remote from reality, but is amenable to empirical analysis. The basic data and estimation results are shown in an appendix to the chapter, and are carefully explained in verbal terms.

The individual chapters are based on articles which have been published in various languages in European and American academic journals. They have been completely rewritten, supplemented and brought up to the level of present day discussion. The first, second and ninth chapters were especially written for this volume.

The initial articles were the result of many years of joint work with present and former colleagues. I am grateful to Dr. Hannelore Weck-Hannemann, Professor Werner W. Pommerehne, Dr. Barbara Krug, lic.oec. Heinz Buhofer and Dr. Reiner Eichenberger for permission to draw on jointly-written articles. Chapters 2 and 12 have been strongly influenced by joint research with two colleagues and friends from psychology, Professor Wolfgang Stroebe (University of Tubingen) and Professor Klaus Foppa (University of Berne).

Acknowledgments

Several chapters draw on material contained in, or are the thoroughly revised and updated versions of, articles published in various scientific journals, and are partly coauthored. I am grateful for permission to use this material.

Chapter 4 is based on "A Statistical Study of the Effect of the Great Depression on Elections: The Weimar Republic 1930–33" which was jointly written with Hannelore Weck-Hannemann and published in *Political Behaviour* 5 (1983): 403–420.

Chapter 5 partly draws on material jointly written with Werner W. Pommerehne: "Art Investment: An Empirical Enquiry" was published in the *Southern Economic Journal* 56 (1989): 396–409.

Chapter 7 includes parts of the article "Fighting Political Terrorism by Refusing Recognition" which appeared in the *Journal of Public Policy* 7 (1988): 179–188.

Chapter 8 draws on an article written jointly with Heinz Buhofer entitled "Prisoners and Property Rights" and which was published in the *Journal of Law and Economics* 31 (1988): 19–46.

Chapter 11 is based on an article written jointly with Reiner Eichenberger entitled "Should Social Scientists Care About Choice Anomalies?" which appeared in *Rationality and Society* 1 (1989): 101–122.

Chapter 12 uses material contained in an article written jointly with Beat Heggli entitled "An Ipsative Theory of Business Behaviour" and published in the *Journal of Economic Psychology* 10 (1989): 1–20.

Economics As a Science of
Human Behaviour

PART A
HUMAN BEHAVIOUR

Chapter 1 discusses the economic approach and in particular the characteristics and potential of the *underlying model of human behaviour*. Broader formulations of motivations (preferences) as well as of constraints generalize the economic approach. The applications of the economic view of the world to various problem areas are shown to be interrelated and some interdisciplinary aspects are worked out.

Chapter 2 shows that the model of human behaviour used in economics is fully compatible with *psychology*. The two social sciences do not mutually exclude, but complement one another, and a bringing-together of the two can be profitable to both. The contribution of economics—with its clear distinction between preferences and constraints—consists mainly in providing a suitable general framework of analysis.

1

1 ECONOMICS AS A SOCIAL SCIENCE: APPROACH, APPLICATIONS AND INTERDISCIPLINARITY

The Economic View of Human Beings

A New Development

During the last few years a new approach has emerged in the social sciences. Originating in economics it has also found supporters in the neighbouring social sciences and beyond. This new development has only partly been recognized in traditional economics. In other sciences, the new view is either unknown to many scholars, or is fiercely attacked. The critique is often based on misunderstandings or distortions which, to some extent, are the result of insufficient knowledge. One of the main reasons for these shortcomings is the lack of a comprehensive exposition of these new developments.

The new approach is characterized by a close integration between *human behaviour* and *institutions*. Human beings stand in the centre: their behaviour is determined by their wishes (preferences) and the constraints they face. The restrictions are mainly imposed by the institutional conditions. Institutions can be regarded as agreements shaping repeated human interactions.

3

It is useful to distinguish three types of institutions:

Decision Making Systems. Institutions are rules or procedures with which decisions are taken in society. The most important systems for reaching decisions are:

the price system or market;

democracy;

hierarchy or other authoritarian procedures;

bargaining.

Each one of these procedures functions in a specific way and influences human behaviour in a systematic and therefore predictable manner. Somebody acting within the price system, for example, has to cope with specific constraints; the possibilities for action are set by income and relative prices for goods and services. On the other hand, somebody acting in the democratic political sphere has to take regularly occurring elections into account.

Norms, Traditions and other Behavioural Rules. Human behaviour is determined by a multitude of more or less constraining prescriptions which can be interpreted as institutions. Many of these norms are explicitly set by the government and other organizations (e.g., laws or regulations). A large part of behavioural norms are not formally laid down, however, but are nevertheless of crucial importance for human beings. Among them are traditional or religious rules and laws (such as the ten commandments) or the way one is supposed to treat friends and family members.

Organizations. Institutions of this third type are the state, interest groups, firms and bureaucracies, but also purely private clubs, families and informal associations.

The three types of institutions are closely related; they may indeed be seen as an entity. The classification used merely stresses particular aspects. What matters is how institutions influence the possibility space available to each human being. One of the main purposes is to show the influence of different or changing institutions upon human behaviour (the *Comparative Analysis of Institutions*).

As a matter of principle, the analysis considers actually existing institutions rather than ideals. A comparison with a perfectly functioning institution—such as, for instance, an ideal state governed by politicians and public officials solely interested in the population's welfare—corresponds to a "Nirwana" approach. It is rejected because it assumes as given what has to be explained. Institutions are not given to man, they are rather the outcome of human behaviour. One of the purposes of economic analysis is to explain how institutions emerge and survive. At a given point in time, human behaviour is determined by the interaction with existing institutions, but the latter have to be explicable by individual action. For this reason the concept of human behaviour used is central.

Properties of the Economic Model of Human Behaviour

Human action can be analysed with the help of five elements:

Individuals Act. What happens on the social level is explained by the behaviour of persons (methodological individualism). This does not mean at all that human beings are considered isolated; rather, their behaviour can only be understood as the result of interactions with their surroundings, other people and institutions.

This approach differs fundamentally from theories in which collectivities act on their own, as is assumed, for example, in the organic conception of the state. No further distinctions are made below the level of the individual (but see chapter 9). This distinguishes the economic approach from several variants of psychology where split personalities are studied, and also from sociobiology where there is a level of genes below the individual person.

To take the individualistic stand also means that a person's evaluations and normative views are accepted. Statements such as "something is socially desirable" are taken to be meaningless because "society" is no behavioural unit which could proffer an evaluation. What counts is how people in society evaluate the various possibilities open to them.

Incentives Determine Behaviour. People do not act randomly but react systematically and predictably when they consider a possibility for action to be more advantageous or more disadvantageous.

Human beings have resources at their disposal; they seek and find solutions, learn and invent (but they are not fully informed); they form expectations about the future; they compare the advantages and disadvantages of the possibilities of action available to them in an implicit and sometimes explicit way.

The economic model of behaviour is thus quite distinct from the view that man is a perfectly informed being acting like an automaton. Homo oeconomicus is characterized by limited knowledge which is extended if found worthwhile.

Incentives are Produced by Preferences and Constraints which are Strictly Distinguished. Changes in human behaviour are attributed (as far as possible) to observable and measurable changes of the opportunity set determined by the constraints. Behavioural changes are thus not attributed to non-observable and non-measurable preference changes. This procedure enables us to develop theoretical hypotheses and to test them empirically.

A simple example may be given for illustration. Assume that an increasing tendency is observed to buy smaller cars than formerly was the case. This change in behaviour could be explained by arguing that the consumers have shifted their preferences and now put a higher value on small cars (e.g., following "post-industrial norms"). Such an explanation is difficult or even impossible to test empirically. What would be needed is an observation of a preference change *independent* of the behaviour observed. There are a variety of methods available for this purpose (see Pommerehne 1987) but they are often not applicable. If the "change in preferences" cannot be observed independently, an "explanation" only consists in a description using different words: a preference change must have occurred because behaviour has changed. Conversely, had there been no change in behaviour, there would be no preference change. An empirical test of such an "explanation" is meaningless because it *must* always be true. Accordingly, no new empirical insights are gained.

The economic model of behaviour proceeds in a different way. It first asks in what way the individuals' *possibility set* has changed. The opportunities for action available to a person are attributed to observable changes in the constraints. Primarily, changes in the *prices* or *costs* of goods and actions are considered which may have caused the change in behaviour. The economist then speaks of a shift in *relative prices* because the price change compared to alternative goods and actions is relevant. To explain the increased purchase of smaller cars one may, for example, refer to the following possibilities: an increase in the fuel price (small cars use less petrol); more favourable taxation or insurance premiums for small compared to large cars; government regulations to the disadvantage of larger cars (such as speed limits); or other changes in environmental conditions (such as smaller public parking lots).

In contrast to changes in values the economic approach based on

frequency

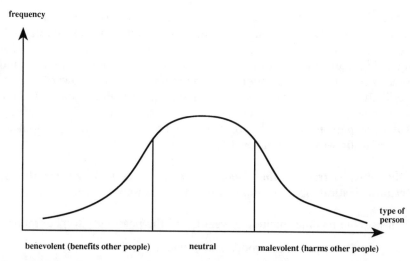

benevolent (benefits other people)　　　　neutral　　　　malevolent (harms other people)

type of person

Figure 1–1. The Distribution of Human Preferences.

changes in constraints is empirically testable. Thus, it is easy to measure a rise in the price of petrol. As may be seen from the example, the notion of "price and cost" is understood in an extensive way. It includes not only monetary prices (such as the price of petrol) or monetary burdens (such as taxes or insurance premiums) but all costs which arise when undertaking an action (smaller parking lots lead, e.g., to greater time loss and more inconvenience).

Individuals Pursue Their Own Interests and Generally Behave in a Selfish Way. This assumption about preferences seems at first sight to represent a negative evaluation of man: an egoist is not likeable. This is, however, a misunderstanding. Selfish behaviour means that it cannot be assumed that every person acts magnanimously towards others—this would certainly be unrealistic. Nor does it mean that every person always endeavours to harm others. Selfish behaviour takes a middle position. Most people are, with few exceptions, neither saints nor criminals. Figure 1–1 illustrates how human preferences or traits are distributed. Most are selfish, while only a few are consistently good or bad.

Human behaviour is thus characterized by neither love, nor hate, nor envy; people act neutrally in this respect (Collard 1978). Selfish behaviour can be relied on, it may as a rule be expected that human beings act to their own advantage.

Selfishness may take quite different forms under varying conditions. In the family or among friends, for instance, to be selfish means that in one's own interest one takes other people's welfare into account. The same holds in recurrent situations such as between regular customers and tradesmen. Those who, under such conditions, act badly towards others are likely to harm their own reputation and interest (Frank 1988). On the other hand, in an anonymous environment selfishness normally means that each person acts in his or her own narrow self-interest, or in an opportunistic way (Williamson 1985, 1986).

Constraints Determine the Human Possibility Set and are Mainly the Result of Institutions.   The most important restrictions are:

disposable income, including wealth and the possibility to get credit;

the (relative) prices for goods and services;

the time required for consuming and acting.

The first two conditions define a person's disposable *real income*. (In simple graphical expositions this income is given by the "budget constraint.") A person's income may be increased by relinquishing leisure hours and working more. As total time is limited to 24 hours per day, from which time needed for sleeping, eating and recreation must be deducted; someone with a given endowment can only reach a certain maximum income, even if he or she does nothing else. A person's possibilities are thus determined by a *full income constraint*. In addition to the monetary and time constraints there are other physical and psychic limits (they will be discussed in chapters 9 and 12).

The Law of Demand.   On the basis of these five elements of the economic model of human behaviour, it is possible to derive a central law— the generalized *law of demand*. Suitably applied, it allows us to theoretically and empirically explain how people act.

The law of demand states: if the price (or cost) of a good or activity rises in comparison to other goods or activities (i.e., if the relative price rises) the particular good is demanded less and the particular activity is carried out less.

This central law is based on the principle of *marginal substitution*. A relative price rise does not provoke a total or abrupt change in behaviour but rather a more or less strong adjustment to changing scarcities. The law only applies provided other influences stay constant (this is the *ceteris paribus* assumption). The influence of other factors on demand must be taken into account separately. To take up again the example of a switch from large to small cars: if the price of petrol rises (which benefits buyers of smaller, petrol-saving cars), but income rises at the same time (which induces the purchase of more expensive, larger cars), it may not necessarily be expected that relatively more small cars are bought (the substitution and the income effects work in opposite directions).

An important property of the law of demand is that the direction of the expected change in behaviour is well determined. The relatively more expensive activity is undertaken to a lesser extent, and the relatively *more expensive* good is purchased and consumed *less*, and *vice versa*. This property does not normally obtain for other influences on demand. In particular, no general theoretical hypotheses exist about whether a higher income raises or lowers demand. The demand for larger cars may increase with rising income, the demand for plain food may decrease. Theoretically, however, the direction of the influence of a higher income is uncertain; it can only be determined by empirical observation.

Differences from Other Social Sciences' Views of Man

In sociology and many parts of political science, but implicitly also in law, a model of human behaviour is generally assumed which differs strongly from the economic concept. Since Durkheim (1885), the "father of modern sociology," and in particular since Parsons (1949, 1951), people's actions are taken to be influenced by moral and social factors. These social determinants of human behaviour are acquired by socialization and internalization processes. Persons deviating from these norms imposed by society are punished, with the aim of restoring a morally desirable behaviour. The model of "homo sociologicus" (see Dahrendorf 1958) consists of three central elements (Opp 1979a, 1986; Lindenberg 1985a,b):

1. Human behaviour is determined by society. Society is an entity from which the behaviour of people derives. Human beings are programmed by their social environment.

2. People act within roles. Society consists of a network of behavioural norms in which an individual is placed. This system of roles provokes behavioural expectations which make coexistence possible. Deviations from roles are only possible if socialization is insufficient.

3. Norm deviations are sanctioned by society. Punishment, mainly in youth and within the family, serves to strengthen and supplement socialization.

This sketch should make it clear that homo sociologicus is not attributed powers which would allow him to learn and to find solutions of his own. He has no possibility to choose between different actions and to substitute, and to decide himself on the most advantageous solution. Constraints are only set by sanctions and role expectations of other people, but not by income, prices, time, physical and psychic factors. As a result, the scarcity of possibilities is insufficiently taken into account.

In empirical social research based almost exclusively on the survey method, a somewhat different model of human behaviour is assumed (see Lindenberg 1985b). Opinions, attitudes and orientations are taken to be social processes which determine people's behaviour. It is accordingly taken for granted that behaviour can be deduced from attitudes.

This sociological model again provides no space for active behaviour based on learning and choosing, and again, there are no constraints on actions due to scarcities of income and time. All that matters is the pressure imposed by other people's expectations. In contrast to the sociological view, the importance of the constraints on behaviour (taken into account in the economic model of man) will be illustrated by an example. When asked in a survey, many people will indicate that they are fond of the theatre, opera and cinema. Empirical social research therefrom deduces that people act accordingly. But empirical analyses of the attendance of artistic events (see e.g., Frey and Pommerehne 1989a, chapter 1) reveal that attitudes and behaviour strongly deviate from each other. Persons with low income and little time, but especially those for whom a visit to a cultural event leads to high cost, do not act in accordance with their attitudes. These costs do not only consist in monetary expenditure for the admission fee. For those living in the country for whom the journey is expensive and time-consuming, or those with young children who have to employ a babysitter (if they are able to get one), the additional non-material costs are particularly high. Total cost in addition to the admission fee is considerable in such cases, resulting in low attendance by such persons to theatres, operas and cinemas. That particular attitudes need not necessarily lead to respective types of behaviour does not only apply in this particular example but holds quite generally. This conclusion by economists is shared by social psychologists who have undertaken extensive research in this matter (see chapter 2 of this book as well as Stroebe and Frey 1980). In areas where income, relative prices and scarcity of time restrict human behaviour to any appreciable extent, the economic approach proves to be superior (for various comparisons see Gäfgen and Monissen 1978, and Opp 1985).

Economics can certainly also learn from sociology. In particular, it is necessary to include the great variety of values, wishes, internalized norms, as well as aspects of perception which are transmitted by social processes into the economic approach. Both views of man have their strengths: economics seems to be better equipped to explain *changes* in human behaviour, while sociology seems to be better equipped to explain historically existing *levels*. In the case of voting participation, economists concentrate on explaining why at a given instance it is higher or lower than average, and sociologists try to explain average participation (Kirchgässner 1980).

Sources and Variants of the Economic Model of Behaviour

The economic approach to human action has already been sketched by the classic authors such as Adam Smith (1776). Methodological individualism, the belief in the existence of laws (nomological orientation), selfishness as a crucial incentive, the importance of constraints (scarcity of means), and, finally, the relevance of institutions for guiding human behaviour, can all be found in classical economic writings (Albert 1985).

So far, there is no unique name for the "economic view of the world." Depending on what aspects are stressed we find

"The Economic Approach to Human Behavior" (Becker 1976);

"The New World of Economics" (McKenzie and Tullock 1975; Kirchgässner 1988);

"Non-Market Economics" (Tullock 1991);

"New Political Economy" (Bombach 1977/78; Boettcher 1983; Lindenberg 1985a);

"Comparative Analysis of Institutions" (Frey 1990);

"Institutional Choice" (Schenk 1983, 1988), or

"New Institutionalism" (Coase 1984; Furubotn and Richter 1984; Williamson 1986).

In sociology, the term "Rational Choice Approach" is dominant, while in political science the terms "Economic Theory of Politics" and "Public Choice" (mostly in the United States) are most often used.

Rationality, Utility Maximization and Survival

To understand man as seen by economics and applied to other areas it is useful to discuss two aspects which are particularly controversial.

Rationality and Utility Maximization

Rational behaviour is not a goal but a means to reach goals. A rational actor should not make logical mistakes; his or her behaviour should be internally consistent (Hirshleifer 1985). The choice of alternatives from the opportunity set should be consistent with specific requirements. As has been shown, especially by psychologists, human beings tend to violate these axioms systematically under some conditions (see the extensive discussion and examples in chapter 11 on "behavioural anomalies"). In the sense of formal decision theory people certainly do not act rationally.

But rationality can more generally be understood as a "reasonable pursuit of one's own interests" (Sen 1988). This is the view of "homo oeconomicus" taken in the social sciences. Some authors assume that people maximize their utility subject to the constraints imposed by the environment (in particular, Becker 1976). It turns out, however, that this strict model of utility maximization is not necessary in order to derive (most of) the theoretical and empirically testable propositions. In many cases it is, however, useful in order to facilitate a mathematical formulation.

The explanation of human behaviour is not based on the assumption of utility maximization but rather on the five characteristics discussed above: individualism; systematic reaction to incentives; distinction between preferences and constraints, changes in the latter determining changes in behaviour; selfishness; the role of institutions. This approach is consistent with "bounded rationality" (Simon 1982; Williamson 1985): Human decisions are divided into a number of partial aspects so that the amount of information as well as the psychic effort are limited. One often acts according to custom which may well be reasonable. A person may, for example, want to reach a goal and be satisfied if it is reached ("satisficing," Simon 1957); in this case no maximization takes place. The concepts of bounded rationality and satisficing should not be interpreted as maximization subject to additional constraints in the form of incomplete information. "Rationality" does not relate to the action's outcome but rather to how people go about acting, that is, it refers to the *cognitive process* (Simon 1978).

Rationality and Survival

Human beings are to some extent forced to act rationally; if not, "natural" selection eventually results in their elimination. Those who optimize are more successful; those not optimizing lose income, wealth and social esteem. In an economy with harsh competition, enterprises which do not maximize profits do not survive but go bankrupt (Alchian 1950; Friedman 1953).

According to this Darwinian view people do not choose to act rationally. Rather, the social environment tolerates rationality only. As a result, one observes outcomes which would not obtain if people did not act in a rational way ("as if" behaviour). This indirect support for utility and profit maximization stresses that people act in a social setting which they have to take into account. The analogy to natural selection in biology should, however, not be drawn too far because the concept is not at all clear in that science (see Dawkins 1982; Maynard Smith 1982; and applied to economics Witt 1985, 1987). If the survival of a group of people is considered, it is well possible that groups deviating from selfishness and supporting altruistic motives are more capable of surviving (Akerlof 1984; Sen 1985; Frank 1988).

The evolutionary process of competing firms does not lead to the same long-run outcome, "as if" they had maximized profits either (Winter 1971; Nelson and Winter 1982). The natural (economic) selection of firms, even in a competitive environment under realistic conditions, (namely, that profit maximization is more expensive than just imitating the behaviour of others), leads to the result that both profit maximization and imitating enterprises coexist. To assume rationality in the form of utility and profit maximization is thus not a necessary consequence of the struggle for survival, there is room for far less limited models of human behaviour.

Applications of the Economic View

Economy

Orthodox microeconomic textbooks dealing with the behaviour of people as consumers and as producers (firms) are often based on a simplified model. People are fully informed, all transactions are free, and the best alternative is found without effort, cost, and in a very short time. For some purposes (for example, the question of whether a general equilibrium exists in principle and whether it is stable and Pareto-optimal) this view of man may be acceptable. In any case, important aspects such as the innovating entrepreneur (Schumpeter 1912; Kirzner 1979) and above all institutional aspects are neglected. Economic affairs take place in a vacuum. Consequently this orthodox type of microeconomics can only contribute in a limited way to our understanding of present day problems.

In macroeconomic theory dealing with the determinants of total production (the national income), employment and inflation, the 1970s saw an intensive discussion of the concept of "rational expectations" (originally Muth 1961; Lucas 1976), but it has since lost some of its glamour. According to this type of rationality, people are assumed to consider all information relevant for their decisions, and thereupon to maximize their utility. They cannot, even in the short run, be fooled by economic policy actions which they can expect. Rational expectations help to explain why Keynesian business cycle policy (to be expansionary in the depression, and restrictive in the boom) was effective in the post-war years (when people did not expect such policies), but does not work nowadays. Some authors quickly jumped to the conclusion that (expected) government policies can never have a real effect on the economy. This overlooks the institutional constraints which make it impossible to adjust rapidly. Moreover, the model's assumptions with respect to humans' rationality is too exacting. Empirical analyses even of firms' behaviour (e.g., Schwartz 1987; De Bondt and Makhija 1988) show clearly that while people act in a quite reasonable way they do not act rationally in the sense of logical consistency and maximization. Macroeconomic theory would also benefit greatly from a more realistic view of man, and in particular from introducing the influence of institutions into the analysis.

Other Areas

This book applies the economic view of the world to areas which have so far been reserved for other sciences:

Chapter 3 is devoted to the *natural environment*. It is asked whether environmental ethics may stop the degradation of nature, and various measures to improve the quality of the environment are discussed.

Chapter 4 deals with *politics*. The fall of the Weimar Republic and the rise of National Socialism are analysed to see what was the role of unemployment, but also of belonging to a particular religion or profession.

Chapter 5 applies economic thinking to a topical subject in the *arts*. The profitability of investment in paintings is analysed.

Chapter 6 analyses the *family* from the point of view of economics, applying it to the position of a patriarch in China.

Chapter 7 uses economic thinking to suggest solutions to social *conflicts*. A new policy to fight political terrorism is suggested.

Chapter 8 deals with *history*. It is explained how and why prisoners of war were treated very differently in different periods.

Economic thinking has also been applied to other areas not treated in this book. Well established are the *economics of education* (Blaug 1968, 1969) and the *economics of health* (Cooper and Culyer 1973; Zweifel 1982). Newer areas are the *economics of women* (e.g., Blau and Ferber 1986; Bergman 1986) and the *economics of sports* (Heinemann 1984; Goff and Tollison 1990). The economic approach has also been used to explain particular areas of human life connected with the *family*: marriage, children, divorce, suicide (Becker 1971, 1973, 1976, 1981, 1988) and even to the determinants of *abortion* (Medoff 1988), *drug addiction* (Winston 1980, Becker and Murphy 1988), *religious practices* (Ehrenberg 1977, Iannaccone 1988, 1991, Anderson 1988), and *lying* and *cheating* (Tullock 1967, ch. IX).

Interdisciplinarity and the Social Science Paradigm

The economic view of the world applies the *same theoretical approach* to many different areas. Interdisciplinarity does not refer to the scientific method but to the topic. The use of a unitary approach makes it possible to look at distinct parts of society from one point of view and to thereby integrate them closely. The social sciences are no longer distinguished according to their dominant field of application—in particular economics is no longer restricted to the study of the economy. The "unity of the social sciences" is achieved.

Some scholars (such as Stigler 1984; Hirshleifer 1985; Brunner 1987) consider it as a matter of course that this unity is to be undertaken under the leadership of economics. The approach explaining changes in human behaviour by changes in constraints may indeed be understood as a *general social science paradigm*: while this procedure is employed in this book one should not dismiss the possibility that another discipline's approach can also fruitfully be applied to various areas. Recently, extending sociological thinking to the study of the economy has been propagated ("economic sociology," Swedberg 1985, 1986; Swedberg,

Himmelstrand and Brulin 1985; see also Etzioni 1988). In both economic as well as sociological "imperialism," the area of application is distinguished from the methodology used.

The type of interdisciplinarity championed in this book—the application of economic thinking to many different topics—differs drastically from what is normally called "interdisciplinarity," namely the mixture of the methodological approaches emanating from various sciences. When this latter type of interdisciplinarity is followed, as a rule the criteria of scientific rigour are given up because it is only possible to unite at the lowest common level. The result is usually a kind of journalistic exposition. Journalism has, of course, its place, but it should not be confounded with scientific analysis.

In this book various sciences beyond economics are touched on. The most important are:

Philosophy. To start with the queen of the sciences, the discussion of the natural environment (chapter 3) and of the price system (chapter 10) can be considered as contributions to ethics or to the moral sciences.

Social Sciences. Various neighbouring sciences of economics are referred to:

1. The analyses of the rise of National Socialism (chapter 4), of terrorism (chapter 7) and of prisoners of war (chapter 8) can be looked at as *political science* topics. One of the most developed variants of the "economic view of the world" is the *economic theory of politics* (see the surveys by Mueller 1989; Frey 1978). The economic methods are applied to aspects of elections and other social decision-making mechanisms (Black 1958; Arrow 1963; Sen 1970); party competition and the behaviour of governments (Schumpeter 1942; Downs 1957); the formation and influence of pressure groups (Olson 1965; Moe 1980), and the behaviour of bureaucracies (Tullock 1965; Niskanen 1971; Breton and Wintrobe 1982). *Constitutional economics* has become of special importance (Buchanan and Tullock 1962; Buchanan 1977, 1987) and deals with the emergence and impact of rules, among them constitutions. This in turn has fundamental consequences for the theory of economic policy (Brennan and Buchanan 1980, 1985; Frey 1983).

The aforementioned chapters also touch upon issues of *international relations theory*. Economics has been applied to this topic in the form of *International political economy* (Baldwin 1985; Frey 1984; Magee, Brock and Young 1989). The *economics of conflict* (Schelling 1960; Boulding

1962; Hirshleifer 1987) has mainly drawn on game theoretic concepts in order to understand this aspect of society better. The *economics of war* (Hitch and McKean 1961; Kennedy 1975) and the *economics of peace* (Boulding 1977, 1986; Isard 1988) are closely related.

2. The analysis of the family (chapter 6), as well as of terrorism and prisoners of war (chapters 7 and 8) comprise *sociological* topics. Various "typically" sociological themes such as the emergence of norms (Ullmann-Margalit 1977; Coleman 1990b), of rules (Heiner 1983) or of institutions (e.g., Schotter 1981; Kliemt 1985; Witt 1987) have been treated employing the economic approach. The same holds for the sociology of deviant behaviour which is analysed within the *economics of crime* (Becker 1968; Ehrlich 1973, 1975; Cameron 1988, and for a comparison of the two approaches Opp 1979b). The rational choice approach has recently been taken to be an essential part of sociology (Coleman 1990a).

3. The discussion on terrorism (chapter 7) and the treatment of prisoners of war (chapter 8) contribute to an area covered by *law*. The *economics of law* (sometimes called *law and economics*, see Posner 1986) deals with its public branch (in the form of constitutional economics), with criminal law (in the form of the economics of crime), but primarily with private law. The way in which particular legal settings influence social actions is analysed, together with how legal norms emerge and how they should look if particular goals are to be achieved. The theoretical basis has been laid mainly in the *theory of property rights* (Coase 1960; Demsetz 1967; Alchian and Demsetz 1972; Furubotn and Pejovich 1974) and in the *theory of transaction costs* (Williamson 1979, 1985; De Alessi 1983).

4. The relationship to *psychology* is particularly close and forms the subject of chapter 2, as well as of chapters 10, 11 and 12.

Other Human Sciences. The economic view of the world contributes in particular to two areas:

1. The rise of Nazism (chapter 4) and the treatment of prisoners of war (chapter 8) are themes treated in *history*. The economic approach has been applied beyond the study of economic history to more general historical events (*new economic history*, see Temin 1973; North 1981, 1988). When in addition to deriving hypotheses from economic theory they are also econometrically tested, one speaks of *cliometrics* (clio is the muse of history; see Fogel 1965).

2. The discussion of art in chapter 5 concerns an area of *art history* or

art science. The *economic analysis of art* (Baumol and Bowen 1966; Throsby and Withers 1979; Frey and Pommerehne 1989a) deals with the demand for, and supply of, art in all its forms, the influence of different institutional settings on people's behaviour (e.g., publicly-subsidized or profit-oriented theatre) being a central topic.

How the Economic Approach has been Received in the Other Sciences

The economic view of the world has been evaluated in quite different ways in the sciences traditionally dealing with the subjects treated. Some think that "economic imperialism" has to be rejected as a matter of principle—but the same "imperialism" undertaken by other sciences is found to be acceptable. Many opponents of the economic approach welcome as a matter of course that sociology, psychology or law are applied to various topics. The sociology, psychology or law of the family, or the sociology, psychology or law of art are taken to be completely legitimate, but not economics of the family or of art. This asymmetric evaluation of the sociological, psychological and legal approaches as opposed to the economic approach suggests that the problem does not lie in imperialism as such, but rather in the economists' way of thinking.

More widespread than an outright rejection of the economic approach is that it is little known, and what is known is often a seriously biased picture. In political science a rejection is still widespread in Europe but less so in America. Nevertheless, the Economic Theory of Politics, the New Political Economy or Public Choice have by now been accepted as useful variants of political science. In sociology this is less the case; the Rational Choice Approach is only applied by a rather small group of scholars (e.g., Opp 1985; Lindenberg 1983; Coleman 1987, 1990a; Vanberg 1988; Friedman and Hechter 1988). Some elements of the economic approach, in particular Olson's (1965) theory of the emergence and stability of interest groups, have been integrated. In psychology the economic model of man stressing the opportunity set as a method of explaining behaviour is largely unknown but there are efforts to introduce it into social psychology (e.g., Stroebe and Meyer 1982). Quite another thing is to take psychological factors in human behaviour into account when it comes to explaining consumption, saving, or paying taxes, where interdisciplinarity exists to some extent (see chapter 2).

In law, the economic view of the world is well-established in the United States. Apart from professional journals (such as the *Journal of*

Law and Economics or the *Journal of Legal Studies*), excellent textbooks exist (Posner 1986; Hirsch 1988; Cooter and Ulen 1988). Elsewhere, acceptance by lawyers is much less widespread, if it exists at all. Finally, in other sciences to which economics can contribute, the situation is similar or even worse. In the history of art, for example, it is almost completely unknown that an economic approach to the arts exists at all.

General References to the Literature

The application of economic thinking to general social problems is due to a large extent to Gary Becker whose most important contributions are collected in

> Becker, Gary S. *The Economic Approach to Human Behavior.* Chicago: Chicago University Press, 1976.

A simple introduction demonstrating applications in the areas of human interactions, the family, crime, politics and learning is given in

> McKenzie, Richard B. and Tullock, Gordon. *The New World of Economics,* 2nd ed. Homewood, Illinois: Irwin, 1975.

A good discussion of the possibilities and limits of the economic approach is

> Hirshleifer, Jack. "The Expanding Domain of Economics." *American Economic Review* 75 (Dec. 1985): 53–68.

Selected articles may be found in

> Radnitzky, Gerard and Bernholz, Peter (eds). *Economic Imperialism. The Economic Method Applied Outside the Field of Economics.* New York: Paragon, 1987.

Recent surveys of two sub-fields are

> DeAlessi, Louis. "Form, Substance and Welfare Comparisons in the Analysis of Institutions." *Journal of Institutional and Theoretical Economics* 146 (March 1990): 5–23.

> Williamson, Oliver E. "Operationalizing the New Institutional Economics. The Transaction Cost Economic Perspective." *Journal of Institutional and Theoretical Economics,* forthcoming (1992).

> Eggertsson, Thrainn. *Economic Behaviour and Institutions: Principles of Neoinstitutional Economics.* Cambridge: Cambridge University Press, 1990.

Important applications of economic methodology to sociological topics, such as the emergence and effect of norms, are extensively treated in

> Coleman, James S. *Foundations of Social Theory.* Cambridge, Mass.: Belknap Press of Harvard University Press, 1990.

2 ECONOMICS AND PSYCHOLOGY: HOMO OECONOMICUS

Opposing Views

In modern economics it is a hotly debated question whether the model of homo oeconomicus is "unpsychological." The arguments advanced to support the contrasting views differ greatly among each other, and correspondingly quite opposing conclusions are drawn.

According to a first view, which cannot do justice to human behaviour, homo oeconomicus is an utterly incomplete figure. Homo oeconomicus guided in his decisions by the principle of maximizing his own utility is taken to be a caricature unable to describe and predict the complexity of human actions, nor keep pace with the modern state of psychology. The total neglect of psychological elements in the economic conception of man is deplored and it is demanded that more insights of psychology be introduced into economics. The psychological model of human behaviour is taken to be vastly superior to the economic view; the shortcomings of homo oeconomicus can only be overcome by integrating psychological elements.

Such a rejection of the model of homo oeconomicus can often

be found in the economic literature. Thus, Scitovsky (1976) states: "How much more realistic and convincing psychological theory is compared to the economists' sweeping assumptions of rational behaviour" (p. xii) and "Psychologists have a much broader view of man's behaviour and motivation than economists do" (p. xiii). Similar views are advanced by other psychological economists such as Katona (1975) or Leibenstein (1976), or earlier by Marchal (1950), Schmölders (1962) or Myrdal (1964).

Another group within economics agrees that homo oeconomicus does not correspond to the concept of human beings held in modern psychology, but considers it to be a decisive advantage of the economic model. Homo oeconomicus is taken to be by far the best model of human behaviour. Psychology is accused of being based on the irrationality of individual decisions, making predictions impossible. As a consequence it is claimed that the introduction of psychological elements is unnecessary or even damaging.

This view has been mainly advanced by American economists (e.g., Alchian and Demsetz 1972, or Becker 1976). Meckling (1976, p. 555) claims, for example: "It is difficult to infer much of anything about social behaviour from the psychological model of man that is not trivial or false."

As these two completely opposing views about homo oeconomicus are part of two important currents in present day economics, it is worthwhile inquiring into the question posed. In particular, we must ask whether economists should concern themselves with psychology, and if so, what the possible and fruitful approaches are.

This chapter advances two propositions:

1. The economic model of behaviour strongly resembles a particular psychological model, one used in social psychology. For this reason, the views discussed above may not be maintained in the form advanced. The common elements of the two models are analysed by sketching the development of the social psychological theories of attitudes in the direction of the economic model of behaviour (section 2). The differences between the two which emanate from particular questions and perspectives are also discussed.

2. Both social sciences can learn from each other and can thereby gain a better conception of human behaviour. A critique of the psychological model of behaviour sketched shows us how psychology can profit from economics (section 3); conversely, economics can learn in various ways from psychological research (section 4).

The Psychological Model Approaches the Economic Model

When comparing the economic and psychological models of behaviour it is straightforward and most useful to look at social psychology because it is that branch of psychology which deals with the same areas as economics. The social psychological model of behaviour has been developed in four steps.

Attitudes Explain Behaviour

In the early phase of social psychological research it was assumed that behaviour can be predicted from attitudes. The concept of "attitude" was introduced by Thomas and Znaniecki (1918) into social psychology and has since occupied a central position. An attitude is a positive or negative evaluation of an attitudinal object, for example, a person, group, type of behaviour, or good (Thurstone 1928). For a long time it was taken as a matter of course that the close connection presumed between attitudes and behaviour is sufficient to predict behaviour. This phase saw the development of most of the methods to construct attitudinal scales, such as those by Likert (1932), Guttman (1944) or Thurstone (1928).

In practical marketing research (an area in which economists and psychologists closely cooperate) it has been clearly assumed that attitudes determine consumers' behaviour. This hypothesis is taken to be well supported by empirical evidence (e.g., Achenbaum 1966, p. 112).

Attitudes Do Not Explain Behaviour

Beginning in the mid-sixties, the connection between attitudes and behaviour has been called into question by a series of research results. A large number of laboratory and field experiments (see Wicker 1969) revealed that it is indeed in many cases impossible to deduce behaviour from attitudes. It has, for instance, been shown that the behaviour of restaurant managers with respect to admission of racial minorities (in the United States the Blacks and Chinese) does not correspond to the attitudes which had previously been established in surveys (Kutner, Wilkins and Yarrow 1952; La Piere 1934). Many other instances have been found in areas such as job performance (Vroom 1964), absence from the place of work (Bernberg 1952; Vroom 1962), the purchase of consumer goods (Sampson 1971), child education (Zunich 1961), behaviour towards other races (Himmelstein and Moore 1963; Katz and Benjamin 1960) and political activities (Sample and Warland 1973). On the basis of this empirical research, Wicker (1969, p. 65) concludes in a survey article: "Taken as a whole, these studies suggest that it is considerably more likely that attitudes will be correlated or only slightly related to overt behaviours than that attitudes will be closely related to actions."

Ad Hoc Theories

The breakdown of the simple model postulating a complete association between attitudes and behaviour contributed to the emergence of ad hoc explanations. They should serve to make the assumption that attitudes determine behaviour compatible with empirical observations. On the one hand, the concept of attitude was enlarged by including not only evaluations but also opinions and tendencies for action (e.g., Rosenberg and Hovland 1960). On the other hand, additional behavioural determinants such as norms, habits and personality characteristics were introduced (e.g., Ehrlich 1969, Triandis 1967, Wicker 1969).

In applied marketing research the buying intention was introduced as a link between attitude and purchasing behaviour. This serves to capture the various specific factors which relate to a consequent purchasing situation. (Somebody may, for example, have a strongly positive attitude to a car of a certain make, but may nevertheless refrain from stating a purchase intention, because he or she knows that the dealer of this make does not offer good service.)

Unified Explanatory Approach

Ad hoc explanations being unsatisfactory, a unified approach was sought which, in particular, takes the social aspects of behaviour into consideration. This constitutes a first step towards separating attitudes as general preferences and externally imposed constraints. Above all, social norms as explicit constraints, and thereby determinants of behaviour, were introduced. The procedure may be illustrated with a simple model by Ajzen and Fishbein (1973) which has recently been further developed (Ajzen 1988). The two authors distinguish two determinants of behaviour: attitudes and normative factors. The observed and the intended behaviour of persons is the result of a weighted sum of these two factors:

$$B_o \sim B_i = A \cdot W_A + (N \cdot M) \cdot W_N$$

The symbols have the following meanings:

B_o: observed behaviour;

B_i: intended behaviour;

W_A, W_N: empirical weights of attitudes and of normative constraints, respectively;

A: attitudes towards an action;

N: assumptions about the existence of a normative expectation;

M: the motivation to conform to a normative expectation.

The symbol $\sim$ indicates that a high correlation between observed and intended behaviour is expected.

This model has been tested in a great number of works. Ajzen and Fishbein (1973), for example, discuss ten research studies in which the identification of attitudinal and normative components made it possible to successfully explain a wide variety of actions (such as premarital sex among students or cooperative behaviour in prisoner's dilemma games).

The four stages of the psychological model of behaviour can be interpreted as a movement towards the economic model of behaviour: (a) An increasingly general formulation in a unified setting is endeavoured, which can be applied to special cases; (b) Attitudes (preferences) are taken to be only one factor to explain behaviour, and constraints (in particular social norms) are accounted for. This means that the strict distinction between preferences and constraints typical for economics is approached.

How can Psychology Profit from Economics?

Starting from social psychology's model of behaviour, three areas may be identified where psychology can learn from the economic view.

Generality of the Approach

The economic view has the advantage of making it possible to derive specific hypotheses about behaviour based on a few basic assumptions.

The theory developed applies to all situations. Psychology, in comparison, does not have such a general model of behaviour. For each particular area, it has developed rather divergent approaches, and the areas to which they apply are often unclearly defined. Over the past years there have been no serious efforts to integrate the various approaches into a general social psychological model of behaviour. In this respect, psychology could gain by looking at and possibly imitating the economists' approach.

Strict Distinction Between Preferences and Constraints

The social psychological model of behaviour differentiates only inadequately between preferences and constraints imposed from outside, the violations of which lead to costs. The social norms introduced by Ajzen and Fishbein (1973), for instance, do not always belong to the constraints. Traditional norms which have been "internalized" by the various persons could enter the preferences. On the other hand, legal norms clearly relate to constraints because they are imposed on people from outside, and when they are transgressed one has to reckon with well-specified costs in the form of fines or even imprisonment.

A Multitude of Constraints

The socio-psychological models of behaviour mainly consider normative demands as constraints. The monetary restrictions representing income and prices (the classical budget constraint) which are in the centre of the economic model of behaviour are, on the other hand, scarcely taken into account. A second type of restriction, the time constraint, is also of much importance in economic analysis because it can also be evaluated in monetary terms. In many psychological experiments the participants have sufficient time to act and to take decisions. Outside the laboratory setting, sufficient time is often not available, which may cause a deviation of real life behaviour from laboratory experiments.

In psychological research which deals with the experimental testing of hypotheses in the laboratory, such constraints are often found to be a nuisance, leading to a deviation between intended and actual behaviour not planned by the researcher. Thus Ajzen and Fishbein (1973, p. 44) complain: ". . . an individual may not be able to perform a given behaviour, despite his intention to do so, if he lacks the required ability or if he is prevented from doing so by circumstances or by other people. When these problems can be avoided, a measure of intention is expected to be highly related to overt behaviour."

Psychologists thus tend to construct their experiments so that such constraints are avoided as far as possible. This means, however, that their impact on individual behaviour is not analysed and is therefore neglected.

The economic view, on the other hand, stresses exactly the monetary and time constraints defining a person's possibility set, therefore fixing what alternatives are feasible and can be chosen. As will be discussed in chapter 12, this objective possibility set need not coincide with the alternatives which a particular person considers to be attainable for him- or herself. This deviation between the objective and the "ipsative" possibility set helps to explain aspects of human behaviour which otherwise would appear to be paradoxical.

What Can Economics Learn from Psychology?

There are three main areas in which economics can benefit from the results of psychological research. The first two areas refer to aspects of content, the third of methodology.

The Importance of Learning Processes

Both economics and psychology assume that the subjective evaluations of benefits and costs are relevant for behaviour. In the economics of crime (see e.g., Ehrlich 1973, 1975), for instance, it is assumed that the subjective estimate of the probability of detection and punishment determine the "supply" of criminal activities. In modern macroeconomic theory subjective expectations play a central role. The trade-off between inflation and unemployment is, for example, taken to be determined by people's inflation expectation. Actual inflation and unemployment are thus mainly the result of subjective evaluations. The same holds for rates of exchange and many other prices (such as the price of oil); their current level depends strongly on what people expect the future price level to be.

In economics it is assumed that subjective perception must adjust to objective conditions: To continuously err is taken to be impossible. The objective factors *enforce* a change in behaviour, at least in the long run, when perceptions deviate from actual conditions. If an entrepreneur continuously overestimates the demand for his or her products, he or she will go bankrupt and will be forced out of the market. This process effects an elimination of wrong expectations. If a person underestimates the crime detection rate and repeatedly undertakes criminal acts, he or she will sooner or later be apprehended and convicted, and the prison sentence makes it impossble to hold to the wrong perceptions and pursue the respective behaviour.

Economic theory does not, however, state how long this process of adjustment lasts. It is only assumed that there must be an adjustment in the long run. Nevertheless, the length of time it takes for a deviation between perception and real conditions to disappear is of great interest for social science. It may well happen that a large discrepancy exists for a long period of time, determining people's behaviour. As a result, the real economic conditions may be influenced in such a way that the long-term adjustment is of little importance.

Economics urgently needs a theory describing the adjustment between perceptions and objective conditions. Such a theory should also allow for the possibility that the difference between subjectively perceived and objective factors continuously widens. Among human beings "perverse learning", that is, learning in the wrong direction, should not be excluded. Such a theory should not be restricted to the level of individuals' behaviour but should also take institutions into account, in particular the mass media. Television, radio and the press can strongly influence the relationship between perceptions and objective conditions by offering or suppressing particular kinds of information.

Psychology can contribute greatly to the development of a social science theory of learning. It embodies various theoretical approaches which explain and predict types of behaviour on the basis of forming preferences and learning with what probability particular types of behaviour affect outcomes. A large part of its studies is concerned with learning from direct experience. Two forms are distinguished: *classical* and *instrumental conditioning*. In the case of classical conditioning, the joint use of two stimuli transfers the reaction which would normally follow a later applied stimulus onto a stimulus earlier applied. Normally, such reactions are autonomous, arising without willingly controlling the organism following the unconditional stimulus. A neutral stimulus may become, for instance, positively evaluated solely because it is associated with a positive stimulus. Veitch and Griffith (1976), for example, show in an experiment that persons find a stranger much more likeable if shortly before they met him they listened to news about positive events, than if they had been confronted with bad news. In clinical psychology, therapies based on classical conditioning are applied, for example, in the case of alcohol-dependent persons. A combination of alcohol with a vomiting stimulus in the form of a medical drug can in many cases successfully deal with alcohol problems (Bandura 1969; Voegtlin 1940). Classical conditioning is taken to be a fundamental process underlying the formation of preferences.

While the organism plays a passive role only in classical conditioning, in the case of instrumental conditioning it must actively produce the behaviour before it can be rewarded or punished. It is analysed how far reward or punishment influence the probability that a particular type of behaviour will occur, and what the effects of irregular rewards are on learning. An individual's knowledge of the probability with which particular behaviour leads to particular behavioural effects is not solely based on our own experience, but is also influenced by observing the experience gained by others. The latter processes have been intensively studied (e.g., Bandura 1973). Psychologists have developed a number of theoretical approaches tested by a great many experiments.

Generally speaking, learning is neither a simple nor an automatic activity, as is normally assumed in economic theory (see Payne 1982, pp. 397–8). Uncertainty, instability in the social and technical environment as well as unsatisfactory attempts to evaluate behavioural alternatives represent serious barriers (Einhorn 1980; Brehmer 1980). Learning is possible only when the feedback is well structured—which rarely obtains in reality. Even then the learning process is usually slow and sometimes incorrect or even perverse (Einhorn and Hogarth 1978, 1981). For practical reasons it is important to have a good knowledge of the determinants and the possibilities of influencing the relationship between the perception of particular persons and objective opportunities. Attempts have always been made, for instance, to influence perceptions in order to reach political goals. One example is the attempt to influence inflation expectations by "moral suasion." It may well be that the most effective way to fight crime is not to increase the rate of apprehension or the size of punishment. Rather, improved information on the risks of carrying out criminal acts may more significantly influence the perception and behaviour of potential law breakers.

Identification of Benefits and Costs

Economics is characterized by "if/then" statements of the following kind: If benefits exceed costs, that is, if net benefits are positive, then there exists an incentive to undertake a particular activity. In the framework of the analysis it is, however, not exactly defined what the particular benefits and costs are. When the theory is practically applied it often turns out that it is far from clear what the benefits and costs are. A theory is required which is able to transfer the observations made into the benefit and cost categories.

In many areas of economic research the benefits and costs are not determined but are attributed on an ad hoc basis, or, even worse, they are attributed afterwards in order to support the particular conclusions reached in the analysis. In the latter case, no testing of hypotheses is possible.

When benefits and costs are insufficiently defined, major problems result. This may be exemplified with a simple example from the economic theory of marriage. Becker (1976, ch. 11) develops the following thesis: Differing preferences between partners are beneficial for marriage as long as these tastes are substitutive. Each family member can then undertake those activities which he or she prefers without unperformed tasks remaining. Thus it is beneficial if one partner likes to cook and the other likes to do gardening, because if both enjoy doing the same work, the other tasks are not carried out, leading to friction. Similar preferences, on the other hand, are good for a marriage if they relate to complementary activities. It is, for example, beneficial for marriage if the two partners have similar tastes with respect to holidays (e.g., they both prefer the sea to the mountains, or vice versa) because a good relationship is thereby supported.

The problem is that for many activities the characterization of activities as complementary or substitutive is not easy to make a priori. Cooking and gardening may be substitutive or complementary activities. To cook jointly or to work jointly in the garden may be more agreeable and may therefore promote the quality of a marriage. Conversely, deviating preferences, for example, with respect to art, may benefit a marriage, as differing views may enrich a partnership.

Already existing psychological research results can help significantly to identify the benefits and costs relevant for human behaviour. In the context of marriage analysis, one can refer back to specific analyses of the relationship between preferences (attitudes), behaviour and marriage stability (see Mikula and Stroebe 1977). The concepts of substitutive and complementary characteristics are filled with content. Psychological research does not end, as economics often does, with formulating general principles, but rather considers its main task to be to concretely identify benefits and costs.

The contribution of psychological research can lead to better predictions of human behaviour by filling the abstract economic concepts with content. It helps to identify incentives which are crucial for explaining people's actions.

Experiments

In economics, including public finance, there is still a tendency to submit theoretical arguments without any empirical analysis. Modern social psychology, on the other hand, has a strong empirical orientation. As a rule, theoretical hypotheses are tested with the help of laboratory or field experiments (for surveys see Aronson and Carlsmith 1968; Stroebe 1978).

Experiments are the main test procedure in psychology because they provide the best possibility to check for, and to vary, the various determinants of people's behaviour. In many areas of economics this advantage may also be made use of, which allows us to employ a wider spectrum of empirical methods to explain and predict human actions. Recently, the experimental approach has been increasingly used by economists (see the surveys by Butler and Hey 1987; Roth 1988 and Smith 1989). Laboratory experiments are presently used on a large scale at some universities in the United States (e.g., Smith 1976; Battalio et al., 1973; Hoggatt, Friedman and Gill 1976). Much earlier, such experiments were carried out in Germany by Sauermann and Selten (1962) (see Sauermann 1967–1972; Tietz 1974), and since then have been used in many studies (e.g., Güth, Schmittberger and Schwarz 1982; Schneider and Pommerehne 1981). Thus, chapter 11 of this book, which is devoted to anomalies in individual behaviour, strongly relies on experimental results produced by both cognitive psychologists and economists. Besides laboratory experiments there are also field experiments in which the variables can (up to a certain extent) be controlled, so that social reality is used as a laboratory (see the extensive survey in Ferber and Hirsch 1982). "Synthetic" studies that analyse what effects a hypothetical change of a variable would have can also be considered to be experiments in a wider sense. Thus the impact of an emission charge on activities causing environmental pollution can be studied by econometrically estimating the reaction of emissions to price changes with the help of multiple regressions, and by introducing the price increase due to the imposition of the emission charge into the estimated supply function (e.g., Griffin 1974).

Division of Labour and Integration

In at least some areas, the two sciences of economics and psychology are approaching each other. It has been shown that

the social psychological model of behaviour is developed in the direction of the economic model of behaviour;

economists have taken up the experimental methods of psychology.

The cooperation between the two sciences was institutionalized some time ago by the foundation of an International Association for Research in Economic Psychology and a *Journal of Economic Psychology*. This movement (though only implicitly) takes up an existing, older tradition (see Stroebe and Frey 1980). The French scholar Tarde published a book entitled *Economie Psychologique* already in 1907. For German speaking countries Münsterberg (1912) should be mentioned, and more recently Schmölders (1962, 1975) who developed a fiscal psychology, Jöhr (1972), who related business cycle movements to "psychological core processes" ("Psychologische Kernprozesse"), and the already mentioned Sauermann and Selten (1962), who made early experiments on psychological aspects of oligopoly theory. In the United States, Duesenberry (1949) introduced psychological aspects into a macroeconomic consumption function, Katona (1975) endeavoured to improve the prediction of consumers' behaviour by using an "index of consumer sentiment," and Simon (1957) emphasized the limits of human capacities in complex decision situations and developed the important concepts of "bounded rationality" and "satisficing behaviour." Over the last few years the emerging field of economic psychology or psychological economics has been covered in textbooks (Furnham and Lewis 1986; Lea, Tarpy and Webley 1987), collections of articles (MacFadyen and MacFadyen 1986; Earl 1988), and handbooks (Van Raaij, van Veldhoven and Wärneryd 1988).

In these works, however, the connection between the two areas is mainly seen in the introduction of psychological elements into consumer and marketing analysis. The mutual enrichment with respect to the underlying model of human behaviour is rather neglected. In this chapter, on the other hand, this aspect has been the focal point. It has in particular been argued that in the field of human behaviour, economics can benefit from psychology, and psychology can benefit from economics. A division of labour is useful. Psychology has a comparative advantage with respect to the determinants of preferences and the analysis of the behaviour of particular individuals. Economics is stronger with respect to the effects of changes in constraints and in institutional conditions on human behaviour. This chapter has pointed out that psychological research can generalize its approach centred on specific cases by taking up the strict distinction between preferences and constraints. Economics, on the other hand, can profit by integrating the differentiated psychological analyses of incentives, and by filling with content the often void concepts of benefits and costs. Economics can also learn much from the psychological theories of perception and learning.

The question whether the model of homo oeconomicus is "unpsychological" must clearly be answered *negatively*. Homo oeconomicus, whose behaviour is systematically determined by incentives and is therefore predictable, is not in conflict with the psychological view. On the contrary: Social psychology's model of behaviour is perfectly compatible with the concept of homo oeconomicus proffered in this book. The economic and socio-psychological model of behaviour goes back to a similar view of man.

However, the question of whether homo oeconomicus is unpsychological is inadequate in one respect. The concept of man which is called homo oeconomicus is neither psychological nor economic. This model of behaviour is common to all the social sciences.

General References to the Literature

Survey books of economic psychology are
> Furnham, Adrian and Lewis, Alan. *The Economic Mind. The Social Psychology of Economic Behaviour.* Baltimore and Brighton: Wheatsheaf Books, Harvester Press, 1986.
> Lea, Stephen E.G., Tarpy, Roger M. and Webley, Paul. *The Individual in the Economy. A Survey of Economic Psychology.* Cambridge: Cambridge University Press, 1987.

A recent article on the subject is
> Earl, Peter E. "Economics and Psychology: A Survey." *The Economic Journal* 100, (1990): 718–755.

A corresponding collection of articles is
> Van Raaij, W. Fred, Van Veldhoven, Gerry M. and Wärneryd, Karl Erik (eds). *Handbook of Economic Psychology.* Dordrecht: Kluwer, 1988.

Areas and approaches of modern social psychology are presented in
> Hewstone, Miles, Stroebe, Wolfgang, Codol, Jean-Paul and Stephenson, Geoffrey M. (eds). *Introduction to Social Psychology. A European Perspective.* Oxford: Blackwell, 1988.

An important contribution to the development of a realistic view of man in the social sciences is due to

Simon, Herbert A. *Models of Man*. New York: Wiley, 1957.

Economic and psychological aspects have been integrated in a particularly original way by

Scitovsky, Tibor. *The Joyless Economy: An Inquiry into Human Satisfaction and Consumer Dissatisfaction*. Oxford: Oxford University Press, 1976.

Leibenstein, Harvey. *Beyond Economic Man: A New Foundation for Microeconomics*. Cambridge, Mass.: Harvard University Press, 1976.

Maital, Shlomo. *Minds, Markets and Money*. New York: Basic Books, 1982.

More strongly neoclassically oriented, but pursuing the same goal, are the contributions by

Akerlof, George A. *An Economic Theorist's Book of Tales*. Cambridge: Cambridge University Press, 1984.

Frank, Robert H. *Choosing the Right Pond*. Oxford: Oxford University Press, 1985;

and by the same author

Passion within Reason. The Strategic Role of the Emotion. New York: Norton, 1988.

PART B
APPLICATIONS TO VARIOUS
AREAS

The model of human behaviour discussed in the first part will be applied in this second part to six different areas and problems. The goal of all chapters is to show how institutional conditions shape the possibility space which, in turn, gives incentives to act in a particular way. Unconventional areas of application have purposely been chosen in order to clarify the potential of the economic approach.

Chapter 3 discusses the limits of *environmental policy* based on changes in human preferences. This policy is suitable only under restricted conditions, in particular in small groups with personal interaction, but not for situations involving a large number of anonymous persons. In most cases there are more effective instruments available for the protection of the environment, among them environmental charges or fees.

Chapter 4 deals with one of the most crucial political developments of the 20th century, *the rise of National Socialism*. The increase in unemployment during the economic depression is closely linked to the inexorable rise of the National Socialists and other extreme parties such as the Communists in the Weimar Republic after 1930. The dependence of vote outcomes on the state of the economy obtains also today, as is exemplified by the American presidential elections.

A topical issue in the *arts* is analysed in chapter 5. The recent dramatic increase in the prices of paintings is often interpreted as an indication that investment in art is highly profitable. Using data from auctions spanning several centuries, as well as modern transactions, the claim that art really is such a good investment is examined.

In chapter 6 the economic model of behaviour is applied to *families in China*. Even though the patriarch takes a prominent position, his behaviour and his ability to retain this position within the family are strongly influenced by economic incentives.

In recent history, politically motivated *terrorism* has played a significant role. The attempts to combat it are, however, often ineffective or even counterproductive. Chapter 7 argues that the incentive to commit terrorist acts is diminished when terrorists are refused publicity, towards which goal appropriate procedures are suggested.

History shows us that *prisoners of war* are treated in distinct ways. The allocation of property rights determines the treatment meted out, as argued in chapter 8; if a prisoner belongs to the captor, he will spare him and ransom him (provided payment is possible). When the property rights shift to the state or to supranational organizations, a soldier has no longer an incentive of his own to spare his adversary or to treat prisoners well.

3 NATURAL ENVIRONMENT: ENVIRONMENTAL PROTECTION AND ENVIRONMENTAL ETHICS

Appeals to Environmental Ethics

Acting in an "environmentally responsible way," or acting according to the "principles of environmental ethics" is taken by most people to be the *most important* and the *only possible* contribution to overcoming the destruction of our natural environment. Such behaviour consists in a person attributing a particularly high value to the conservation of nature, and believing that the "right attitude" only is able to guarantee a solution to environmental problems.

The view that behaving according to environmental ethics is centrally important has often been brought forward. The practically oriented environmental movement relies quite heavily on environmental ethics. Politicians are also fond of resorting to such appeals.

Environmental Ethics and Selfishness

Persons acting according to environmental ethics are expected to forgo private advantages for the sake of contributing to the conservation of the natural environment. A car emitting less exhaust fumes, but otherwise

37

with the same characteristics as another car, will be more expensive; housewives are asked to do without the convenience of plastic carrier-bags which they receive free of charge. The expected behaviour would, however, occur automatically if people benefited therefrom, that is, if cars with little exhaust were cheaper to buy and run. In this case there would be no reason to appeal to environmental ethics. It would be a pure *information problem*. The population should therefore rather be asked to pursue its self-interest because this would at the same time solve the environmental problems.

Selfish behaviour also meets environmental requirements if the price to be paid for the product or the service includes all *social costs*. These costs do not only refer to the damage done to the environment when consuming the product, for example when car exhaust fumes pollute the air. They also include the environmental costs which arise from the inputs used in the production process (e.g., the air and water degradation caused by the production of steel which is used in cars). Finally, the price of a good taking care of all environmental damages has to include the cost of disposal. In environmental economics (e.g., Baumol and Oates 1979; Siebert 1987) it has been shown in which way such (external) costs imposed on the environment can be internalized into prices. The proposal to burden those who damage nature with environmental charges (or emission fees or taxes) has so far only rarely been put into practice. A major reason for the inadequate use of this instrument to preserve the environment is that exactly those producers and consumers who damage nature most know that they would have to bear a high cost, and would have to drastically change their behaviour if the environmental charge were introduced. This environmental measure is most strongly opposed politically precisely because it is so effective. For this reason, this chapter considers situations in which the environmental costs are not, or only inadequately, internalized, and where *selfish behaviour therefore damages the environment*.

Many important areas of nature such as pure air, clean water, a beautiful landscape and tranquillity are characterized by the fact that all persons (of a particular region) may benefit to approximately the same extent. Not everyone values these environmental amenities equally, but what matters is that they may be consumed irrespective of whether one has contributed to the supply and the cost or not. Even those, for example, who are not prepared to stop driving a car benefit from the improvement in the quality of the air if all other people were to do so. In the case of environmental goods, the "price" for their supply often consists in not carrying out an activity which causes damage but from which one would have benefited *personally*, that is, the "price" paid is the cost of not exploiting an opportunity (opportunity cost).

Goods which are, in this sense, indivisible and from whose consumption nobody can be excluded have been called "public goods" (Samuelson 1954; Musgrave 1969) because they have basically different behavioural consequences from the normal, "private" goods. In a market, private goods can only be consumed by those persons who contribute to the cost of supply by paying a price. This is different with public goods: they can be consumed by everyone even if no price is paid. People in this case tend to behave in an "unsocial" way; they take advantage of such goods even if they have not contributed to their supply. As environmental goods as a rule have the typical characteristics of public goods, it must be expected that *individually* rational, that is, selfish, behaviour conflicts with behaviour which accords with environmental ethics.

Evaluations of Social States

In order to answer the question of whether behaviour following environmental ethics can be expected to solve our environmental problems, we have to make assumptions about how a person evaluates various possible social states. Three categories may be distinguished:

1. The rest of society acts according to environmental ethics.
(a) In an ideal world the person considered *as well as all other members of society* follow Kant's categorical imperative, that is, everyone behaves in an environmentally responsible way.
(b) From a particular person's selfish point of view (an assumption which we have to realistically make), an even better situation exists: all *other* members of society behave according to environmental morality but the person considered opportunistically pursues his or her own interests. The "others" produce the supply of environmental goods while the person considered—who benefits in any case from these public goods—undertakes activities which increase his or her utility and which damage the environment (even if only marginally).
2. The rest of society behaves selfishly.
(c) The opposite of an ideal world is one in which the person considered *as well as all other members of society* act in an egoistic way. Obviously, the environmental damages will be great.
(d) From a particular person's standpoint, an even worse state exists: all *other* people behave selfishly, and only the person concerned acts

according to environmental ethics. He or she forgos a possible increase in private utility while the others go on damaging the environment. In this case one may rightly speak of an exploitation of the environmentally responsible person.

3. One part of society acts according to environmental morals, and one part acts selfishly.

The behaviour discussed under headings (1) and (2) constitute extreme cases. Between these exists any amount of combinations. For illustration, consider in the following the case in which half the population acts according to environmental ethics, and half acts selfishly. The environment will be in a better state than under (2), but in a worse state than under (1). Under these circumstances, it is again to be expected that the person considered experiences a state (e) in which he or she also acts in an environmentally responsible way to be less preferable to a state (f) in which he or she acts in an opportunistic way.

In line with these considerations a person will order the states mentioned in the following way (the sign > indicates that the state on the left hand side is preferred to the state on the right hand side):

(1) b > a: good environmental conditions
(3) f > e: acceptable state of the environment
(2) c > d: bad environmental conditions;

as we have in addition (1) > (3) > (2), the complete ordering is:

$$b > a > f > e > c > d.$$

This preference ordering, taken to be relevant for all persons, will be illustrated by numbers in the following (table 3–1). The absolute size of the numbers is of no consequence, what matters is their relationship to each other. (Thus, each number could be multiplied by any (positive) factor, or the same absolute number could be added anywhere.)

The assumptions underlying the ordering of the states and the numbers in table 3–1 can be summarized in the following way:

Assumption A: A well-conserved environment is highly valued. It is more likely to be attained, the greater the share of people who act according to environmental ethics.

Assumption B: Selfish behaviour, that is, the pursuit of one's own private utility, is preferred to behaviour following environmental norms, all other conditions being equal.

Table 3–1. Preference Orderings With Respect to Various States of the Environment.

		"Other" Members of Society Act:		
		All Selfishly	Half (50%) According to Environmental Morals	All According to Environmental Morals
Person considered acts	According to environmental morals	1 (d)	4 (e)	8 (a)
	Selfishly	2 (c)	6 (f)	12 (b)

Assumption C: The greater the share of people who follow the norms implied by environmental ethics, the greater will be the advantage gained by a person who acts according to his or her private interests.

While assumption A is undisputed, the individual behaviour contained in assumption B is often rejected. However, it is based solely on the premise that a person prefers a state in which his or her utility is higher, to a state in which it is inferior. Assumption B is certainly *not* proposed normatively, but seeks to describe in a realistic way what behaviour has to be assumed *as a rule*.

Assumption C is not necessary for the following discussion, but it is nevertheless assumed to hold, as it characterizes well the conditions typical for the environment. If, for example, all members of society act according to environmental ethics, opportunistic behaviour becomes particularly attractive for the person considered, as driving a car, for example, would offer many advantages by way of pure air and empty streets. State (a) is therefore attributed the index number 8, state (b) the number 12. If, on the other hand, the environment is in a bad condition because nobody observes the norms of environmental ethics, a person acting selfishly only makes sure that he or she is not exploited. Therefore, state (c) is accorded the index number 2 which is only slightly better than state (d) with index number 1.

Table 3-2. Behaviour in a Large Group.

		"Other" Members of Society Act		
		All Selfishly	Half (50%) According to Environmental Morals	All According to Environmental Morals	Expected Value for Person Considered
Person considered acts	According to environmental morals	1 [0.33] (d)	4 [0.33] (e)	8 [0.33] (a)	4.29
	Selfishly	2 [0.33] (c)	6 [0.33] (f)	12 [0.33] (b)	6.60

Social Interaction with Large and Small Groups

A Society with a Large Number of Members

A person who is a member of a large group must assume that his or her choice of behaviour does not affect the behaviour of the others. A typical individual has so little weight in a large group that the behaviour of other people can be considered part of the *given* conditions (Olson 1965). As it is generally unknown how the other people in society will act, table 3-2 assumes that each one of the three types of behaviour of the other members occurs with a probability of 33% (indicated by the numbers in parentheses), following Laplace's rule.

As may be seen from table 3-2, the expected value (i.e., the sum of the index numbers weighted by their probability of occurrence) of selfish behaviour (with 6.6 points) is higher than the behaviour according to environmental ethics (with 4.29 points). Following our assumptions (1 and 2), a person will then act selfishly. As these conditions apply to everyone, the outcome will be that *all* members of the group will act selfishly. Though the persons constituting the society all value a good environment highly, and though all are well aware of the relationship between selfish behaviour and environmental degradation, the result is a situation *bad* for all (cell c with a strongly damaged environment).

This paradoxical outcome is, as shown by table 3-2, *completely in-*

dependent of what particular persons expect with respect to the behaviour of other members of society. Even if someone is certain that the others will act according to environmental norms, society ends up in an unfortunate state where everyone acts in a selfish and environmentally noxious way. The strategy of selfish behaviour *dominates* the alternative strategy: behaviour following environmental ethics will not arise under the (realistic) behavioural assumptions made.

Society with a Small Number of Persons

As soon as a person makes a choice between ethical and selfish behaviour within a small group, he or she must expect the decision to influence the behaviour of the other members of society (see Buchanan 1965). The context has basically changed compared to a large group because the other group members react to one's own behaviour.

Among the many reaction patterns we focus on three:

"Imitative" behaviour. The person considered expects the others to imitate his or her behaviour. If he or she acts in an environmentally responsible way, the other members are likely to do the same. If, on the other hand, he or she acts without regard to the environment, the other persons are also likely to do so. This so-called "tit for tat" behaviour has proved to be relevant and successful in experiments, and thus conforms to rational action (Axelrod 1984). In table 3-3 it is assumed that the probability of imitative behaviour is 60%.

Under these conditions, behaviour according to environmental ethics proves to be the best strategy for every actor: the expected value is 6.1 points compared to 4.2 points with selfish behaviour. Setting a good example is advantageous for everyone as the others tend to follow it. This constellation is beneficial for society as a whole because the quality of the environment is preserved based on people's voluntary behaviour.

"Contrary" behaviour. A person expects the other members of society to be likely to act (the probability is 60%) in a way which is exactly the contrary of his or her own actions. The person thus assumes a kind of defiant reaction from the others. As may be seen from table 3-4, under these conditions selfish behaviour has a higher expected value than behaviour according to environmental ethics. Taking care of the environment is not worth while for any person, especially because the others do not follow the example set anyway, but rather burden him or

Table 3–3.   "Imitative" Behaviour.

| | | "Other" Members of Society Act | | |
		All Selfishly	Half (50%) According to Environmental Morals	All According to Environmental Morals	Expected Value for Person Considered
Person considered acts	According to environmental morals	1 [0.1] (d)	4 [0.3] (e)	8 [0.6] (a)	6.1
	Selfishly	2 [0.6] (c)	6 [0.3] (f)	12 [0.1] (b)	4.2

her with all the costs of preserving the environment. If, however, a person acts selfishly, he or she expects the others to carry the costs of environmental protection.

"Compensatory" behaviour. In this case the other members of society want to convert the person considered to act according to environmental ethics. They protect the environment most strongly when the other person does not do so. Such behaviour may be observed under particular conditions: "Some people believe that their contribution to a public good"—here the preservation of the natural environment—"will of itself and in some unspecified way lead others to contribute" (Dawes 1988, p. 197). Table 3–5 assumes that if the person considered acts in a way corresponding to environmental ethics, the others will also do so with a probability of 60%, but if he or she acts selfishly, the others compensate this by acting in an environmentally responsible way with a probability of 80%.

Again, the best strategy from the point of view of a particular person is to behave *selfishly*. The compensatory behaviour of the other members of the small group results in the environment being preserved, so that a deviation to selfish behaviour is particularly advantageous. In this case the majority of the small group is exploited by the person considered. But as according to our assumptions every member of the group has the

Table 3-4. "Contrary" Behaviour.

		"Other" Members of Society Act		
		All Selfishly	Half (50%) According to Environmental Morals	All According to Environmental Morals	Expected Value for Person Considered
Person considered acts	According to environmental morals	1 [0.6] (d)	4 [0.3] (e)	8 [0.1] (a)	2.6
	Selfishly	2 [0.1] (c)	6 [0.3] (f)	12 [0.6] (b)	9.2

Table 3-5. "Compensatory" Behaviour.

		"Other" Members of Society Act		
		All Selfishly	Half (50%) According to Environmental Morals	All According to Environmental Morals	Expected Value for Person Considered
Person considered acts	According to environmental morals	1 [0.1] (d)	4 [0.3] (e)	8 [0.6] (a)	6.1
	Selfishly	2 [0.0] (c)	6 [0.2] (f)	12 [0.8] (b)	10.8

same considerations, nobody will follow the norms of environmental ethics. The mutual interaction of behaviour results in a destruction of the environment and therefore leads to an unfortunate situation for all, *precisely because* of the attempt to convert the others.

What are Environmental Ethics Good For?

Our discussion has shown that there is often a conflict between the behaviour of persons pursuing their own interests and the welfare of society as a whole. As long as particular persons are selfish, it may not be generally assumed that the natural environment reaches a state satisfactory to all. The model developed is not designed to reflect reality directly but serves to limit over-optimism. It is not sufficient to demand environmental morals and to assume that the destruction of nature is thereby called to a halt. In other words, the environment is *too important* to leave its rescue solely to environmental ethics. According to the economic model of behaviour, one has to take into account the fact that particular persons do not generally act in the best interests of the environment provided; (1) he or she acts in the context of a large, anonymous group, characteristic for modern societies based on division of labour; (2) there is antagonistic behaviour in small groups causing environmentally responsible behaviour to be answered by environmentally reckless behaviour; and (3) some members of a small group offer a "compensatory" behaviour motivating other members to exploit it by pursuing their self-interest and to thus act in a detrimental way towards the environment. For these reasons ethical behaviour towards nature can not, in many and important cases, be expected to provide a solution to the environmental problem.

There are several other reasons why behaviour according to environmental ethics is able to contribute only little toward preserving nature. One is the *time problem* (many environmental problems need urgent action; to make a large number of people and firms environmentally conscious requires considerable time). Another is the problem of *recognizing* environmental degradation (in addition to the direct damage it is also necessary to recognize the indirect damage contained in the goods entering the production process through semi-finished goods and natural resources). The indirect damage is, as a rule, difficult or impossible to see in the final product, so that it remains open which behaviour is in line with environmental ethics.

As has already been pointed out, environmental economics offers several instruments designed to overcome the conflict between self-interest damaging the environment and the "public interest" preserving the environment. In particular a number of methods exist with which persons are given the required *incentives* to act in an environmentally responsible way out of self-interest. One such instrument is environmental charges on those who burden the environment through their production and consumption activities. (They are also called environmental taxes, emission charges or environmental fees.)

Another is the introduction of tradeable environmental certificates which only allow the burdening of nature up to an amount specified in the certificate to be acquired. Both instruments should be compared to today's situation in which the environment can be damaged *free of charge*. Introducing prices means that damaging nature involves cost to a particular person. Self-interest ensures that an effort is made to evade these costs, which means that people behave in an environmentally responsible way.

Why is it then that environmental ethics plays such a prominent role in the discussion? What is the importance of environmental morals as an *effective* instrument of environmental policy?

Acting according to environmental norms is attributed so much importance because it corresponds to the personal experience of the largest number of people: The family is a small group in which imitative behaviour is important. This experience is transferred to the level of society as a whole in a mostly unconscious and unquestioned way. However, most of today's environmental problems are within the setting of a *large number* of actors. They comprise not only persons but also *enterprises* which—with few exceptions—must be assumed to clearly pursue their selfish interests (they are forced by competition to pursue the goal of profit making). Very few environmental goods with a public good character refer to small groups of personal actors.

It is often argued that appealing to environmental ethics serves to sharpen the *perception* and *consciousness* of the problems faced in the preservation of nature. There is little to be said against this view. Indeed, acting according to environmental norms is often the only way to improve nature's quality in those areas where the environment is damaged by many small acts of a large number of individual persons, and when the damage to the environment is obvious. The population can, for example, up to a certain degree be educated to collect the rubbish after a picnic and to be careful when making a fire in the woods. In times of emergency, especially in the context of catastrophes, moral appeals to preserve nature may be quite successful over a limited period of time. When there was an acute shortage of water in New York in the mid-sixties, appeals were able to reduce the use of water by a considerable amount during some weeks.

When launching appeals for environmental ethics, one should recognize that not much has been achieved thereby and that the quality of the environment is unlikely to improve to any significant degree. One should also see that there are other ways in which the population can be made aware of environmental problems. In the long run, the interest in nature evoked by repeated appeals may again diminish, or even become counter-productive. When those who take the appeals seriously become aware that little or nothing is thereby achieved and that they are exploited by other members of society not following the environmental morals, it may well be that they renounce their ethics and also act in an environmentally detrimental manner.

Appeals to environmental ethics must be accompanied by *behaviour* which is likely to result in an improvement of environmental conditions. The model developed here may suggest some useful avenues. The conflict shown between the self-interest of particular persons and an outcome desired by the population as a whole can be overcome by using the *political mechanism*. Though only few people are really ready to give up behaviour harmful to the environment, they may nevertheless be prepared to act in an environmentally responsible way, provided that all other persons act in the same manner (Baumol 1965). As this happens in a spontaneous way only in the special case of a small group with imitative behaviour (as shown in the model developed), individuals can rationally demand that all members of society are *forced* to act in an environmentally responsible way. Thus, political action can make it possible to achieve "imitative" behaviour which would result in a quality of the environment desired by society as a whole. According to our model, such a contract can even transpire voluntarily by mutual consent. The well-intended activities to promote behaviour consistent with environmental ethics should change direction and resort to the political process. This would help to avoid disappointment and to achieve an effective protection of our environment.

General References to the Literature

Introductions into environmental economics are
> Baumol, William J. and Oates, Wallace E. *Economics, Environmental Problems and the Quality of Life.* Englewood Cliffs: Prentice-Hall, 1979.
> Siebert, Horst. *Economics of the Environment: Theory and Policy.* Tübingen: Mohr (Siebeck), 1987.

Related problems in resource economics are discussed in
> Dasgupta, Parta. *The Control of Resources.* Oxford: Blackwell, 1982.

A somewhat sceptical view of the use of environmental charges is provided by

Kelman, Steven. *What Price Incentives? Economists and the Environment.*
Boston: Auborn House, 1981.

The incentives and limits of free riding in the presence of public goods are
discussed in

Olson, Mancur. *The Logic of Collective Action.* Cambridge, Mass.: Harvard
University Press, 1965.

which also contains several applications. Experimental results on the
conditions for, and the extent of, free riding are collected in

Dawes, Robyn M. and Thaler, Richard H. "Anomalies: Cooperation."
Journal of Economic Perspectives 2 (Summer 1988): 187–197.

4 POLITICS: UNEMPLOYMENT AND NATIONAL SOCIALISM

Background

The role of the Great Depression as a causal factor in the fall of the Weimar Republic has been and still is controversial. Was the rise of the National Socialists and other totalitarian parties due to the high rate of unemployment in the years 1930 to 1933? Would the historical development have been different if the economic crisis had not worsened after 1930? Three answers to these questions may be found in the literature (see Bracher 1964; Hentschel 1978; or Jasper 1968):

1. Some authors stress the political and institutional difficulties with which the first German democracy was faced. The Weimar Republic was identified with what was felt to be the shameful conditions of the Versailles treaty. Moreover, the Weimar constitution itself had basic shortcomings. The founding fathers of the Federal Republic of Germany considered these weaknesses of the constitution to be a very strong factor in the Weimar Republic's fall, so they introduced quite different institutional provisions into the 1949 constitution (Grundgesetz) of the Federal Republic, for example, the indirect election of the chancellor by parliament.

51

2. Other authors consider the nature of the then existing socio-demographic and religious groups to be the main reason for the Weimar Republic's breakdown (e.g., Pollock 1944; Lipset 1960). It is maintained that the Nazi party was strongly supported by the rural population, which was heavily hit by the agricultural crisis, and by the bourgeois middle class, which had been impoverished by the preceding hyperinflation and which felt that its social position was threatened. The Catholics and workers, on the other hand, resisted the Nazi movement until 1933 (see Brown 1982). A great number of first-time voters in the period 1930 to 1933 had no clear party identification and therefore became easy prey for the National Socialists (e.g., O'Lessker 1968).

3. A third group of authors sees the main reason for the fall of the Weimar Republic in the economic depression that took place in the period under study (e.g., Helbich 1968; Borchardt 1979). The economic crisis is considered to have been an extremely important factor, if not the only one.

There is little in the literature about the relative importance of these three sets of factors. In order to understand this crucial period in history, it is important to know what the *relative* effect of the various determinants was. This chapter looks at the impact of the sociodemographic determinants and the economic depression on the outcome of the parliamentary elections and evaluates the relative importance of these factors for the vote shares of the parties; in particular, those of the National Socialists separately and the totalitarian parties taken together. Special emphasis will be laid on the role of unemployment. The influence of the Versailles treaty and the specific characteristics of the Weimar constitution cannot be quantitatively studied within the context considered here because these conditions did not vary over the period 1930 to 1933 and consequently cannot be related to *differences* in vote shares over time and regions. After determining the relative importance of socioeconomic factors and the depression, a *Gedankenexperiment* is performed in order to determine what would *hypothetically* have happened if the economic crisis had not worsened after 1930. This experiment may also be considered as an ex post scenario of possible events.

Elections in the Weimar Republic have been the subject of various quantitative studies (e.g., Mellen 1943; Heberle 1945; Bendix 1952). One of the most important is by Kaltefleiter (1966), who studied the influence of economic conditions on the vote shares of various parties. He proceeded by choosing precincts that were similar in all respects except the one whose influence was to be studied. His analysis is mainly verbal, with no statistical inferences being drawn with the help of correlation or regression techniques. Despite its great merits, Kaltefleiter's work can no longer be considered satisfactory from today's point of view because he did not employ the modern econometric methods now at everybody's disposal. His choice of precincts was not based on objective criteria, and the economic and sociodemographic influences were considered in sequence, not simultaneously.

Another important and more recent contribution is by Shively (1972), who tests the theory of party identification, arguing that the shorter the period of time that someone was able to vote, the more likely it was that he or she would vote for Hitler. Shively's analysis is open to the same criticism as Kaltefleiter's, because he uses the same criteria for choosing the precincts and also compares them by nonreproducible methods. A study closely related to our work is that by Brown (1982) who analyzes the simultaneous influence of occupation (or class), religion, and voter participation on the Nazi vote share in July 1932. In a logit regression analysis he uses cross-sectional data of the districts covering the whole area of the Weimar Republic. However, the possible influence of the economic depression (unemployment) on voter decisions is totally ignored. Another study is by Wernette (1976), who explains the *change* in votes for the National Socialists from one election to the next, based on a cross-section study of 1,100 precincts. Wernette introduces a great many (16) explanatory variables in a rather ad hoc manner and without any clear pattern, using a curious mixture of levels and changes in independent variables. The depression is measured by the absolute number of unemployed, not as a percentage share of the working population. The specific functional forms of the test equations are not explained. No theoretical hypotheses are explicitly developed and tested; the author includes those explanatory variables that give the best fit. In the end, Wernette concludes that "the findings show that the benefits of unemployment for the Nazis are limited to the 1930 election. Economic distress gives initial impetus to the growth of a fascist movement. Beyond that point its effects are insignificant." In our *Gedankenexperiment* we will test exactly this conclusion.

The data indeed suggest a connection between the vote share of the National Socialists (Nationalsozialistische Deutsche Arbeiterpartei, NSDAP) in the election to the Reichstag (German parliament) and the state of unemployment. In Figure 4–1 the four last elections to the Reichstag of the Weimar Republic (1930–1933) are marked by vertical lines. (More extensive data on the economic and political situation are presented in tables 4–A and 4–B in the appendix to this chapter.)

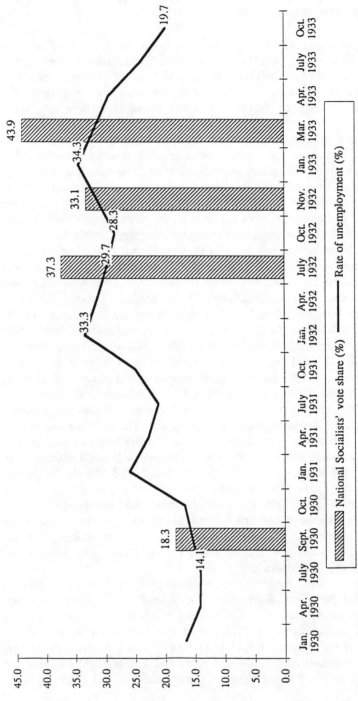

Figure 4–1. Rate of Unemployment and Vote Share of the National Socialists. Elections to the Reichstag in the Weimar Republic, 1930–1933.

The Nazi share in total votes rose dramatically from 18.3% in the Reichstag election of September 14, 1930, to 37.3% in the election of July 31, 1932. The rate of unemployment rose equally dramatically from 14.1% (July 1930) to 29.7% (July 1932) of the work force. The vote gain of the National Socialists was thus in line with the escalating economic crisis. When the second election in the year 1932 took place (November 6), the height of the slump seems to have been passed: it had reached a maximum with 6 million unemployed in the first quarter of 1932. By October 1932 the rate of unemployment dropped to 28.3% of the work force. Again we observe a parallel development of the Nazi vote share as the NSDAP got "only" 33.1% of the total votes in the November 1932 election. The improvement of economic conditions proved, however, to be only temporary. The rate of unemployment rose again to 34.3% in January 1933. On January 10, 1933 Hitler was appointed chancellor (Reichskanzler) so that the elections of March 5, 1933 already took place under Nazi rule. The vote share of the National Socialists rose in line with the unemployment rate to 43.9%. This election took place under special conditions. Though it seems that the Nazis did not commit any outright manipulation of the election outcome, the population was terrorized by National Socialist groups (such as the Sturm-Abteilung, SA), and the political opponents were intimidated by arrests, the euphemistically called "protective imprisonment" (Schutzhaft), and psychological pressure. The right to assemble and the freedom of the press were restricted, while the National Socialists could freely agitate and received election support by government institutions.

The importance of the aforementioned structural factors (the specific behaviour of the farmers, the Catholics and the workers) and of the business cycle factors are analyzed here with the help of econometric methods in order to explain the vote share of the National Socialists and of other parties in the Weimar Republic. A particular effort is made to adequately explain the influence of the rate of unemployment on election outcomes. The period covers the years 1930 to 1933 because it saw the rise of the National Socialists and the breakdown of the Weimar Republic. Attention is focused on the vote share of the NSDAP, but the vote shares of other parties, in particular the other totalitarian parties, the Deutsch-Nationale Volkspartei (DNVP, an extreme right-wing party) and the Communist Party (KPD), are also considered.

In the following section the analysis of voter behaviour in an empirical political economy (politometrics) is applied to the present time (American presidential elections) and to the historical period mentioned (Weimar Republic). The third section discusses the theoretical hypotheses used to explain the rise of National Socialism, and explains the estimation approach and data used. The estimation results are presented in section four; the fifth section draws some conclusions. (The econometric estimates are shown and interpreted in the appendix to this chapter.)

Estimation of Vote and Popularity Functions

The General Approach

One of the most important determinants of clcction outcomes is the state of the economy. Voters tend to make the government responsible for the economic conditions obtaining, as they assume that the government can influence them. When unemployment and inflation rise, the support for the government drops. A higher rate of growth of the economy benefits the government's vote share. The vote share of the opposition parties changes in the opposite way. The voters' behaviour can be measured by the vote share or by popularity indices which are collected by public opinion surveys.

The vote and popularity functions not only consider economic influences in the form of the rate of unemployment, the rate of inflation, and the rate of growth of real disposable income but also sociodemographic and more narrowly political factors. The latter are composed of those influences on voting behaviour depending on the current political situation, such as scandals (e.g., Watergate under President Nixon) or foreign policy events (such as wars).

The research undertaken for industrial countries of the post-war period strongly suggests that unemployment, inflation and real income growth have a systematic effect on government popularity (see e.g., the survey by Schneider and Frey 1988). For the Federal Republic of Germany in the period 1957 to 1975 an estimate (see Frey 1983) gives the following results: A rise of inflation by one percentage point reduces (all other influences being equal, i.e., ceteris paribus) the marginal vote share (or more exactly, the popularity share) of the government by 1.5 percentage points; a rise in unemployment by one percentage point reduces the vote share by 1.7 percentage points, and a rise in the growth rate of real disposable income by one percentage point increases the government's vote share by 0.6 percentage points. The influences prove to be statistically significant.

Popularity and vote functions mainly serve to empirically show the influence of the state of the economy on politics, and to give an indication of the magnitudes involved. In particular when such evaluation functions are estimated with short-run (quarterly or even monthly) data, they can also be used for forecasting purposes.

Election of the President of the United States

The American presidential elections over the period 1916 to 1984 were the object of an econometrically estimated vote function (Fair 1987). The estimates shown and interpreted in Table 4–C of the appendix to this chapter yield the following results:

the basic vote share of a Democratic candidate amounts to 40.7% of the total vote (keeping all other influences constant). This constant picks up all sociodemographic influences;

the vote share of the Democratic Party tends to grow over time, which is captured by a trend variable;

when a Democrat runs for the succession of a Democratic president, he has a vote advantage of 0.5 percentage points;

when a Democratic president is the incumbent, he has a vote advantage of 4.5 percentage points;

when the growth rate of real GNP (Gross National Product) per capita rises by one percentage point in the second and third quarters of an election year, the vote share of a candidate whose party was in power before the election rises (ceteris paribus) by 1.0 percentage points;

when inflation rises by one percentage point in the two years preceding the election, the vote share of a candidate whose party was in power before the election falls (ceteris paribus) by 0.3 percentage points.

This estimate can be used to predict ex post the outcomes of the presidential elections. As is shown in table 4–1, the deviations between the politicoeconomic forecast and the actual election result is regularly smaller than two percentage points.

The estimated election function also performs well in the case of a "true" (ex ante) forecast. Shortly before the presidential election of November 1988, in which the Republican Bush and the Democrat Dukakis were running for the succession of the retiring Republican president Reagan, the survey research institutes predicted (and announced in the Wall Street Journal and on the television network ABC)

Table 4-1.   Results of U.S. Presidential Elections Predicted on the Basis of an
Election Function and Actual Outcome. Share of the Democratic Candidate in
Percent. (1968-1984 ex post forecasts, 1988 ex ante forecast).

			(ex post)			(ex ante)
	1968	1972	1976	1980	1984	1988
Predicted on the basis of an election function	50.2	39.6	49.7	44.7	42.5	46.0
Actual result	49.6	38.2	51.1	44.7	40.8	46.0
Difference	+0.6	+1.4	−1.4	0	1.7	0

Source: Fair (1987) and own calculations.

that the Democrat Dukakis would get 43% of the votes. The margin of
error indicated was 4 percentage points. Using the election function
estimated over the period 1916 to 1984, and introducing the growth rate
of real income of 4% (2nd and 3rd quarter of 1988) as well as the rate of
inflation over the two years before the election (also amounting to 4%)
the vote share of the Democratic candidate for the election in 1988 was
predicted to be 46% of the total vote. The actual vote share indeed
turned out to be 46%!

When an econometric estimation is applied, one of course also has to
take into account the variance around the estimate. Nevertheless, the
good *ex post* predictions presented in table 4-1 for 1968 to 1984, and the
good *ex ante* prediction for 1988 strongly suggest that the American
presidential elections are not only determined by personal factors (such as
the candidate's television appeal) or by the election strategies (as often
claimed in journalistic accounts) but also by the state of the economy:
Good economic conditions benefit the candidate of the party that had
previously been in power.

Elections to the Reichstag in the Weimar Republic

The general hypotheses underlying the vote and popularity functions
can be transferred to the conditions obtaining in the Weimar period
1930-1933. The voters, dissatisfied with the state of the economy, tended
to turn away from the parties in government and to increasingly support
the opposition parties. This implied a decision *against* the Weimar
Democracy because the opposition was mainly composed of extreme
parties of the right (NSDAP, and the much smaller DNVP) and of the

left (DKP). The existing democratic order was supported by the parties in the centre of the ideological spectrum. The hypothesis may therefore be advanced that the increasing rate of unemployment reduced the vote share of the "Weimar Parties" of the centre, and increased the vote share of the National Socialists and of the Communists. The empirical test of this hypothesis is the subject of the politometric analyses of the following two sections.

Estimation Approach

Hypotheses

Among the variables serving to account for the vote shares reached at the four elections studied are business cycle (rate of unemployment), sociodemographic (share of Catholics, of farmers, and of workers in the total population) and political (vote participation rate) factors.

The following vote shares are to be explained:

Among Totalitarian parties:

National Socialists (NSDAP);

Deutsch-Nationale Volkspartei (DNVP);

German Communist Party (DKP);

Among the Weimar parties:

Deutsche Volkspartei (DVP);

the Catholic Centre (including the Bayrische Volkspartei);

Deutsche Staatspartei (DStP);

German Social Democratic Party (SPD);

The vote shares of these parties in the four Reichstag elections 1930 to 1933 are given in table 4–A in the appendix.

On the basis of the literature briefly reviewed above, the following theoretical hypotheses may be formulated:

1. When economic conditions worsen, the vote share of the National Socialists and of the totalitarian parties rises overall, and the vote share of the parties supporting the Weimar Republic falls;

2. When the vote participation increases, the National Socialists may gain from the votes additionally mobilized;

3. The more Catholics there are in a precinct, the higher is the vote share of the Weimar parties (in particular of the Catholic Centre), and the smaller the vote share of all totalitarian parties;

4. The more persons there are in a precinct who have agricultural occupations (farmers), the larger is the vote share of the National Socialists (and of the ideologically related DNVP), and the smaller the vote share of the Communists and the Weimar parties.

5. The more workers there are in a precinct, the more votes are received by the Communist Party, and the less by the extreme parties of the right, NSDAP and DNAP.

Data and Estimation Method

A time series analysis of the four elections between 1930 and 1933 provides too few observations to study the influence of economic, socio-demographic and political factors on elections. A larger number of observations are reached if the election results in the various regions of the Weimar Republic are considered. Such a cross-section analysis requires that the statistical data for the political (vote share), the economic (rate of unemployment) and sociodemographic factors which were collected according to different geographic criteria, are harmonized. The complete data set resulting is available for 13 regions. (The economic and political data for each of these regions are given in Frey and Weck 1981, 1983.)

The rate of unemployment in the labour force of the 13 regions strongly differs. In July 1932, for example, when average unemployment in Germany was 29.7% overall, in Eastern Prussia it was "only" 15.7%, in Pomerenia 19.9%, and in South-West Germany 21.3%, while in the Rhineland it amounted to 34.0% and in Saxony 36.4%.

Among the 13 regions distinguished there are also great differences with respect to the sociodemographic structure:

Share of Catholics: it is highest in Bavaria with 70%, and in the Rhineland with 66.8% of the total population, and it is lowest in Saxony and Pomerenia with 3.6%.

Share of farmers: the rural regions, East Prussia with 55.7%, Pomerenia with 50.7% and Bavaria with 43.7% of the population in farming. Saxony with 12.4%, Brandenburg with 18.4% and the

Rhineland with 19.3% have a relatively low share of farmers in the population.

Share of workers: this share is highest in Saxony and Westfalia with roughly 54% of the work force. Lower shares obtain for Hessia, Bavaria and South-West Germany with 36–40%.

The differences between regions were also large for the vote shares of the various parties. In the first election considered (September 1930), for example, the National Socialists received 23.4% of the votes in the Nordmark, 22.8% in Pomerenia, 22.5% in East Prussia, and 22.3% in Saxony. Their vote share was, on the other hand, only 13% in Westfalia, 15.3% in South-West Germany and 15.9% in the Rhineland. But they also received only 17.4% of the votes in protestant Brandenburg.

Estimation Results

The *pooled* cross-section and time-series analysis yielding $13 \times 4 = 52$ observations allows us to reach results for the overall period. It is implicitly assumed that the influences across regions may be interpreted in the same way as over time. Due to the sufficiently large number of observations the estimates are statistically trustworthy.

The results of the econometric estimates are presented and explained in table 4–D of the appendix. The table shows the estimated parameter values and their statistical significance. This multiple variable approach allows us to capture the simultaneous influence of economic, socio-demographic and political factors on the vote share of the various parties in the Weimar Republic, and to assess their quantitative importance.

The empirical estimate is able to account for a significant part of the differences in the vote share of the various parties in the 13 regions and elections. The share of the regional and temporal differences of election outcomes (i.e., the variance) explained is 91.4% for the National Socialists, and even 97.8% for the Catholic Centre. The share of the variance explained by the model employed lies between 63% and 98%. The signs of the parameters derived empirically correspond to a large extent to the theoretical hypotheses advanced. The results for selected parties are:

National Socialists

The expected highly positive influence of rising unemployment on the vote share of the NSDAP is clearly borne out (see estimation equation

(1) in table 4–D). A rise in the rate of unemployment by 10 percentage points (over time or between regions) is accompanied by an increase in the National Socialist vote share of 10.1 percentage points. Unemployment makes the most important contribution to explaining the NSDAP vote share. The Nazis also benefited from a higher vote participation. A greater share of Catholics in a region leads, on the other hand, to a significantly lower vote share of the National Socialists. The more farmers there are in a region, the more votes the Nazis received. This is an important factor explaining the vote share of the National Socialists. The influences mentioned correspond to the theoretical hypotheses advanced. However, a larger share of workers in a region does not, as expected, lower the Nazi vote share in a statistically significant way (but the corresponding coefficient points to a negative relationship).

The Communist Party

Unemployment benefited the KPD (see estimation equation (3)) significantly, but the corresponding parameter value of 0.18 indicates only a quantitatively small effect. A rising vote participation rate affected it negatively in a significant and extensive way. While the Communists could count on the continued support of some voters, new voters tended more towards other parties. It also corresponds to our theoretical expectation that a high share of workers in a region significantly increased the Communist vote share. Catholics and farmers, on the other hand, tended not to vote for this extreme left-wing party.

The Parties of the Weimar Coalition

The Deutsche Volkspartei (estimation equation (4)) was negatively affected by rising unemployment. In regions with a higher share of people in agriculture its vote share was significantly lower. The Catholic Centre (equation (5)) received its votes mainly from the Catholic population, as theoretically proposed. This factor explains by far the largest part of the Centre's election results. A higher participation rate by voters, on the other hand, implied vote losses. The Deutsche Staatspartei (estimation equation (6)) also lost votes with rising unemployment. It also experienced a significant vote loss in regions with a higher share of Catholics, farmers, and workers. The Social Democratic Party (equation (7)) was made responsible by voters for the escalating economic crisis; the higher the rate of unemployment was, the lower was its vote share. In contrast to the other Weimar parties, the SPD could profit from a higher vote participation; when this rate increased by 10 percentage points, the SPD vote share rose by 3.1 percentage points. As expected, the vote share of the Social Democrats is smaller (ceteris paribus), the larger the share of Catholics and farmers.

What Would Have Happened Without Economic Depression?

The theoretical hypotheses advanced have been well supported by empirical analysis. The *economic crisis*, captured by the rise in unemployment, had a *dominant influence* on the vote share of the various parties and groupings in the elections to the Reichstag. There is strong evidence that increasing unemployment significantly contributed to the rise of National Socialism and to the fall of the Weimar Republic. The vote share of the totalitarian parties opposed to democracy was strongly pushed up by unemployment, and the vote share of those parties supporting the Weimar Republic was appreciably diminished.

On the basis of the econometric analysis it is possible to calculate the hypothetical vote share that would have been reached by the National Socialists if the economic situation had not worsened after 1930. Estimation equation (1) in table 4–D suggests that an increase in the rate of unemployment of one percentage point caused the NSDAP vote share to rise by 1.01 percentage points. Between the election of September 1930 and the election of July 1932, the unemployment rate grew on average by 15.6 percentage points in the German Reich. Keeping all other influences constant, the rise in the rate of unemployment increased the National Socialist vote share by 1.01×15.6 (percentage points) = 15.8 percentage points. With unchanged economic conditions (i.e., an unemployment rate of 14.1%) the vote share of the NSDAP in the July 1932 election would have been around 21.5%, and not 37.3%. In an analogous way the National Socialist vote share can be computed for the other two elections. Overall, we have the following comparison (table 4–2):

This comparison indicates that the spectacular increase of the Nazi vote in the 1930s can mainly be attributed to the high unemployment rate. Under better economic conditions, the vote share of the National Socialists would not have exceeded 29%. It is also shown that the high vote share of 43.9% of the NSDAP in the election of March 1933 is

Table 4–2. Actual and hypothetical vote share of National Socialists, 1930–33.

	Elections			
	Sept. 1930	July 1932	Nov. 1932	March 1933
Actual	18.3%	37.3%	33.1%	43.9%
Hypothetical (no worsening of economic conditions since 1930)	18.3%	21.5%	18.8%	28.5%

mainly due to the increase in unemployment to 43.3% (January 1933), and—according to our calculations—less to the fact that the population more strongly supported the chancellor Hitler for ideological reasons, or that it was intimidated strongly by the terrorist activities of the Nazis.

The state of the economy is a most important, but certainly not the only factor explaining election outcomes in the Weimar Republic. The *sociodemographic influences* also matter. The hypotheses taken from the literature are supported; the larger the share of Catholics in a region, the higher is the vote share of the Weimar parties, especially of the Catholic Centre. The vote share of the totalitarian parties, on the other hand, is significantly lower. In regions mainly composed of an agrarian population the vote share of the NSDAP and the DNVP is particularly high, while a high share of workers mainly benefited the Communists and the DNVP.

One hypothesis found in the pertinent literature, and discussed in the first section of this chapter, can be rejected. It can no longer be claimed that unemployment was not a major cause for the fall of the Weimar Republic. The analysis undertaken here does not state whether the votes going to the Nazi and other totalitarian parties were cast by the unemployed themselves. What has been shown is that the totalitarian parties greatly benefited from unemployment, in particular the NSDAP. The votes they received may have come from people who were (still) employed but who, worried by the high unemployment and the bad economic conditions, turned to the radicals of the right and left.

Using popularity and vote functions, it has been demonstrated empirically that unemployment had in principle the same effect on the party (or parties) in government in representative democracies of the postwar period. The vote loss suffered by the parties supporting the Weimar Republic, and the vote gain made by the totalitarian parties, as a result of the economic depression, may in this sense be considered a "normal" event, not necessarily reflecting the special situation of the Weimar Republic.

The cyclical development of the vote share of the various parties—and above all the rise, decline and renewed rise of the National Socialists— can only be explained by cyclical, and not by structural, factors. It has been shown in this chapter that business fluctuations are one such cyclical factor influencing vote shares in a statistically significant way. This suggests that long-run structural influences (such as the short-comings of the Weimar constitution, the burden of the Versailles treaty, but also sociodemographic factors) should be considered *indirect* causes for the short-run fluctuations in vote shares. Historical research should be concentrated on explaining *in what way* the structural factors have motivated people hit, or at least frightened, by the economic depression to vote for totalitarian parties. This includes the question of why such voters favoured more strongly right wing and not left wing extremist parties.

Politometrics is only *one* of many possible and useful avenues to study a particular historical period. The method of multiple regression based on pooled cross-section and time series data allows an approach to aspects so far little analyzed in historical research. It is not a substitute for a detailed study of socio-economic processes using the instruments normally used by historians. Rather, it constitutes a useful complement which may help to elucidate the relationships involved more clearly and gain a better understanding of the quantitative magnitudes involved.

General References to the Literature

The application of economics to politics, i.e., the Economic Theory of Politics or New Political Economy, is presented in

> Mueller, Dennis. *Public Choice II. 2nd ed*. Cambridge: Cambridge University Press, 1989.
>
> Frey, Bruno S. *Democratic Economic Policy*. Oxford: Blackwell, 1983.

Econometric estimates of the influence of the state of the economy on the popularity and election results of the government are presented and discussed for various countries and time periods in

> Schneider, Friedrich and Frey, Bruno S. "Politico-Economic Models of Macroeconomic Policy: A Review of the Empirical Evidence." In: Willett, Thomas D. (ed.). *The Political Economy of Money, Inflation and Unemployment*. Durham and London: Duke University Press, 1988, pp. 240–275.

Hibbs, Douglas C. *The Political Economy of Industrial Democracies.* Cambridge, Mass.: Harvard University, Press 1987.

The historical background of the Weimar Republic and National Socialism is portrayed in

Bracher, Karl Dietrich. *Die Auflösung der Weimarer Republik. Eine Studie zum Problem des Machtzerfalls in der Demokratie. 4th ed.* Villingen: Ring, 1964.

Heberle, Rudolf. *From Democracy to Nazism.* Baton Rouge: Louisiana State University Press, 1945.

Halperin, William S. *Germany Tried Democracy.* New York: Crowell, 1946.

Political science studies of voting in the Weimar Republic which may be useful for a comparison of approaches are, for example

Brown, Courtney. "The Nazi Vote: A National Ecological Study." *American Political Science Review* 76 (1982): 285–302.

Shively, W. Philips. "Party Identification, Party Choice, and Voting Stability: The Weimar Case." *American Political Science Review* 66 (1972): 1203–1224.

Appendix

Table 4–A. Vote Shares and Seats of Reichstag Elections, 1930–1933.

Parties	Sept. 14, 1930 Votes (%)	Seats	July 31, 1932 Votes (%)	Seats	Nov. 6, 1932 Votes (%)	Seats	March 5, 1933 Votes (%)	Seats
NSDAP	18.3	107	37.3	230	33.1	196	43.9	288
DNVP	7.0	41	5.9	37	8.5	52	8.0	52
DVP	4.5	30	1.2	7	1.9	11	1.1	2
Z	14.8	87	15.7	99	15.0	90	14.0	92
DStP	3.8	20	1.0	4	1.0	2	0.8	—
SPD	24.5	143	21.6	133	20.4	121	18.3	125
KPD	13.1	77	14.3	89	16.9	100	12.3	81
Totalitarian parties: NSDAP DNVP KPD	38.4	225	57.5	356	58.5	348	64.2	421
Weimar parties: DVP Z DStP SPD	47.6	280	39.5	243	38.3	224	34.2	219
Remaining parties:	14.0	62	3.0	9	3.2	12	1.6	7

NSDAP	Nationalsozialistische Deutsche Arbeiterpartei
DStP	Deutsche Staatspartei
SPD	Sozialdemokratische Partei Deutschlands
DNVP	Deutsch-Nationale Volkspartei
DVP	Deutsche Volkspartei
KPD	Kommunistische Partei Deutschlands
Z	Zentrum und Bayerische Volkspartei

Source: Statistische Jahrbücher des Deutschen Reiches, 1930–1934.

Table 4–B. Economic Development in the Weimar Republic, 1930–1933.

	1930				1931				1932				1933			
	Jan.	April	July	Oct.	Jan.	April	July	Oct.	Jan.	April	July	Oct.	Jan.	April	July	Oct.
National income (real, purchasing power as of 1928 in Mill. RM)			72320				64142				56795				59428	
Number of unemployed per 1000	3218	2787	2765	3252	4887	4358	3990	4623	6042	5739	5392	5109	6262	4761	4417	3260
Rate of unemployment in %	16.6	14.2	14.1	16.7	25.9	22.7	21.0	24.9	33.3	31.4	29.7	28.3	34.3	29.3	23.9	19.7

Source: Statistische Jahrbücher des Deutschen Reiches, 1930–1934, and own calculations.

Table 4–C.   Election Function for U.S. Presidential Elections, 1916–1984 (quarterly data).

Share of the Democratic Candidate (in percent) =	
40.7 (11.7)	Constant
+0.3·t (1.8)	t = time trend
+0.5·I (0.3)	I = 1, if a Democratic candidate follows a Democratic president, I = −1, for a Republican incumbent; I = 0 in all other cases.
+4.5·DPRES (2.7)	DPRES = 1, if a Democratic president runs for re-election; DPRES = −1, if a Republican president runs for re-election; DPRES = 0, in all other cases.
+1.0·g·I (5.0)	g = growth rate of real national product per capita in the 2nd and 3rd quarter of an election year.
−0.3·p·I (−1.13)	p = rate of inflation over the last two years before an election.
$\bar{R}^2$ = 88.7%	

Note: The vote share of the Republican and of the Democratic candidates sum to 100 percent, i.e., the small parties with extremely small vote shares are neglected. Figures in parentheses indicate the t-values.
Source: Fair (1987, p. 3).

Notes for Interpreting Table 4–C

The figures listed (no parentheses) show the parameter values estimated by multiple regression analysis. The figures below these values in parentheses show the t-values. An (absolute) t-value exceeding 2 indicates with an error probability of 5% that the corresponding value differs in a statistically significant way from zero. A positive figure shows that the respective explanatory variable has a positive effect on the vote share of the Democratic candidate running for the U.S. presidency.

In the estimate reported in Table 4–C, three parameter values have a positive sign:

1. If a Democratic candidate follows a Democratic president, the voters give him a bonus, that is, he profits from the popularity of the

predecessors of his own party. According to the estimate, this bonus is 0.5 percentage points but does not deviate in a statistically significant way from no bonus (the t-value of the parameter 0.5 amounts to 0.3 and is clearly below the significance level of 2).

2. If a president runs for re-election, he profits from a sizeable bonus by the voters, quite independent of the state of the economy. According to the econometric estimate, this bonus amounts to 4.5 percentage points and is statistically significant (the t-value is 2.7 and therewith lies clearly above the significance level of 2).

3. A rise in the growth rate of real GNP benefits a Democratic candidate who follows a Democratic president (i.e., the dummy variable I = 1). When the real growth rate increases by one percentage point (e.g., from 3% to 4% per year), his vote share rises by 1.0 percentage point (e.g., from 50% to 51%). This relationship is statistically well founded; the t-value of 5 is well above the significance level.

In an analogous way a Republican candidate benefits from good economic conditions if he strives to follow a Republican president. In this case, the dummy variable is I = −1: the *Democratic* candidate's vote share (explained by the equation) *falls* by 1.0 percentage point when the real growth rate rises by one percentage point.

If, however, a Democratic candidate wants to follow a Republican president, or a Republican candidate a Democratic president, that is, if I = 0, he does not benefit from better economic conditions.

One parameter of estimation equation table 4–C has a negative value: The higher inflation, the worse are the election prospects of a candidate running for the succession of a president of his own party. When the rate of inflation rises by one percentage point (e.g., from 5% to 6% per year), the vote share falls by 0.3 percentage points (e.g., from 50.3% to 50% of the vote).

The test statistic $\overline{R}^2$ indicates to what extent the equation can trace the vote share of the (Democratic) candidate based on the econometrically estimated model (i.e., based on the explanatory variables listed). $\overline{R}^2$ can achieve a maximum value of 100%. Estimation equation table 4–C is capable of tracing a high share (88.7%) of the election outcome of the various presidential elections.

Table 4–D. The Influence of Business Cycle, Sociodemographic and Political Factors on the Vote Share of Selected Parties. Four Elections to the Reichstag, Weimar Republic, 1930–1933. (Pooled cross section/time series estimate).

Equation Party	Constant	Explanatory Variables					$\bar{R}^2$ %
		Rate of Unemployment %	Election Participation %	Share of Catholics %	Share of Farmers %	Share of Workers %	
(1) National Socialists NSDAP	-30.5	1.01* (14.4)	0.44* (2.7)	-0.17* (-7.7)	0.53* (10.4)	-0.21 (-1.8)	91.4
(2) Deutsch-Nationale Volkspartei DNVP	3.2	0.08 (1.3)	-0.28* (-2.2)	-0.08* (-4.9)	0.24* (5.8)	0.46* (4.9)	63.4
(3) Communist Party KPD	68.7	0.18* (4.7)	-0.77* (-8.5)	-0.05* (-4.0)	-0.22* (-7.7)	0.29* (4.4)	83.5
(4) Deutsche Volkspartei DVP	4.9	-0.23* (-10.1)	0.11* (2.2)	-0.01 (1.5)	-0.09* (-5.4)	-0.06 (-1.6)	74.5
(5) Centre Z	23.4	0.00 (0.02)	-0.18* (-2.1)	0.45* (40.4)	-0.07* (-2.5)	-0.13* (-2.2)	97.8
(6) Deutsche Staatspartei DStP	11.1	-0.16* (-7.8)	0.06 (1.2)	-0.02* (-2.4)	-0.09* (-6.3)	-0.15* (-4.3)	69.6
(7) Social Democratic Party SPD	16.4	-0.29* (-4.9)	0.31* (2.3)	-0.16* (-8.7)	-0.14* (-3.3)	-0.10 (-1.0)	74.2

Note: The figures in parentheses indicate the t-values.

Notes for Interpreting Table 4−D

To facilitate understanding, some of the figures listed in this table are interpreted by way of illustration:

1. Parameter 1.01* (second figure in the first estimation equation) indicates that an increase in the rate of unemployment by one percentage point (e.g., from 20% to 21%) increased the vote share of the National Socialist Party (NSDAP) by 1.01 percentage points (e.g., from 30% to 31.01%). A rise of unemployment by ten percentage points thus increased the Nazi vote share by 10.1 percentage points. This parameter value is statistically significant; its t-value of 14.4 (shown in parentheses below the parameter estimate) lies clearly above the level of significance of 2.

2. Parameter −0.17* (fourth figure in the first estimation equation) shows that in a precinct in which the share of Catholics is one percentage point higher than elsewhere, the vote share of the National Socialists is lower by 0.17 percentage points. This vote share reduction is statistically significant, the t-value in parentheses being −7.7. Keeping all other influences constant, the difference in the share of Catholics between Bavaria (70%) and Eastern Prussia (15.1%) amounting to 54.9 percentage points explains a reduction in the Nazi vote share of −0.17 · 54.9% = 9.3% in Bavaria.

3. The estimation equation for the vote share of the National Socialists (equation (1)) is able to trace 91.4% of the differences between regions and elections. In the case of the KPD (estimation equation (3)), the share of the variance "explained" amounts to 83.5%.

4. Parameter −0.29* (second figure in estimation equation (7)) indicates that a rise in unemployment by one percentage point reduces the vote share of the Social Democratic Party (other things being unchanged) by 0.29 percentage points, which is statistically significant (the t-value is −4.9).

5 ARTS: INVESTMENTS IN PAINTINGS

Record Prices

The demand for art today is higher than ever before. Auction houses report record turnovers and absolute top prices are paid in increasingly rapid sequence. Only some years ago, Turner's *Seascape: Folkstone* had an auction price of $9.8 million at Sotheby's London. A little later van Gogh's *Landscape with Rising Sun* was sold for $9.9 million at Sotheby's New York, and Mantegna's *Adoration of the Magi* sold at Christie's London for $10.4 million. Enormous publicity greeted the sale in April 1987 of van Gogh's *Sunflowers*, which was sold at Christie's London to the Japanese insurance company Yasuda for $39.9 million. In 1907, 17 years after van Gogh's death, *Sunflowers* was offered at an exhibition in Mannheim for DM 12,000 (roughly $3,000). Two years later, again in Mannheim, it was offered for DM 28,000 (roughly $7,000). Edith Batty is said to have acquired it in 1934 for DM 63,000 (about $24,000) from the Parisian art dealer Paul Rosenberg. After the deduction of all costs involved, the investment of DM 63,000 yielded a *yearly* rate of return of 11.4%. This return is far above the rate of inflation which was approximately 6.7% per annum in that period. The *real* rate of return of 4.7%

73

per annum is also higher than the return from most kinds of financial investment, say in gold or in securities. Wendell Cherry, the last owner of Picasso's self-portrait *Yo, Picasso*, a 1901 post-impressionist painting, did even better. In 1981 he bought the painting at an auction for $5.83 million; he sold it by auction in 1989 for $47.85 million, achieving a real net rate of return of 19.6% per annum.

Over the past few years, the list of record prices paid at auctions changed ever more rapidly. The enormous prices fetched for some paintings create a widespread belief that the rate of return on investments in paintings and art is in general very high. Especially in the United States, an increasing number of investors believe that purchasing art provides not only aesthetic pleasure but also financial remuneration. American banks, and recently also auction houses, strengthen the trend of viewing art as an investment by extending credit and by hiring "art investment counsellors" thus suggesting that it is financially rewarding to buy art. While such tendencies can also be seen in some financial circles in Europe, art lovers and investment advisers are more hesitant. Many warn that art objects are unsuitable for portfolio diversification. Most art collectors share this feeling, arguing that art should be owned for its intrinsic value rather than for financial reasons.

Who is right? Does investment in paintings yield a higher rate of return than comparable forms of investment? Should paintings be bought for financial profit? The following section discusses the specific features of returns and risk in art auctions. The result of empirical studies for extended time periods are presented in the third section, and the fourth section considers the question of whether it is possible to predict future art prices.

Art Auctions

In principle, the rate of return and the risk inherent in buying and holding paintings is calculated in the same way as for investments in financial markets. However, paintings differ significantly from shareholdings, in various respects.

Returns

Prices of paintings bought and sold are not generally available; information is generally restricted to auctions. However, auction prices play an important role in art markets, because collectors and professional art dealers take these prices as guideposts. The rate of return is calculated by taking the continuous compound rate of interest resulting from the difference between (gross) buying price and (net) selling price. The rate of return thus is net of all cost connected with buying and selling a painting in an auction. These transaction costs vary between countries, periods and prices of the paintings traded, but they are usually substantial. Insurance costs amount to something like 0.5% of the object's value. A typical auction fee amounts to more than 10% of the value reached, for both buyer and seller. The sales commissions (including indirect taxes) for both sides of the market are currently close to 20% in the United States, 25% in the United Kingdom and Switzerland, up to 32% in France and about 35% in Germany.

Due to these insurance premia and auction fees, the price of a picture must rise steeply simply in order to cover these costs, provided the owner intends to make a profit when selling. In addition, inflation must be taken into account. Though rather obvious, this fact is frequently not sufficiently borne in mind.

In order to envisage the magnitudes involved, consider the painting *Yo, Picasso*, which was sold for $47.85 million on May 9, 1989 at Sotheby's New York. Merely in order to make up for inflation (assumed to be the same as in the period 1970–1988, that is, 6.2% per annum), the value must rise to $65 million in five years' time (by 1994). Moreover, if the present owner wants to cover the auction fees (assuming them to be 10% for buyer and seller) as well as insurance premia, the selling price in 1994 must rise to $81 million. Thus, already in five years, the monetary value of *Yo, Picasso* must appreciate by not less than $33 million before the owner breaks even. If, moreover, he wants to earn a profit—assume the real annual rate of return of three percent on U.S. government securities obtained over the period 1970–1988—the price of the painting must rise to $94 million by 1994. If, however, the present owner expects to gain the same real return as the previous owner of the painting— 19.6% per annum in real terms—*Yo, Picasso's* value would have to appreciate by $168 million to not less than $216 million by 1994. It is not surprising that such price increases required to compensate for inflation, plus auction and insurance fees, are often not realized.

Risks

An investment in the art market is subject to various kinds of risk beyond the uncertainty of future prices.

Despite all efforts to establish clarity, the problem of authenticity sometimes remains tricky. Jan van Eyck's *St. Francis*, for instance, was bought for £8 in 1828 by Sir William O'Court as a painting by Albrecht Dürer, but when it was identified as having been painted by van Eyck it reached a price of £700 in 1884. The opposite case is Rembrandt's *Saskia as Minerva*. In 1931 this picture was bought in Munich for RM 80,000 (about £6,700), and in London in 1965 it reached a price of £125,300. Thereafter, Horst Gerson, a Dutch art expert, wrote in his list of works of Rembrandt about the "Minerva" (no. 469) that "personally I doubt the attribution [to Rembrandt]." When the picture was auctioned in 1975 in Paris by Ader, Picard and Tajan, it reached a price of only FF 1.3 million (£144,000), a clear loss in real terms. Similarly, Peter Paul Rubens' *Daniel in the Lions' Den* was auctioned in 1882 for £1,680 by Christie's of London, and was resold in 1885 for £2,520. In 1963, having been attributed in the meantime to Jacob Jordaens, it was auctioned for a mere £500; but in 1965, now acknowledged as a school piece by Rubens, it was acquired by the Metropolitan Museum of Art in New York for £178,600.

There is a similar problem with fakes and forgeries. Even art experts cannot *guarantee* that a painting is original. While the technical means for detection continue to improve, the forgers also steadily employ the newest technologies for their purpose. So it has been claimed that there are 8,000 paintings by Camille Corot in the United States alone. This is an astonishing number, considering that there are only 3,000 authentic works by that master (Harris 1961). The situation is similar for various other painters, in particular for pictures by Antony van Dyck and Maurice Utrillo (Cole 1955; Graner 1976).

Finally, there is a purely material risk as well: the painting may be destroyed by fire, damaged by war or stolen. This happened, for example, to the *Gran Canal Venice* by Richard Parkes Bonington, which sold for £409 in 1834 and for £3,150 in 1878, but was partly mutilated by fire in 1902; it then reached only £84 in an auction. Although for the last two centuries at least most English and American collectors were spared the risk caused by wars and revolutions, art thefts have increased over time as auction prices have risen. According to the International Foundation of Art Research, the number of reported art thefts tripled during the last decade of strongly rising picture prices, while the number of recoveries declined from 22% to 5%. However, when a painting bought solely for financial reasons is kept in a bank vault, these costs can be significantly reduced. Maintenance and restoration costs of paintings, which can be substantial, are also often ignored. For these reasons, the calculated rate of return on investments in paintings is likely to be biased in the upward direction as only financial risks are considered.

Empirical Studies

Long Period Returns

Art historian Gerald Reitlinger, in his three volume *The Economics of Taste* (1961, 1970), has collected auction prices for paintings over more than three centuries. He only considers "important works of the best-known painters of the world" and concentrates on auctions in London, and later also in New York (mostly at Sotheby's and Christie's).

Baumol (1986) has studied the price changes of pictures that have changed hands at least twice between 1652 and 1960, utilizing Reitlinger's (restricted) data set. The real rate of return on paintings that he calculates for this period is 0.6% per annum. The corresponding real rate of return for government securities amounts to 2.5% per annum. A representative investor would therefore have experienced a loss of nearly 2% per annum. Baumol finds that investment in paintings is quite risky. On average, the real rate of return ranged between −19% and +27% per annum. In 40% of all transactions there was an absolute loss in real terms, while 60% of all transactions yielded a rate of return lower than that received for government securities.

Another study (Anderson 1974) also includes the decade 1960 to 1970, and considers additional sources of data. He finds that the *nominal* rate of return on paintings is 3.3% per annum on average, which is roughly half as high as the return for financial assets. The standard deviation of the rate of return on the two assets, paintings and stocks is 56% and 12% respectively.

A third study (Stein 1977) concentrates on auctions held in the United States and Great Britain between 1946 and 1968. He finds that the *nominal* rate of return on paintings is 10.5% per annum, compared to 14.3% for financial assets in the same period. In real terms, a representative investor would have lost 3.8% per annum. Stein, too, shows that the prices of paintings fluctuate much more than prices in financial assets, which suggests that art investment is riskier than investment in financial assets.

Frey and Pommerehne (1989b) have extended Reitlinger's data up to 1987, and have included auction data from France, Germany and the Netherlands. As there is a consensus that short-term speculation in art is financially unprofitable (partly due to the high commission fees and other transaction costs connected with auctions) only holding periods of 20 years or more between buying and selling a picture are considered. The sample includes over 2000 observations over the period 1635–1987. The prices paid are deflated by a price index, and the considerable costs involved in the transactions (which vary according to period, country and auction house) are also taken into account. A typical auction fee would amount to more than 10% of the value for both the buyer and the seller.

According to these calculations, the average *real* rate of return for investment in paintings amounts to 1.5% per annum over this 350 year period. As a comparison, an investor into best credits, in particular government securities, would have enjoyed a long-term real rate of return of a little more than 3% per annum. Thus, an investment into paintings (as opposed to financial assets) would have incurred a real opportunity cost of somewhat less than 2 percentage points a year. This is a sizeable amount: the real rate of return on paintings is half the real return on public securities.

It may be argued that financially motivated investments in paintings began on a large scale only after the Second World War. For this reason, the rate of return before and after 1950 was calculated. The real rate of return on paintings for the period 1635 to 1949 amounts to 1.4% per annum. This rate of return is clearly lower than the corresponding real returns on government securities, which would be about 3.3% per annum. A representative investor in paintings would thus have suffered a real opportunity cost of nearly 2 percentage points by not investing in public securities in the period before 1950.

From 1950 to 1987 the real rate of return on paintings was 1.6% per annum. An investor in financial assets in this period would have reaped a real return of almost 2.5% per annum. In this more recent period the representative investor in paintings would thus have incurred a real opportunity cost of a little more than half a percentage point per annum. The main reason why investments in paintings have become *relatively* more attractive than those in financial assets (the real opportunity cost has fallen from 2 to half a percentage point) is not so much an increase in the real return on paintings as an increase in the rate of inflation, which rose from half a percent per annum before 1950 to over 5% per year after 1950, and which has not been fully reflected in the nominal rates of interest on long-term credits. As a result, investments in long-term credits have become less attractive (the real return falling from 3.3% to 2.3% per annum). A lower rate of inflation would produce the opposite effect: If in the future inflation returned to pre-1950 levels, investors in paintings (as opposed to financial investments) would presumably incur even higher real opportunity cost than they do today.

Not only are the rates of return on investment in paintings surprisingly small; they also fluctuate widely and hence are quite risky. In the postwar period the average real rates of return ranged between −19% and +16% (for the period 1635–1950 between −16% and +26%). In real terms, nearly one third of all transactions resulted in an absolute loss. For more than half the transactions (55%), the profitability was lower than would have been the case had one invested in public securities. Similar results characterized the period before 1950. For both periods of time, there is more volatility in the rates of return for paintings than for financial assets.

The average results may be illustrated by reference to some individual paintings and painters. Who are the big winners and losers? The highest real rate of return (above 26% per annum) in the sample was reached by Frans Hals' *Man in Black*, which in 1885 was auctioned for a little more than £5 at Christie's in London, and in 1913 reached £9,000 at Sotheby's in London. Other pictures by Hals have achieved rates of return of approximately 10% in real terms in the last two centuries. Similar high rates of return could have been realized by investors in paintings by well-known artists such as Cézanne, Gauguin, van Gogh, Manet, Matisse, Monet and Renoir. Even with these famous painters, however, some transactions have resulted in low, and sometimes even negative, real rates of return.

The worst investment in financial terms revealed in our sample is John Singer Sargent's oil sketch *San Virgilio* which in 1925 was sold for £7,350 but in 1952 was auctioned for only £105 at Christie's of London. The real rate of return to the unfortunate owner was −19.3% per annum. Other painters who produced works that were sold at great real financial loss include Sir Lawrence Alma-Tadema, Carlo Crivelli, John Hoppner, William H. Hunt, Sir Edwin Landseer, Frederick Lord Leighton, Sir John Millais, Sir Joshua Reynolds and David Roberts. Not surprisingly, most of these painters are not generally known among today's art lovers because their art went out of fashion. Some of these artists, however, have met with increasing interest recently, so their works have produced positive real rates of return in the last few years.

Collections

It may be argued—and quite rightly—the what matters in investment is not the return on individual items but rather on the portfolio as a whole.

In the case of investment in paintings, the question is thus whether *collections* are financially profitable.

Consider the case of the American art investor Gerald Guterman. In the years 1981 to 1986 he acquired 47 Dutch and Flemish Old Masters with the intention of selling them shortly thereafter in order to achieve a high rate of return. The "collection" was sold in January 1988 at Sotheby's New York, a major media event. But 17 of the 47 paintings could not be sold at the stated minimum price. More than one third of the paintings thus did not reach a price expected by Guterman; from a speculative point of view this must be considered a bad investment.

The buying prices for 14 of the 30 paintings auctioned were publicly available. Guterman had invested $2.7 million in these 14 paintings; in 1988 they sold for $4.8 million (including selling fees). The real net rate of return was 3.2% per annum. While this return is fairly good, Guterman would have done much better if he had invested in U.S. government bonds. With minimal transaction fees he could have reached a yearly real return of 6.9%. If he had bought industrial shares instead, the appreciation in their value would have brought him a real return of 7.7% per annum (to which dividend payments could be added). In the case of the Guterman collection, an alternative investment in purely financial assets would have been more profitable than speculating in Old Masters.

In 1979 a whole collection was sold by the Swiss textile producer Hans Mettler. His paintings were acquired between 1915 and 1979 and were then sold at Christie's in London for SFr. 9.6 million. The 24 paintings auctioned were mainly impressionist works by Matisse, Toulouse-Lautrec, Pissarro, van Gogh, Cézanne, Renoir and Utrillo, but also Dufy and Hodler. The average rate of return of this investment—weighted by the corresponding initial expenditure for each painting—amounts to 4.9% in nominal, and 2.8% in real terms, after deducting auction and insurance fees. If Mettler had invested the same amount of money in Swiss federal bonds he would have earned 1.2% in real terms, which is significantly less than the financial return on his collection. If he had invested in shares, their value would have appreciated by 1.9% per annum in real terms, to which the dividends could be added. The latter would have amounted to (at least) 1%–2% per annum, so that the real total rate of return on shares would have been between 3% and 4% per annum, which is higher than the return on the collection of paintings.

The highest financial return on Mettler's collection was reached by Odile Redon's picture *Fleurs éxotiques* which in 1923 was acquired for SFr. 7,000 and sold in 1979 for SFr. 966,680. The nominal value rose by nearly SFr. 960,000, or 138 times the initial price. Nevertheless, the real net rate of return is "only" 5.8% per annum. A somewhat lower real net return (5.3% per annum) was reached by Henri Matisse's *Concour sur le tapis bleu et rose* (bought in 1918 for SFr. 7,000, and sold in 1979 for SFr. 706,440). Corresponding returns of 4.6% and 4.5% were achieved by Kees van Dongen's *Yung Ting couchée* and Redon's *Fleures assorties dans une cruche*, respectively.

Two paintings in Mettler's collection yielded a return of less than 1% per annum: Maurice Utrillo's *La rue Lépic, Montmartre avec le moulin de Galette et le Sacré Coeur* was sold with a nominal gain of SFr. 104,480 but the real net return was only 0.8% per annum. The same applies for André Derain's *Vue sur Bandol* which in 1922 was bought for SFr. 6,010, and in 1979 was auctioned for SFr. 53,910.

The decision of the British Rail Pension Fund to invest in art attracted great attention in the world of art. This is the first institution which included art in its portfolio for purely financial reasons and with the explicit purpose of selling it at a profit. In the last two decades, nearly $90 million were invested in art (but this was less than one percent of the total investment of this Pension Fund). In addition to Asian art, impressionists, modern art, British painters and old masters were bought.

Starting in 1987, in British Rail Pension Fund began to sell at Sotheby's London. The auctions of old masters and Asian art brought satisfactory returns. Some of the paintings appreciated even sensationally in value, in particular Thomas Gainsborough's *A Boy Leading a Donkey on a Hilly Path*, which in 1978 was acquired for £10,000 and in 1987 was auctioned for £140,000. The total return of the first sales was nevertheless rather modest. After deducting the rate of inflation (which in Britain was high in this period) the real net rate of return was only 3% per annum.

In April 1989, 25 impressionist paintings, drawings and sculptures were auctioned at Sotheby's, arousing the interest of the media. This part of the "collection" was acquired between 1975 and 1979 for £27.9 million and was now sold for £38.2 million (in both cases excluding auction fees). The highest annual net return was reached by Picasso's *Le garçon bleu*, which was bought for £26,400 and sold for £3,96 million, yielding a net rate of return of almost 36% per annum. Claude Monet's oil painting *Santa Maria della Salute*, with a return of 23.5% per annum in real terms, was financially also very rewarding. In 1979 it was bought for £253,000, appreciated dramatically in value thereafter, and was auctioned for £6.7 million. High returns were also reached by Matisse's sculpture *Deux Negresses* (18.8% per annum) and Camille Pissarro's *Paysage* (16% per annum). A huge price increase was also experienced by Auguste Renoir's *La Promenade*, which was bought by the Getty Museum for £10.3 million, but for which the British Rail Pension Fund in 1976 had had to pay only £682,000. The real net rate of return amounts to 10.9% per annum.

In several cases the Fund made investments in art objects which turned out to be unprofitable from the financial point of view. The watercolour by Paul Cézanne *Baigneuses* brought a small real loss of minus 0.2% per annum. Eugène Boudin's painting *Trouville, Scène de Plage* could just be auctioned without incurring a loss in real terms (the real net return was 0.5% per annum). Similar low returns were reached for works by Manet (*Les Vieux Musiciens* and *Vue du Port de Le Havre*).

The average annual rate of return in real terms, after deducting all expenses, of the British Rail Persion Fund's impressionist collection amounts to 9.9%, which is quite remarkable. This return is considerably higher than the one reached by the collections of Mettler (2.8% per annum) and of Guterman (3.2% per annum). The high financial profit is, however, mainly due to the few paintings mentioned above with enormous returns (Picasso, Monet, Matisse and Pissarro); one could also say that a good deal of luck was involved.

The British Rail Pension Fund's *overall* real net return on its art collection amounts to 6.9% per annum. Due to the great success in the sale of the impressionist part of the collection, the previous rather low annual return of 3% could be raised to almost 7%. As has been calculated by the auction house Sotheby's London, the Fund would have done better to buy shares at the London Stock Exchange. According to the Financial Times Index the real return would have in this case amounted to 7.5% per annum.

Unpredictable Fashions

The studies on the monetary returns of collections mentioned, as well as the analysis taking longer time periods and a larger number of transactions into account, all come to the same conclusion: Investment in paintings is financially less profitable, and moreover more risky, than investments in traditional financial assets.

A similar result has been reached for modern prints, that is, for works by Chagall, Picasso, Miró, Matisse, and others (Pesando 1990). In the aggregate, the mean real rate of return from 1977 to 1988 amounts to 7.7% per annum, while the profitability of stocks over the same period was 10.6% per annum. Prints by Picasso did somewhat better; their real return was 9.7%. However, compared to paintings, the risk as reflected by the standard deviation of prices was lower than for stocks (in the aggregate 18.6% for prints and 25.5% for stocks).

There is evidence suggesting that in the long run the price changes in paintings follow a *random process* (Baumol 1986). This finding is not inconsistent with the view that the recent dramatic price increases for auctioned paintings can be interpreted as a "bubble" where, based on particular expectations of speculators (which are beyond explanation), higher and higher prices chase each other. The random element here is that such a price bubble sooner or later is bound to burst—but it is not possible to predict when this will happen. Interpreting the price movements on the art market as basically a random process means that the real rate of return on investments in paintings is difficult or impossible to attribute to any systematic or identifiable factors.

The finding that the changes in the prices of paintings tend to be the result of random influences allows us to draw two conclusions:

1. The alterations in price and the rate of return of a painting *cannot* be predicted.
2. Information and any specific knowledge about the market for art in general, and about any paintings in particular, does not allow a person, *on average*, to reap higher rates of return than he or she might have if the paintings had been bought without special knowledge.

It follows that art experts are not, on average, able to invest more successfully in the art market, their superior knowledge and experience notwithstanding. The price movements, that *in retrospect* are termed "fashions," are not predictable even by art experts, and therefore cannot be anticipated and exploited in a systematic way.

There are many examples to support these findings. Vermeer was held in low regard for a long time and his paintings accordingly fetched low prices; today his paintings are among the world's most expensive. The same can be said of El Greco. Turner's paintings at first were sold at very high prices; then the prices fell sharply. Today his paintings fetch record prices again. Similar price movements characterize Pre-Raphaelite paintings which are becoming increasingly popular. Conversely, there are many artists who were previously highly esteemed, but who nowadays are little known, such as van Ostade, Berchem, Wouvermans. Alma-Tadema also comes to mind. His works were initially highly priced, but by the time of his death in 1913 the prices of his paintings had been falling for a decade. The decline in price could hardly have been steeper: in 1960 one of his most famous paintings could not find a buyer at 5% of the price paid in 1904. Art experts are, of course, able to provide explanations for such dramatic price falls in retrospect; they cannot, however, predict which and when fashions will arise and when they will begin and end.

Price movements are random, but this does not mean that no investors make large profits by buying paintings. But it is equally true that *some* investors suffer huge losses. One who bought a Vermeer or a Pre-Raphaelite when it was out of fashion can sell at a profit today; but one who bought a Berchem, van Ostade or Alma-Tadema in the past, and sold it recently, probably incurred a severe loss. The important point is that winners and losers are apparent only with hindsight; successes and failures cannot be attributed to identifiable causes, and therefore cannot be predicted.

The visualized possibility of making a profit in the art market is exaggerated for various reasons. One is that auction houses only accept paintings which they expect to reach high prices, the others are rejected. Also, little notice is paid to the fact that many pieces are withdrawn during the course of an auction. At two auctions of old masters on June 17 and 18, 1989, for example, 15% of Sotheby's lots, and 37% of Christie's, were withdrawn. These shares of withdrawals are quite normal. The would-be sellers cannot realize their price expectations, and would suffer large losses in real terms if they insisted on selling. The visible sales and record prices highlighted by the press give an exaggerated notion of opportunities in the art market.

Those who aspire to make a killing in the art market should ask themselves the following questions. Why exactly should *this* market alone provide extraordinarily large profits? Why should some paintings be financially undervalued today without other investors knowing, buying, and pushing up the current prices? The second question is particularly relevant today, when art investment is in vogue, and when investors are well informed about market conditions. There is an obvious analogy between investments in the stock and securities markets: if someone is sure that a financial asset's price will increase, he or she will buy it and thereby push up the price until all super-normal profit opportunities are exhausted.

Promises of high profits in the market for art are misleading. Theoretical arguments, as well as all serious empirical studies, indicate that it is no easier to make speculative financial profits in art than anywhere else.

Art should be bought for enjoyment, because people derive intrinsic benefits from its possession. For such buyers, investing in art is always profitable. The sceptical view of experienced art traders and collectors is thus supported by scientific studies. It is reassuring that objects of art are more likely to provide aesthetic than financial satisfaction.

General References to the Literature

The classic contribution to the economics of the arts is

Baumol, William J. and Bowen, William G. *Performing Arts—The Economic Dilemma*. Cambridge, Mass.: Twentieth Century Fund, 1966.

More modern books are

Throsby C. David and Withers, Glenn A. *The Economics of the Performing Arts*. London and Melbourne: Edward Arnold, 1979.

Frey, Bruno, S. and Pommerehne, Werner W. *Muses and Markets. Explorations in the Economics of the Arts*. Oxford: Blackwell 1989.

A discussion of auctions is provided by

Ashenfelter, Orley. "How Auctions Work for Wine and Art." *Journal of Economic Perspectives* 3 (Summer 1989): 23–36.

The returns and risk of investment in paintings are more fully discussed in

Baumol, William J. "Unnatural Value: or Art Investment as Floating Crap Game." *American Economic Review* 76 (May 1986): 10–14.

Frey, Bruno S. and Pommerehne, Werner W. "Art: An Empirical Inquiry." *Southern Economic Journal* 56 (October 1989): 396–409.

Pesando, James E. "Art as an Investment: the Market for Modern Prints." *Mimeo*. Toronto: University of Toronto, Institute for Policy Analysis, 1990.

Similar results for other areas of art investment have been found. The return and risk for specific violins are, for example, calculated by

Ross, Myron H. and Zonderman, Scott. "Capital Gains and the Rate of Return on a Stradivarius." *Economic Inquiry* 27 (July 1989): 529–540.

6 FAMILY: PATRIARCHY IN CHINA

The Family in Developing Countries

The economic literature on the countries of the Third World rarely deals with the family in an adequate way. In most cases the family is not mentioned at all, mainly because it is assumed that households do not produce for the market (e.g., Eckstein 1968). If the economic role of the family is taken into account, its behaviour is explained in terms of sociological categories, that is, in terms of "values", "roles" and "tradition" (see e.g., Parsons 1966; Eisenstadt 1973).

The *economic* theory of the family as mainly developed by Becker (see the collection of articles in Becker 1976, as well as in Schultz 1974 and the survey by Pollak 1985) has, on the other hand, rarely been applied to developing countries but has (implicitly) considered the conditions in industrial countries. The contributions by Sen (1981, 1983) analysing families in India are major exceptions. The economic theory of the family has thus either remained abstract, or has been restricted to industrial societies.

Despite this neglect by economists, the family is of great economic importance in virtually all developing countries. This also applies to China, both *before* and *after* the communist takeover. The family as a

87

unit of consumption *and* production needs to be studied in order to comprehend the past and future economic development of China. In the course of the liberalization after Mao Zedong's death in 1976 and the (partial) introduction of market elements, the role of state enterprises decreased in favour of private or collective firms. It has been reported that in mid-1985 there were more than 8 million private enterprises, many of them in the agricultural sector. Most of these enterprises, both inside and outside agriculture, have been established and are run by families (see e.g., Croll 1983, p. 28).

Families in China, as well as in other Asian countries, have a patriarchal structure. In China, this type of family has existed for thousands of years, the beginnings can be traced back to 2000 B.C. (Granet 1976, p. 19). From the time of the Middle Kingdom until the first phase of industrialization at the beginning of the twentieth century, the family under the leadership of a patriarch was the dominating economic unit in which production and consumption took place. The patriarchal family only seemed to lose its ground with the communist takeover in 1949. In reality, this basic form of the organization of individuals has survived and has been responsible for a considerable share of productive activities, especially in agriculture. Collectivization has not been able to destroy the patriarchal families who have been able to adjust to the conditions set by the Chinese Communist Party. Even if, for instance, family members were working in state collective units (or were forced to work there), the remunerations were given to the patriarch who then distributed total household income among his family members (Parish and Whyte 1978, pp. 207, 238). It is also notable that the working places in the factories were the property of the families; sons inherited them from their fathers (Shirk 1981, p. 593), daughters from their mothers (Croll 1983, p. 43).

Anthropologists and sociologists usually talk about *the* family, referring to the Chinese ideal, in which every family attempts to assemble four generations under one roof. They concentrate on different forms of families, like clans, extended families, kinship, lineages etc., without being able to explain why families differ in size, centralization of power and economic behaviour. Normally, changes in family size are attributed to intrafamily "tensions" (see e.g., Yang 1959; Eberhard 1962). The following model, however, proposes explanations why such conflicts occur. This is done, not by referring to "quarrelsome" wives (the common Chinese explanation) or competitive brothers, but by introducing external constraints which determine the behaviour of individual family members. Thus, the term family can be applied to every type of family whenever the patriarch assumes the function as described below.

This chapter intends to develop a theory of the patriarchal family on the basis of the economic approach, and to present empirical evidence for the case of China. The following section outlines an economic model of the patriarchal family. The third section derives testable propositions about the behaviour of such families and confronts them with "sociological" hypotheses. It will be shown that the descriptive literature on China tends to support the economic model. The final section comments on the contribution of the economic approach.

The Patriarchal Family: A Model

In the patriarchal family, as is indicated by its name, the male head (jiazhang) is dominant. He (1) allocates the tasks among the members of his family, (2) distributes the family income among its members by implicitly and explicitly imposing taxes and paying out transfers, (3) determines the size of the household. Following the economic theory of human behaviour, changes in the behaviour of the patriarch are attributed to empirically observable changes in his *opportunity set*. Behaviour is thus explained by changes in the constraints determining the opportunity set, and not by nonobservable preference changes. The patriarch is taken to pursue his *own* utility. This assumption deviates from Becker (first in his "theory of marriage," 1973/1974) in whose model altruism among family members results in the patriarch acting *as if* he were pursuing the family's interest.

The patriarch's opportunity set is determined by two groups of constraints—family organization and economic conditions. In China, *family organization* restricts the patriarch in four different ways:

1. If the family unit as a whole is not sufficiently productive, the family is dissolved by a collective decision of its members (fenjia) so that the head loses his position. There is an obvious analogy to a loss-making firm which is closed down.

2. If the sons consider the family's productivity achieved under the patriarch to be considerably lower than what could be achieved by a more efficient management, the head is forced to retire prematurely.

3. If the sons find the level of taxation imposed by the patriarch to be too burdensome, and his consumption to be too high, they (also) break the intergenerational contract and set a low pension for their father. The sons take this action when the patriarch's marginal productivity in organizing the family's economic activities is considerably lower than his

rate of consumption. The sons thus redistribute lifetime consumption in their favour after the patriarch has resigned.

4. Individual members can leave the family unit if the benefits of belonging to it are smaller than the taxes imposed by the patriarch. This is especially done by emigrating from the villages to the cities.

The first three constraints of the patriarch's opportunity set constitute a *collective* resistance (or voice) by the other family members, the fourth restriction is based on *individual* reactions (or exit) (see Hirschman 1970). The patriarch's opportunity set is finally constrained by

5. the budget constraint. In the long run, the family's consumption must not exceed its income. (Over the short run, the patriarch may borrow from his clan.)

These constraints are not totally independent of each other. But even if their impact is analysed bit by bit it is possible to derive relevant and empirically testable propositions of the behaviour of a patriarchal family. It will be shown how the five restrictions affect the possibility set of the patriarch. A change in these restrictions imposed by the family organization or by the economic conditions can be interpreted as a change in relative prices or relative cost. Following the fundamental law of demand, a more costly activity is performed less (holding other influences constant).

Allocation and Distribution in the Patriarchal Family

The Family's Total Productivity

The patriarch knows that the family may be dissolved by a collective decision if he is unable to reach a sufficiently high productivity by a suitable allocation of the family members' labour input. When the sons are able to achieve higher production than within the patriarchal family by each setting up an independent household (jointly with their respective wives and children), the family head loses his function (has no marginal productivity). The seemingly almighty patriarch is thus forced to arrange an *efficient allocation* of the resources of his family:

Hypothesis 1. The family's factors of production (labour) are allocated according to their *relative productivities* in the various activities.

It follows that when the relative productivities of the family members undergo a change (thus affecting the patriarch's possibility set), the allocation of the family members' work is systematically changed.

A "sociological" view of the patriarchal family in China would propose a competing hypothesis:

Antithesis 1. The economic allocation within the family is determined by the family members' roles as prescribed by tradition.

According to this sociological antithesis, the sons, daughters and daughters-in-law have to perform traditional functions. The patriarch and his wife enforce the traditional division of labour. The eldest son is trained for taking over the role as head of the family; the daughters who marry out will get only the minimum education, since they are regarded as a mere financial burden to the family budget; the daughters-in-law are trained to do most of the household chores (Wolf 1968, pp. 40–1; Wolf 1972, pp. 32–41).

Consequently, a change in the relative labour productivities of each family member does not affect this allocation of labour, at least in the short and medium run. The sociological approach may allow for economic influences to affect traditions in the long run. Such changes in tradition, however, do not follow short-term changes in utilities and costs.

The economic hypothesis 1 is supported by empirical evidence collected from the descriptive literature on both classical and modern China. Three types of reaction to changes in relative labour productivities are discussed.

1. The traditional occupation for men in Chinese peasant families has always been to work in the fields where they have a higher labour productivity due to their physical strength, while the women did household work, including gardening, where they were more productive. When, in the eighteenth century, silk worm breeding and the spinning of raw silk became profitable sideline productions, this work was allocated to the *women* because they proved to be more productive than the men. Silk worm breeding and the production of raw silk do not require physical strength but rather specific manual skills which make women relatively more productive in this occupation than in farming. The influence of tradition forcing women to stay in the house could be sustained by the fact that they provided only 16% of the work force engaged in wheat production (Buck 1937, p. 303) even in regions where no sideline production was possible. However, the traditional role attributed to women in the household was given up when sideline production changed the

relative labour productivities in the family. The adjustment of labour allocation to the new productivity ratio was undertaken by the patriarchs when the women began to contribute the main share to the family income, also leading to an increase in their influence (see Topley 1975, pp. 72–84; Stacey 1983, pp. 100–101).

2. With the beginning of Chinese industrialization, daughters were sent to work in the factory. They therewith could contribute relatively more to family income than if they performed work in the household. Again, this change in relative labour productivity led to a radical change in the traditional distribution of tasks. The daughters were allowed (or even forced) by the patriarch to leave the family home but remain in the family unit. Above all, they have to give a large part of their income to the head of the family who then redistributes it among the members of his family. (For the interrelationship between female wage earning power and influence within the family in our times, see Mitchell 1969, pp. 39–42, 121–131). A further consequence of the change in relative labour productivity is that the patriarch and his wife help more in caring for the children of their working daughters and daughters-in-law (Wolf 1975, pp. 126–127).

3. The patriarch supports the most talented son and not the eldest. The most talented son receives more education because he is expected to contribute more to family income in the future. For a long time educational investments were restricted to male descendants. As soon as the women were able to take up work outside agriculture it became worthwhile for the patriarch to invest in the education of female descendants, too. (For an example see Seagrave 1985, pp. 109–139). In particular, the patriarch decides which of the sons is going to be apprenticed and which is going to embark on a career as an official (Mandarin) by studying for the classical examinations according to expected success; he also decides which degree he should aim at (Loewe 1965, p. 149; Rozman 1981, pp. 165–166). Chinese merchants had no entry to the imperial examination system. One of the reasons given was that "they travelled constantly and did therefore not perform properly the services for the living and dead parents." In other words, they could evade the taxes imposed on them by the central government or by the patriarch (Eberhard 1962, p. 239). When, at the beginning of the twentieth century, it became profitable to let their sons be trained in international trading, they started modern (Western) schools.

These examples indicate that the roles within the family are not fixed by tradition. Rather, the distribution of tasks among family members is decided by the patriarch according to the changing labour productivities in order to maximize total family income (including household work).

In addition to an efficient allocation of work among a given number of family members, the patriarch must also determine the *size* of the (extended) family so that the maximum consumption per head is achieved.

Hypothesis 2. The number of self-produced (children) and acquired (daughters-in-law) family members is controlled by the patriarch to ensure maximum consumption per head.

According to this hypothesis the patriarch adjusts the size of his family to changing external conditions. In particular, the family size is increased when the addition of a new member adds more to the total family income than that consumed by him or her and decreased when a member consumes more than he/she contributes.

Antithesis 2. The size of the family is determined by tradition, following the rule that the more sons, the happier the family. It is also concluded that the more traditional a family, like peasant or gentry families, the more sons they will raise and the earlier they will take in daughters-in-law (Eberhard 1962, pp. 188–191; Wolf 1968, p. 130).

In China, the patriarch chooses the number of natural children by using the means of abortion, adopting daughters in or out, conscious neglect or even infanticide (Eberhard 1962, p. 131; Fei 1939, pp. 33–34). It should be remembered that killing infants was not illegal until the marriage law of 1930/1931.

The total output of labour in an agrarian society is strongly determined by the size of the farm. The larger the cultivated area over which a patriarch commands, the more profitable it is to have a large family (for China see Myers 1970, pp. 132–133; for Taiwan, Tai Yen-hui 1959, p. 28). The patriarch may adjust the family to the desired size by letting the sons marry earlier than usual, thus enlarging the family by one member, and by accepting more children per woman. Moreover, the patriarch may take more concubines the larger the area cultivated (Fei 1939, p. 29; Marsh 1961, p. 71).

That family size in China is strongly affected by economic utility and cost evaluations, and is not simply determined by tradition, as has been found in many studies. A survey in the People's Republic of China in 1982 revealed, for instance, that the population living in cities aims at a smaller number of children than the one living in the country. The reasons given are that raising children in a city is more expensive and that the children are able to contribute to family income only later. The main determinants of the number of children quoted were provision for old age (50% of the respondents) and contribution to the family's work force (20%). Surprisingly enough, only one quarter of the respondents quoted the more traditional aim of continuing the family line (*Renkou Yanjiu* 5, Sept. 1982; see also Platte 1984, pp. 655–659).

A Hongkong study shows that the number of children is strongly negatively correlated to the female work-participation rate and the educational level. This indicates that not only the pure raising costs of children are taken into account, but the opportunity costs (foregone income) of the mothers (Mitchell 1969, p. 258).

These findings suggest that the heads of Chinese families are able to distinguish between *marginal* effects (namely improved old age security and higher family income) and *total* effects on the benefits and costs of having children (such as the continuation of the family line as such), thus supporting the economic approach to the family.

The Patriarch's Relative Productivity

The head of a Chinese family may only keep himself in charge as long as he is capable of leading the family successfully, in particular with respect to economic matters.

Hypothesis 3. The less productive a patriarch is compared to his sons, the earlier and the more fully he is forced to retire.

Antithesis 3. The patriarch exerts total control up to a traditionally fixed age of retirement (60 years), or up to his death. When sons or daughters do not comply with his authoritative rule such behaviour is attributed to differences in temperament or family background and incompatible ambitions of the various family members. Age, poor health or a weak personality are also factors which make the patriarch lose his control (Eberhard 1962, p. 35; Wolf 1968, pp. 43–44).

In Chinese agriculture the most productive son is first employed in farming, then the other sons and the patriarch, according to their relative productivity. Correspondingly, the sons working in the fields take over some of the tasks, and therewith power, of the patriarch. This may go so far as to reduce the (nominal) patriarch to a mere adviser. The more productive the sons are in relation to the patriarch, the smaller is the latter's influence, leading to a partial or full retirement (Fei 1939, p. 38; Lang 1968, p. 165).

More recently, the sons' and daughters' productivity has been strongly determined by the education and income gained outside the agricultural family unit. In old China, where a high rate of illiteracy was characteristic, the experience of the elders constituted a comparative advantage in relation to the younger generation. The larger the share of monetary income contributed to the family by the sons and daughters, the earlier and more fully the patriarch loses power. That the loss of power was not limited to the patriarch's financial control only can be seen in the following: As soon as the Japanese war economy in Taiwan in the early 1920s and 1930s offered enough full-time workplaces to male workers, the sons rebelled against the *sim-pua* form of marriage. According to this tradition girls were adopted in a family at a young age in order to marry one of the sons later. Thus the usual high bride-price was avoided. Obviously, many of the sons felt incestuous about marrying a foster sister. When they could earn enough money they threatened their fathers with their moving out. Subsequently, the percentage of adopted-in girls dropped from 77% (1910) to 44% (1931), and this tradition has by now almost completely disappeared (Wolf 1972, pp. 180–181.)

The tendency for the gradual dissolution of the extended family in the course of industrialization may be attributed to this economic influence (see Yang 1959, p. 91; Myers 1970, p. 165).

Break of the Intergenerational Contract

The level of consumption available to the head of a patriarchal family is restricted by his descendants acting in the context of the family organization. He is not free to set his consumption level independent of the consumption level of the following generation.

Hypothesis 4.   If the patriarch taxes his descendants too highly compared to his own consumption standard and his own productivity (thus breaking the implicit intergenerational contract), his consumption level will be lowered after his resignation or he is no longer supported at all.

Antithesis 4.   The Chinese family is required under all circumstances to guarantee the patriarch a life long consumption standard set by tradition. Exceptions to this rule are again explained by conflicts between parents and children, or by the modernization process in which old traditions fell apart. (Wolf 1972, pp. 217–221.)

It is difficult to find direct evidence for this hypothesis. The breaking of the intergenerational contract by the sons violates the duty to support the parents which is also contained in the Chinese constitution of December 4, 1982, article 49, stating that ". . . children who have come of age have the duty to support and assist their parents." This holds even if the patriarch has previously broken the intergenerational contract by consuming more than is due to him relative to his own (marginal) contribution to family income and the consumption standard of his descendants. The Chinese are therefore unwilling to reveal information in surveys about the frequency of breaking the intergenerational contract by the sons, as well as about the processes involved therein. There is, however, evidence indirectly supporting the economic hypothesis:

1. In the Chinese empire, the clans binding together various extended families had to act as arbiters when the patriarch abused his powers over his children. They also served to arbiter the complaints of the parents vis à vis their children. This function of the clan was formally fixed in the Chinese marriage laws of 1930–1931 (article 1090).

2. After the foundation of the People's Republic of China, conflicts about the economic support of the parents had to be brought to the bar. Some cases have become known (Yang 1959, pp. 101–104). The Chinese press also publishes complaints that the descendants neglect to support their parents and treat them unfairly (see e.g., *Renmin Ribao* [People's Daily], February 5, 1985). This shows that the moral and legal duty to support the parents is not automatically fulfilled, but that it depends on circumstances.

3. The breaking of the intergenerational contract is not only a feature of today; the well-known reformer K'ang Yu-wei (published in 1974) complained in the 1920s that "In my village hardly one out of 1,000 people provides for his father, hardly one out of 100 provides for his mother."

Exit of the Family Members

The patriarch redistributes income between the family members in order to keep the family functioning and to maximize family income; prerequisites for maintaining his own position. The members gaining income outside the family are taxed, while the other family members, in particular the women doing the housework and raising the children, receive a transfer. Taxation and transfers can be monetary or in the form of consumption goods, explicit or implicit. In the case, for instance, of a son who lives in town and who transfers a share of his income to the patriarch living in the countryside, "taxation" is explicit and monetary. A son, on the other hand, working on the family farm who receives part of the product contributed in the form of housing and food only, is taxed implicitly and in kind (see Lang 1968, pp. 159–160, for various forms of taxation).

The patriarch endeavours to raise the taxes necessary to support the nonincome receiving family members as *efficiently* and "fairly" as possible. If he is successful, he maximizes the support by his family as well as the consumption standard enjoyed by himself and the other members. He is confronted with the same problem as that treated in the *theory of optimal taxation*: a given amount of tax revenue has to be raised in order to maximize a social welfare function (see the surveys by Bradford and Rosen 1976; Atkinson and Stiglitz 1980). The essential point of the theory of optimal income taxation is to take into account the disincentive effects and, therefore, the dead weight loss of taxation. In the context here considered, the social welfare function is replaced by the welfare function of the family.

The optimal tax rates derived from the neoclassical theory of taxation do not, however, only depend on the welfare function chosen, but on a variety of special properties of the goods and activities involved, such as partial elasticities of substitution. It is hence difficult to deduce any general result. One may, however, draw an analogy to the *Ramsey Rule* (Ramsey 1927) stating that those goods are to be taxed the highest which have a low price elasticity of demand (disregarding cross elasticities of demand), and vice versa. This rule ensures that the efficiency losses are minimized. Accordingly, the dead weight losses are smallest when the income of those persons with the highest price elasticity of labour supply is taxed the lowest, and the income of price inelastic persons is taxed the highest (see Sandmo 1976, p. 32).

Following this theory the patriarch endeavours to reduce the work incentives due to the redistribution of income as little as possible. He will take into account that the price elasticities of supply of labour by the the various members of his family differ one from another. Those family members who find it easy to evade family taxation (in particular by "emigrating" into anonymous large cities) are taxed lightly. On the other hand, family members who have little or no chance to evade family taxes are taxed more highly.

Hypothesis 5. The rate of taxation of the income of family members is set by the patriarch to be inversely related to their respective price elasticities of the supply of labour.

Antithesis 5. The rate of taxation among family members is determined by traditional demographic characteristics such as sex, age or seniority within the family. This means an increasing tax rate in the following order: The patriarch's wife, his eldest son, other sons, eldest son's wife, other daughters-in-law (according to seniority), adopted daughters (see Wolf's vivid description of the Lim-family's conflict about intrafamily taxation as fought out by the female family members [Wolf 1972, pp. 115–131]).

Hypothesis 5 allows us to draw more specific conclusions for which empirical evidence may be found:

1. Sons living with their parents are taxed more heavily than sons who no longer live and work within the family context. Thus, for example, considerate mothers were rather reluctant to let their daughters marry an eldest son. This meant more unpaid (more heavily taxed) work for their daughters and higher contributions to the retired patriarch and his wife (Wolf 1972, p. 143). The sons living outside have a much better chance to evade family taxation by hiding a part of their income or by leaving the family unit altogether; their price elasticity of the supply of labour in favour of the family is thus high. The patriarch therefore has to tax those sons lightly in order to reduce the incentive to leave the family unit and to induce them to make at least some contribution to family income (instead of possibly none at all).

2. Sons living outside the family and having a high price elasticity of family labour supply are only asked to contribute to the patriarch's and his wives' old age support if these services cannot be provided by the sons living within the family and having a low price elasticity of labour supply (Parish and Whyte 1978, pp. 212–213).

3. The son chosen to continue the ancestral worship is taxed highest in the form of personal services to his parents by having his mobility restricted. He is prevented from profiting from the chances the market offers outside the family context. Due to this "enforced" immobility his price elasticity of labour supply is low and he is therefore taxed more heavily than the other sons (see Granet 1976, pp. 181 and 193).

4. In traditional families the women in particular are heavily taxed because they have little opportunity to leave the family by their own will. However, as soon as income opportunities opened up outside the family in the course of the industrialization of China, exit became more easily possible. The increase in the price elasticity of supply of women leaves them a higher share of their income for personal disposal (see Lang 1968, especially p. 205). It has also been shown for Taiwan (Wolf 1975, p. 127)

that the improved possibility for women to gain income resulted in a lower implicit family taxation of the daughters-in-law; they now have to perform less personal services for their parents-in-law.

5. Women who do not personally care for their children but who can send them to kindergartens are taxed less heavily than women solely concerned with child rearing (Wolf 1975, p. 127). They are more independent and can more easily vary their work input in favour of the family (Yang 1959, pp. 150–152). Such women have a higher price elasticity of the supply of work than pure housewives.

6. Women who have the possibility to leave their marriage and go back to their natural family or found their own household are taxed less by the patriarch of the family into which they entered by marriage. This explains the miserable life of adopted daughters (sim-pua). Since they could not rely on their natural family, from where they were adopted out, they could be taxed most heavily (Wolf 1968, pp. 99–114; see also Parish and Whyte 1978, pp. 193–195). The price elasticity of work supply of such women is lower than for those women who can leave their husband's family (see, for examples, Lang 1968, pp. 266–269).

Contribution of the Economic Approach

The patriarchal family has not only been the dominant form of organization for individuals in the past but is also of great importance in the People's Republic of China even today. It is to be expected that the patriarchal families increasingly create their own enterprises and thus embark on production activities.

The family led by a patriarch is analysed in this paper with the help of economic theory. The patriarch is taken to obey a self-interested utility function having present and future consumption (including the old age pension provided by his descendants) as arguments. His possibility space is restricted by the members of his family (in particular by his sons) via voice and exit as well as by the budget constraint.

The theory of the patriarchal family allows us to derive five testable hypotheses:

1. Family members are allocated various work tasks according to their relative productivities.

2. Family size is restricted in order to maximize per capita income in the family.

3. A patriarch who proves to act inefficiently compared to what his sons would acquire independently, is forced to retire.

4. The consumption level of the retired patriarch is lowered by his sons if he breaks the implicit generational contract by taxing the family members too heavily in comparison to his personal consumption and to the consumption level the sons could achieve by themselves during the time he is in charge of the family.

5. Family members who find it easy to evade family taxation and who thus have a high price elasticity of supply in favour of family work are taxed lightly. Conversely family members with a low price elasticity of work supply are taxed heavily.

These hypotheses are supported by evidence found in the literature on the effect of changes in the opportunity set on behaviour. It can be shown that systematic reactions in the hypothesized directions take place. Such changes in behaviour do not conform with sociological hypotheses built on the concepts of role and tradition. In many popular literary as well as scientific accounts of family life in China the patriarch is regarded to be almost almighty. The economic view, on the other hand, stresses the restrictions he is subjected to and specifies in what way and for what purposes he uses (or is forced to use) his seeming "discretion." Patriarchy is thus not considered so much a special kind of power but a specific institutional setting under which the head of the household acts.

The economic theory of human behaviour that builds on the pursuit of self-interest and on the restrictions of the opportunity set proves to be capable of making a useful contribution to a better understanding of the Chinese family and the Chinese economy.

General References to the Literature

The economic view of the family is developed in
> Becker, Gary S. *A Treatise on the Family*. Cambridge, Mass: Harvard University Press, 1981.

This approach is criticized by
> Hannan, Michael T. "Families, Markets, and Social Structures: An Essay on Becker's A Treatise on the Family." *Journal of Economic Literature* 20 (March 1982): 65–72.

A somewhat different approach is used in
> Pollak, Robert A. "A Transaction Cost Approach to Families and Households." *Journal of Economic Literature* 23 (June 1985): 581–608.

The particular aspects of family in developing countries are discussed by
> Sen, Amartya K. "Economics and the Family." *Asian Development Review* 1 (1983): 14–26.

For the recent history of China see, for example

Rozman, Gilbert. *The Modernization of China.* New York and London: Macmillan, 1981.

The Chinese economy is treated in

Eckstein, Alexander. *China's Economic Development. The Interplay of Scarcity and Ideology.* Ann Arbor: University of Michigan Press, 1976.

Family traditions and the position of the patriarch in China are discussed by

Lang, Olga. *Chinese Family and Society, 2nd ed.* New Haven: Yale University Press, 1968.

Croll, Elisabeth. *Chinese Women since Mao.* New York: Sharpe, 1983.

7 CONFLICT: FIGHTING POLITICAL TERRORISM BY REFUSING RECOGNITION

Helplessness

Over the last dozen years political terrorism has become more widespread than ever. The incidents range from kidnapping individuals and hijacking collective means of transportation (planes, ships and even trains) to bombings. Kidnapping of prominent individuals such as the president of the German Employers' Association, Hanns Martin Schleyer, in 1977 or of the Italian former prime minister Aldo Moro in 1978 have had deadly outcomes, and many innocent bystanders have been killed in other acts of terrorism. Accordingly, terrorist acts have received great attention in the media: there is "virtually a 100 percent probability of achieving world-wide or at least national publicity" (Jenkins and Ronfeldt 1977, p. 1). The estimated worldwide media audience of a significant terrorist act is 500,000,000, that is, terrorists can count on "a public opinion prize probably unmatched in history" (Watson 1976, p. 195). Signs of hysteria have appeared. The fight against political terrorism has had considerable repercussions in most societies: new police forces have been established, and new techniques of investigation and search have been introduced. As a result human rights and civil liberties have been curtailed, and in times of acute terror have been openly violated.

The reaction of the authorities to this wave of political terrorism can be described as inadequate, and even helpless (see e.g., Crelinston and Szabo 1980, pp. 81–83). The fact that not more people have been killed seems to be more the result of luck than of good management of the crises by the authorities. The authorities have tended to resort to illegal or at least illegitimate means in fighting terrorism. Moreover, they have allowed the terrorists and their causes to get prominent attention (and thus have helped to achieve one of the main goals of political terrorists), and have even gone so far as to negotiate with the terrorists on an equal footing, violating the constitutional principle that the state has to maintain the monopoly of force in society.

This chapter suggests a new strategy to deal with political terrorism which avoids some of the major disadvantages of current policies. In particular, the civil liberties of the population remain intact, while terrorist acts may be expected to decrease significantly. Terrorists' behaviour and the workings of the new strategy for fighting them are discussed in the following II. Possible objections are dealt with in the third section. The fourth section compares the new strategy to the one currently in use, and the final section offers concluding remarks.

The Strategy Outlined

The Behaviour of Terrorists

Terrorists do not act without purpose, rather they are goal-oriented actors (Stohl 1979, pp. 6–7). Political terrorists want to draw public attention to their cause, and/or want to achieve specific political demands (such as the release of imprisoned members of their group). Media recognition is absolutely crucial; the success of a terrorist act depends mainly on the media coverage it enjoys: "Terrorist action is nothing, publicity is everything" (Laqueur 1977, p. 105; 1978, p. 225). A "vital factor [for the proliferation of international terrorism] is the impact of modern communications media. Terrorists are today given free worldwide publicity" (Wilkinson 1974, p. 124). One may even speak of an "implicit theatrical nature of terrorism" (Corsi 1981, p. 48) in which "the mass media take a vital role" (Crelinston and Szabo 1980, p. 89). Terrorists act to achieve their goals by considering the benefits and costs associated with alternative actions. When there are two actions available (say kidnapping a prominent politician or throwing indiscriminately a bomb in a gathering of people) they will choose the one which yields higher benefits in terms of achieving the goals, or which entails lower costs in terms of material needed and risk of being captured, wounded or killed.

In this limited sense terrorists may be taken to act "rationally." Terrorists are neither madmen nor is their behaviour random, rather it is systematic and, in principle, predictable. This view of terrorists accords well with reality; terrorists are known for careful preparations of their acts, gathering information and meticulously planning the procedure. It has been shown in careful investigations (Mickolus 1980; Gurr 1979) that political terrorists systematically react to changes in factors such as risk and the probability of a clash with the authorities. Terrorist activities with high risk like hijacking and hostage-taking occur the least often while activities with low risk like bombings and assassinations occur the most often.

Refusing Recognition

Based on this view of terrorists' behaviour, they can be discouraged from acting by reducing their utility of goal attainment. The authorities in charge must in particular ascertain that a particular group of terrorists do not receive the credit and therewith the public attention for committing a terrorist act. The authorities must see to it that the terrorist act is not attributed to those people who might have undertaken it and who might have made the respective effort and taken the risk. There are two strategies for refusing to attribute a terrorist act to a particular group:

1. All information on terrorist activities is suppressed; the authorities behave and talk as if no such terrorist act has happened. In an open and free society it is extremely difficult, if not impossible, to withhold such information in which the public is highly interested. In effect, the freedom of the press is seriously limited either by "voluntary" agreement or by law. As the foreign press and news media are not bound by such agreements and laws, it is, at least in a democracy, most likely that the news leaks out. The terrorists can easily inform foreign news agencies who, due to the competitive pressure to provide interesting news, will normally be ready to inform the international public about the terrorist act. This first strategy must therefore be rejected as being ineffective and incompatible with democracy.

2. The information available to the public may be "thinned" by supplying much of it. This can be done by making it known that *several*

terrorist groups *could* be responsible for a particular terrorist act. The authorities have to reveal that they never know with certainty who has committed a terrorist act. Even when it seems obvious which terrorist group is involved, the police can never be sure because it may be a politically opposed group who has committed the act in order to incriminate the more "obvious" groups, and invite police action against the latter. Rather the authorities have various hypotheses to which they attach various degrees of belief. They must communicate this probability distribution of possible actors to the public. They have to refrain from attributing a terrorist act to any particular group as long as the truth is not established. In a lawful country, this is the privilege of the courts, but not of the police.

Usually, there are several groups claiming to have committed a particular terrorist act. There are cases in which the media have attributed it to some innocent terrorist group, as it later turned out (Laqueur 1977, p. 106). The authorities have to stress that any one of them may be the responsible one. As a consequence, the various media draw the public's attention to many different, and possibly conflicting, political goals. In the unlikely case that only one group claims to have committed the terrorist act, the authorities responsible have to point out that such a claim is not substantiated and that experience shows that several different groups *may* have undertaken the act, but choose to be silent. They may point out that many cases are known where groups have claimed to have committed particular terrorist acts in order to draw the attention of the mass media to themselves. Thus, even in the case of only one claimant, those having committed the act receive only part of the publicity involved, and possibly a small part only.

Effects

The information strategy outlined has systematic and hence predictable effects on the behaviour of both terrorists and responsible authorities. The benefits derived from having committed a terrorist act decreases for the group having undertaken it because the group does not reap the public attention hoped for. The political goals it wants to publicize are not propagated as much as desired. This reduction in publicity makes the terrorist act (to a certain degree) senseless: "all modern terrorist movements require publicity" (Laqueur 1977, p. 106). Terrorists who are ready to take the high risk—and even the risk of death—in order to put forth their political beliefs feel deeply dissatisfied. The frustration is intensified by the feeling that other political groups who were not as "brave" as to have run the risk to undertake terrorist acts are free riders and reap benefits in terms of increased publicity free of charge. This frustration is often intense because terrorist groups tend to be in a state of strong competition even when they have similar political beliefs. None of them is ready to accept that it undertakes dangerous actions but that another group receives the credit for it. Most terrorist groups would prefer that no one is credited than that the publicity is shared by a competing group. The authorities in charge of fighting terrorism may exploit this competition among terrorist groups by pointing out to the media that among the likely authors of a particular terrorist act there may be terrorist groups known to be in competition with each other.

The authorities' strategy resulting in a strong decrease in the rewards for terrorist acts, the terrorist groups concerned may react in three possible ways:

1. The terrorists make an effort to establish the authorship in a terrorist act by providing appropriate "proofs". This can, for instance, be done by providing photographs (e.g., showing a hostage with a newspaper of a particular date as was done in the case of the kidnapping of Schleyer in Germany). The authorities, knowing well that such photographs are easy to fake, will have to point out that this is no adequate "proof," and in many instances they can indicate that similar "proofs" have been presented by other claimants. While the initial attempt to establish authorship undoubtedly receives public attention, this will also be true for the possible counter-evidence provided by the authorities. Terrorists may also try to establish a proof by getting into direct contact with journalists. Such action involves considerable risks because the terrorists have to partially come out into the open and this renders them an easier target for normal police activity. The terrorists cannot, for example, discount the possibility of one of the journalists making contact and informing the police of a planned meeting. The authorities have, moreover, counterstrategies available. They can reveal what evidence they possess, suggesting that a competing terrorist group may well have committed the terrorist act concerned.

2. The terrorists switch to a more overt type of terrorist activity in order to make sure that its authorship is established beyond doubt. Such behaviour increases the risk of being caught by the police.

3. The terrorists desist from further terrorist activity because it does not pay and switch to a nonviolent way of publicizing their demands.

It may be noted that each one of the three types of reaction results in a decrease of terrorism either because the terrorists choose to so act or because the police are in a better position to detect and overwhelm them.

The strategy suggested here also leads to a change in the behaviour of the authorities. Most importantly, as long as the authorship of a terrorist act is not clearly established, they do not have to yield to the demands made. As long as they can argue that they do not know which of the conflicting demands should be fulfilled, they do not even have to reject the demands. In the case of kidnappings this means that there is little risk that the terrorists respond by killing the hostages as they would not gain anything by doing so. Thus no ransom has to be paid. If political terrorists demand that some announcement is read on TV or published in newspapers, this may even be granted, provided several announcements by different terrorist groups are arranged, thus strongly reducing the effect of any particular announcement.

To summarize, the following results may be expected from applying the strategy suggested: The authorities take the initiative by actively taking steps to reduce the attention the terrorists receive from the public. The terrorists become frustrated by the missing reward from the risky terrorist acts, desist from further activities, or increasingly expose themselves to ordinary counter-terrorist methods by the police. The amount of terrorism will decrease; the dissatisfaction with existing political and social conditions will be expressed in different, less violent ways.

Possible Objections

The strategy of refusing recognition by supplying more information than desired by the terrorists may be objected to on various grounds.

Cost of Noncommitment

The public expects, and has a right, to be truthfully informed by the authorities on public affairs, including terrorism. The strategy of refusing recognition by leaving all possibilities open until the truth is established on court may possibly appear to the citizens as if information were withheld, because no particular terrorist group is presented as the author of a particular act. In order to overcome this (mistaken) feeling, the authorities must make it clear that there are by necessity always a number of different suspects and that in a democratic society it is the courts' sole authority to establish who is guilty. The fact that there are more or less likely authors does not allow concentration on only one of them.

Limited Applicability

The strategy based on refusing recognition is relevant for clandestine terrorist acts such as kidnapping with an *unknown* hiding place, and bombings. This is an advantage rather than a disadvantage because "most expert knowledge to date deals with hostage situations in which the site of the hostage is known. Where the site is unknown, operational strategies and tactics are much less clear-cut and well-developed" (Crelinston and Szabo 1980, p. 81). The strategy is not as applicable for overt kidnapping where the hostages are kept at a publicly known place. The authorities can still argue that the hijackers, say of a plane or ship, are not fully identified, and that there are competing claims on who they really are and what cause they really champion. However, the possibility of using such a stragegy is more limited than in the case of clandestine terrorist activities. The strategy suggested is complementary, and not substitutive, to ordinary police activities. Open terrorist actions can be fought by classical police methods such as attacks by appropriately trained and armed forces.

The strategy is also inapplicable if terrorists' behaviour were solely motivated by creating chaos. In that case terrorists derive no utility if their movement and their political goals are identified. The literature on terrorism does not indicate, however, that such a utility function is widespread, if it exists at all.

Unwillingness to Use the Strategy

The politicians and the police chiefs responsible may be reluctant to apply the strategy of refusing recognition because it gives the impression to the public that the authorities are incompetent as they do not appear to know which group is responsible for the terrorist act concerned. The politicians and public authorities in charge prefer to state that they are well informed and that they will soon be able to capture the terrorists, even if this is more wishful thinking than reality. The strategy has, moreover, the disadvantage that the decline in terrorism brought about by the deliberate decision of formerly terrorist groups is not directly attributed to the police and other public authorities. Both would, of course, prefer to be directly credited. The small incentives for the official decision-makers to apply the strategy is a serious problem. A competent government may, however, be able to attribute the success of the antiterrorist policy to their actions and particularly by pointing out its *success*. In times of crisis, which often obtains when terrorism mounts, the parties in a democracy tend to have an implicit or even explicit consensus with respect to antiterror policy; the government is insulated during this period from usual party competition and can, if it desires, pursue the strategy suggested. The government can also show its determination to fight terrorism by pointing out its use of classical police methods.

It is, however, not necessary to rely only on the enlightened self-interest of the government. Laws prohibiting an unproven accusation of having committed a terrorist act may be introduced or strengthened, and it must apply also to the public authorities, including the police. As a result, the authorities would be more careful to attribute a terrorist act to a particular group but would be forced to also indicate other possible actors. The laws would firmly establish that only the courts may establish who is guilty. Once the courts have decided, the group who actually committed the crime gains the undivided publicity—but this is long after the terrorist act has taken place. In a world characterized by many news items and among them many atrocities, the amount of attention paid by the mass media and the public is considerably smaller than it would have been at the time of the terrorist act.

Comparison to Current Antiterrorist Policy

There are six major differences between the strategy of refusing recognition and the policy currently used:

1. The strategy is active, the authorities force the terrorists to react. The currently used antiterrorist policy is, on the other hand, reactive, the terrorists dictate the procedure and the terms under which the interaction takes place.

2. The strategy refuses to give terrorists the rewards going with public attention. The current policy tends to publicize and "officially" acknowledge the existence of the terrorist group and therewith its cause.

3. The strategy allows the authorities not to yield to the demands raised by the terrorists without running an increased risk. The current policy seeks a favourable outcome by negotiating the terms of the demands with the terrorists on an equal level. The consequence tends to

be that the terrorists commit further violence in order to ensure that their demands are met.

4. The strategy lowers the rewards of terrorist actions which also reduces the incentives to terrorists for future terrorism. The current terrorist policy invites future terrorism in so far as it has met terrorist demands in the past.

5. The strategy does not touch the freedom of the press and of the other media. Current antiterrorist policy is usually accompanied by a suppression or reduction of free reporting.

6. The strategy does not infringe on human rights and civil liberties. The current antiterrorist policy with its emphasis on heavy use of police power and on modern methods of investigation and surveillance is bound to reduce citizens' rights.

Concluding Remarks

The discussion suggests that a fight of terrorism based on the refusal to acknowledge terrorists by oversupplying information may be a useful extension to existing policies. It has become clear that it is not an alternative in the sense that it would make police action unnecessary. It is, however, a clear alternative with respect to how information is to be handled. Antiterror practitioners would have to find the exact ways to implement the misinformation policy put forward theoretically. The strategy may be openly discussed, its effect does not depend on the fact that the opponents (the terrorists) do not know about it. Rather it is one of the remarkable features that it is largely immune to counterstrategies.

General References to the Literature

Extensive literature on terrorism exists. Surveys on the phenomenon are given, for example, by
Wilkinson, Paul. *Terrorism and the Liberal State*. New York: Macmillan, 1977.
Jenkins, Brian M. *Terrorism and Beyond: An International Conference on Terrorism and Low-Level Conflict*. Santa Monica: Rand, 1982.
Laqueur, Walter. *The Age of Terrorism*. Boston: Little, Brown, 1987.
Statistical facts on terrorism are provided in
Mickolus, Edward F. *Transnational Terrorism: A Chronology of Events*. Westport, Conn.: Greenwood Press, 1980.
Wilkinson, Paul. "Trends in International Terrorism and the American

Response." In: Royal Institute of International Affairs (ed.). *Terrorism and International Order*. London: Routledge and Kegan Paul, 1986.

More strongly analytically orientated is the quantitative study by

Im, Eric I., Cauley, Jon and Sandler, Todd. "Cycles and Substitutions in Terrorist Activities: A Spectral Approach." *Kyklos* 40 (1987): 238–255.

Publicity aspects of terrorism are dealt with in

American Legal Foundation. *Terrorism and the Media*. Washington, D.C. 1990.

The political effects of terrorism are discussed in the reader

Stohl, Michael (ed.). *The Politics of Terrorism*. New York: Dekker, 1979.

Economic analyses of terrorism have been provided by

Landes, William M. "An Economic Study of U.S. Aircraft Hijackings, 1961–1976." *Journal of Law and Economics* 21 (April 1978): 1–32.

Atkinson, Scott E., Sandler, Todd and Tschirhart, John. "Terrorism in a Bargaining Framework." *Journal of Law and Economics* 30 (April 1987): 1–22.

8 HISTORY: PRISONERS OF WAR

Throughout history, defeated enemies have been treated in strikingly distinct ways. Many instances are known in which they were treated with utmost brutality and massacred in large numbers. In his history of the crusades Runciman (1955, p. 274) tells us, for example, that when the Persians conquered Jerusalem in the year 614, 60,000 Christians were murdered regardless of sex or age. The crusaders conquering Jerusalem 500 years later (1099) butchered men, women and children in the city (among them Christians) for an entire afternoon and throughout the following night. During the French Revolution which was based, after all, on the ideal of fraternity among men, all prisoners taken by the revolutionaries in the Vendée (1793–1795)—more than 150,000 in all—were massacred (Hetzel 1889, p. 8). Snow (1981, p. 164) reports that the Japanese killed more than 42,000 men after having conquered Nanking in December 1937. Chinese sources quote much higher figures: 300,000 people are said to have been murdered by the Japanese, among them 30,000 disarmed soldiers in the northern part of the city (*China aktuell*, October 1985, p. 672).

On the other hand, history provides many examples of humane treatment of defeated enemies. In the European Middle Ages, they were

nearly always spared and ransomed (Erler 1978, p. 25). The battles
between the mercenaries in Italy at the time of the Condottieri were
relatively humane: "Battles when they did occur, were often very blood-
less affairs" (Fuller 1961, p. 16). In many battles, only two or three
combatants lost their lives, but hundreds of defeated adversaries were
taken prisoner. At the end of the 16th century, a particularly harmless
form of war emerged. When two opposing armies met, the respective
number of soldiers were counted, and the side with the lower number
simply surrendered to the other (Hochheimer 1967, p. 83). Ransoming
prisoners was a widespread practice up to the seventeenth century, and
it continued, to some extent, thereafter. In the relationship between
Christians and Saracens, it went on up to the nineteenth century.

In this chapter, a comprehensive explanation of the striking differences
in the treatment of conquered enemies is proposed. This explanation is
based on the economic model of behaviour, in which it is assumed that
expected benefits and costs determine individual behaviour. It is shown
that the institution of property rights is a major determinant in the
decision of whether a defeated adversary is brutally or humanely treated.
Two points will be looked at: (1) the conditions for the emergence,
existence and change of particular property rights, and (2) the effects
of particular property rights on the behaviour in war. The influence
of expected benefits and costs on the individual is essential for explaining the treatment of defeated enemies and prisoners. These individual benefits and costs depend on the allotment of the property right
over prisoners.

Three assignments of property rights will be distinguished: that of the
individual soldier who takes a prisoner and thereby owns the property
right over him (discussed in the following section); the property right
belonging to the state (discussed in the second section); and the property
right over prisoners that is transferred to a supranational entity (third
section). These types of property rights are associated with typical periods
in history. For reasons of limited space, only circumstantial evidence can
be provided.

Property Rights Belong to the Captor

Emergence of Property Rights

The assignment to the soldier of the property rights over prisoners must
be consonant with the *technological* conditions of war and the existing

social organization. Assigning the right to individuals is an appropriate form when battles are fought man against man and when it is possible to determine who is taken prisoner by whom. When a ruler has limited or no means of extracting taxes from the population in order to pay his or her soldiers, and if he or she has limited power to force them to serve, other incentives must be used. An effective form is granting each individual soldier the right in the spoils of war he secures for himself, be it goods or prisoners. Individual property rights thus serve to motivate men to participate in war and to fight effectively.

Consequences of Individual Property Rights

A soldier who voluntarily participates in a war may be assumed to act rationally. He also acts rationally when he decides either to kill or to spare a defeated soldier striking back. The advantage of sparing a defeated enemy, on the other hand, is the monetary benefit of selling him at a price determined by the prisoner himself, his family, or whoever else is interested in his release. A higher willingness to pay can be expected from a rich prisoner than from a poor one, from a healthy prisoner than from a wounded or sick one.

There are various costs involved in keeping an adversary prisoner. There is always the risk of his attacking the captor; he must therefore be appropriately guarded, which is costly. Moreover there are costs of feeding and housing the prisoner, and of providing medical treatment if necessary. Finally, transaction costs arise in the process of ransoming, including the risk that no monetary compensation will be secured for freeing the prisoner.

The (net) *value* of a defeated enemy thus depends on a number of empirically observable factors which influence benefits and costs, given the particular form of property rights. The general proposition advanced here is that an individual soldier is more inclined to spare, treat well, and exchange a defeated enemy when the costs of doing so are low and/or the expected benefits are high, and that more defeated enemies are killed when the expected benefits of sparing them are low and/or the costs high.

Ransoming in History

In antiquity, death was generally the fate of the vanquished (see e.g., Flory 1942; Scheidl 1943). Greek law gave the conqueror absolute power, which frequently resulted in the entire slaughter of the defeated nation. However, cases of ransom being paid are known from the Homeric Age and the Punic Wars: Priam prevails on Achilles to deliver up the dead body of Hector on payment of a ransom, to enable his due burial. During the First and Second Punic Wars Roman and Carthaginian generals exchanged prisoners, a sum of gold being paid by the recipient of the greater number (Walker 1899, p. 55). The Romans were the first to perceive the economic value of captives taken in war, and consequently some of the prisoners were sold as slaves by the state, the proceeds being distributed as booty to the soldiers or put into the general treasury. The "practice of enslavement . . . probably produced an improvement in the position of prisoner of war" (Flory 1942, p. 12). Nevertheless, in most cases they were put to death as criminals for having offended against the majesty of Rome. Conditions were similar in Northern Europe. Between the fall of Rome and the Middle Ages war practice remained brutal and savage.

In Europe in the Middle Ages, conditions obtained that made it efficient to assign property rights over a defeated enemy to the *individual* soldier. The rulers had but limited means of extracting taxes from the population. Under these circumstances, no wars could have been undertaken since the combatants (in most cases, knights and their subordinates) could neither be forced to participate (over a period extending beyond the feudal obligations), nor could they be paid. The promise of material compensation in the form of goods and ransom was therefore the only way of inducing combatants to participate in a war. In the Middle Ages the predominant incentive for the individual "soldier" to participate in a war was the expectation of spoils (see Erler 1978 and Hochheimer 1967). Incidentally, the same applied to tournaments. The not-so-wealthy knights especially participated because of the prospect of material gain which consisted partly in the ransom from the defeated participants, partly in the value of the armament, clothing and horses of the losers (Bumke 1986, pp. 350–373). Therefore, "any mercenary would insist on a clear statement of the bounty (including ransoms) being written in his contract" (Glover 1982, p. 159). The custom of ransoming prisoners both *during* and *after* wars was considered by such eminent lawyers as Grotius to be a step toward a more humane society. The property right over a defeated adversary was well established in law, and could even be bequeathed (see in detail, Keen 1965, ch. IX). The individual's right to his booty was so generally accepted that "it was usual to go to court for the settlement of economic disputes between the prisoner (and his family) and the captor . . ." (Rosas 1976, p. 48). The following incident which occurred in the battle of Poitiers in 1356, is reproduced in extenso because it is a good illustration of how far the property rights over defeated enemies *extended* and how some of the transaction cost problems that arose were solved.

"There on all sides you could see the French scattered, and the English running and making prisoners," says Chandos Herald. Among these Frenchmen stood the Count of Dammartin, dismounted, it would appear, and probably more or less immobile in his heavy armour. First, as he stood thus, an esquire of the Black Prince's household called John Trailly came up and demanded his faith, which he gave him "in such wise that he should save me." Trailly took his bacinet and his gauntlets, and while he was doing so another man rushed up and cut the strap of his sword, which the count asked Trailly to keep, as he preferred him, rather than any other, to have it. Trailly then handed him over to a yeoman of his, who however quickly disappeared in quest of private gain. After this a Gascon came up, to whom also the count gave his faith, and who took an escutcheon of his armour. He too then moved on, and as he went the count called after him that since he was leaving him, he would give his faith to anyone else who might appear and would offer to save him. Finally, a man of Sir John Blankmouster arrived on the scene, who stayed with him and took him to his master and the Earl of Salisbury.

When Salisbury and the Black Prince both claimed the count as their prisoner before the Constable, it was thus not at all easy to decide to whom he had pledged his faith. He had been much too liberal with it for that. To avoid this sort of problem, the courts demanded better evidence than conflicting memories of verbal promises. The first man to receive the faith of a prisoner, they ruled, was in law his captor, but on two conditions. Firstly, he ought to establish his capture in the proper way; he should be the first man to seize the prisoner's right gauntlet, and to put his right hand in his. Thereafter, the gauntlet served as a token of his right. Secondly, he must have made some attempt to fulfil his contract to his prisoner, to protect his life. If he simply abandoned him on the field, he lost his right to him. He must therefore either put the prisoner in the charge of someone who would look after him, or he must escort him to a safe place behind the lines. Otherwise the prisoner was still a free man, and to protect his life might give his faith to whom he chose. No doubt it was on this last ground that the Count of Dammartin was in the end adjudged the prisoner of the Earl of Salisbury (Keen 1965, pp. 165–166).

The prisoners' names had to be made public (Keen 1965, p. 148) in order to provide the information necessary for potential demanders to become active. Prominent prisoners, including women, were at the disposition of the commander in chief. This does not mean, however, that the soldier taking the prisoner lost his property right; he had to be appropriately compensated by the commander (Glover 1982, p. 160).

In the Middle Ages, noteworthy institutional techniques were used to *reduce* the transaction cost in the market for prisoners.

1. One such device was the rule that the prisoner had to assess his *own value* (Keen 1965, p. 169). The captor might overestimate the "value" of a prisoner, in which case the ransom was not paid and the imprisonment was drawn out. This happened to Miguel de Cervantes Saavedra who was taken prisoner by corsars in 1575 and was sold on the slave market of Algiers. Because he carried a letter of recommendation to the King of Spain from his chief commander, Don Juan d'Austria, the Algerians thought that they could ask 1,000 gold thalers for his release. His family could not raise this sum. Only in 1580 were the monks of the Order of Trinity (see below) able to arrange for a reduction, so that the ransom could be paid by his family.

The prisoner had an incentive to indicate a ransom without too many strategic distortions: to indicate too low a value would increase the risk of being killed because the expected benefits to the captor might well be lower than the cost; to indicate too high a value would ruin him or her financially, or if the sum was not paid the prisoner ran the risk of being killed.

2. Another means of reducing transaction costs in the market was the rule of releasing the prisoner by *word of honour*. Giving *parole* was advantageous for both captor and captive because the former did not have to carry the cost of guarding and feeding, while the latter enjoyed freedom of movement. This procedure had the added advantage that the ransom could be raised by the prisoner himself, reducing the cost of communication and decision making. The terms of parole were usually kept, because the person (or members of his family or household) might possibly be recaptured. Moreover, in medieval society, breaking one's word of honour was considered untrustworthy, which also had negative effects on economic dealings (Best 1982, p. 170). When, for example, the imprisoned French King François I broke his word to the Emperor Charles V in the year 1525, he had to bear the cost of a lower reputation. The behaviour of the French King John II, who was taken prisoner by the English in the battle of Poitiers in 1356, was quite different. Having undertaken to pay three million écus d'or as ransom, he was allowed to return to France but had to furnish hostages. When one of them, his own son, fled, John II returned to England and died in captivity in 1364.

3. A third way to reduce transaction costs was the use of specialized *institutions* serving to establish contact between the demanders and suppliers in the market for prisoners. Obviously, a prisoner's value

dropped to zero if the captor was unable to transmit his demands to those willing to pay for his release, and the same held if those willing to pay did not know to whom they could make an offer. This problem may be of little relevance in many markets, but it is crucially important in the market for prisoners.

In the Middle Ages, two types of institutions emerged for the purpose of helping to clear the market:

1. *Individuals* acting as professional dealers in prisoners. This function was often performed by Jews because under medieval law only non-Christians were allowed to lend money on interest. As bankers (or being closely connected to banks) Jews could act effectively because they were able to advance the ransom from their own means, thus profiting from price rebates. The dealers had a right, supported by the courts, to recover the outlays and corresponding costs from the released prisoner (Erler 1978, pp. 55–56, 62–68). There was indeed competition between the professionals working for the benefit of both sides of the market.

2. *Private organizations* specializing in the ransom of prisoners. Two religious orders were prominent in this field up to the French Revolution (see Erler 1978, pp. 29–36). The Mercedarian order (Ordo Beatae Mariae Virginis de mercede redemptionis captivorum) was founded in 1218 as a knightly order, but in 1318 was transformed into a purely religious order in order to improve its position as a neutral intermediary, especially in dealings with the Saracens. Over a period of 500 years, roughly 70,000 prisoners are said to have been ransomed by this order. The Trinitarian order (Ordo SS. Trinitatis redemptionis captivorum), founded in 1198, seems to have achieved even more: it is reputed to have arranged the release of 900,000 prisoners (in both cases mostly from the hands of the Saracens). In addition to these orders, cities also acted as neutral intermediaries.

The general proposition that a defeated enemy's fate depends on the (net) value of the prisoners to the captors allows us to derive specific theoretical propositions for the case of well-defined property rights of the individual captors over the prisoners. They can, in principle, be empirically tested. As appropriate data is lacking, no econometric tests are possible. The propositions are therefore illustrated by examples.

The following seven ceteris paribus hypotheses are advanced, with the first four referring to factors on the demand side, and the last three referring to the supply side.

Hypothesis 1.   The higher the disposable material wealth of a prisoner and/or of other demanders, the more likely it is that he will be spared and ransomed. Poor, vanquished soldiers have a higher risk of being killed on the battle field.

This hypothesis is not trivial. It could also be plausibly argued that the military leaders of the enemy (who tended to be more prosperous men) were made responsible for the war and were accordingly punished by long imprisonment or death. The common soldiers (who were generally less wealthy), on the other hand, could not be made responsible for the war and were soon released. This view would predict a type of behaviour in contrast with hypothesis 1. In legal literature (e.g., Delessert 1977, p. 22) it is often argued that the prices asked were "too high," so that only the wealthiest prisoners could ransom themselves. This is a misunderstanding of the price system. Prices asked for poorer prisoners were indeed much lower than for rich ones (see e.g., Flory 1942, p. 111), but while the cost of sparing, guarding and keeping them was similar for all kinds of prisoners, the expected profit to be gained from ransoming a wealthy captive was higher, so that a larger number of them were exchanged. Historical literature is rich in evidence speaking for hypothesis 1. Thus Sultan Bajazet is reported (Glover 1982, p. 158) to have selected twenty of the richest prisoners for ransoming after a victorious battle and to have had the remaining 3,000 prisoners put to death. It is often said (e.g., Contamine 1981, p. 244) that the Swiss soldiers habitually killed all defeated enemies. In actual fact (Schaufelberger 1952, p. 181; Bernoulli 1921, p. 128), the vanquished enemies were spared, provided it was materially rewarding to hold them to ransom. The asymmetric kind of behaviour observed in the Peasants' War (Bauernkrieg) in Germany (1524–1525) is also consistent with hypothesis 1: the winning nobility brutally tortured and killed more than 30,000 poor peasants, but when the peasants, on the other hand, got hold of a rich nobleman, they tended to hold him for ransom, despite the heavy grievances they held against their oppressors.

Hypothesis 2.   The higher a prisoner's human capital value (that is, the better his abilities and education are, and the younger and healthier he is), the better are his chances of being spared in battle and held for ransom.

This hypothesis is, of course, closely related to the preceding hypothesis, but the emphasis here is not only on market income but also on the expected nonmarket output that one such political or religious leader might have. An example is King Richard I (Lionheart) of England.

He was seized by the Austrian Duke Leopold on his return from the First Crusade and sold to the German Emperor Henry VI for 50,000 marks, a sum which enabled the latter to build the wall around Vienna. Henry VI then sold Richard for three times the sum (150,000 marks) to England, thereby financing his costly campaigns in Sicily (Erler 1978, pp. 37–44). The English were prepared to pay this enormous sum because of Richard's performance as an able ruler (a fact vividly illustrated in Sir Walter Scott's Ivanhoe).

According to this hypothesis, defeated enemies were also spared if they were able to perform valued labour services for the individual victors. Coerced labour services, closely akin to slavery, were a perfectly legal treatment of prisoners in the Middle Ages, and for centuries one of the purposes for warfare was to secure such services.

Hypothesis 3.   The more effectively the demanders can act in financial respects, the better a prisoner's chance of being ransomed.

Most of the prisoners of war in the Middle Ages were men. The wives therefore had to be given the right of disposing of the family property. The law, for example, permitted the wives to use the property they had brought into the marriage, which they otherwise were not allowed to dispose of, thus contributing to a (ceteris paribus) upward shift of the demand curve.

Hypothesis 4.   The higher the demand for ransoming is, the less the family members can appropriate the assets and other sources of income of the captured relative.

This hypothesis suggests that it is not *solely* family ties that determine how much effort is made to have a family member released. There are also material aspects involved that influence this effort. The law knew of this trait of human nature. There was *no legal duty* to ransom any relative. However, care was taken that there were no positive incentives for opportunistic behaviour. One of the rules was that children could not inherit from their parents unless they had made a definite effort to ransom them from captivity (see Erler 1978, p. 21). Under certain conditions the relatives automatically *lost* their share in the testator's wealth if they failed to have him released. This was, for instance, the case when the prisoner owned titles and privileges (for example monopoly rents) *ad personam*, which conferred benefits on the relatives.

Hypothesis 5.   The more costly it is to spare a defeated enemy, the more enemies will be killed and the worse they will be treated in captivity. In the Middle Ages the victors often killed prisoners simply because

they found it difficult to nourish them. The massacres of the Christian
crusaders among the Saracens (and also Christians) in Palestine may be
attributed to the high cost of providing food and water. There is evidence
that when the prisoners were able to carry the cost of imprisonment
themselves (which was quite often the case), they were treated more
mildly (Schaufelberger 1952, p. 180).

Hypothesis 6. No unconditional right (or insurance) to be ransomed
from captivity is granted.

In the Middle Ages, some guilds, knightly orders, cities and even small
states had in their statutes the provision that they would ransom their
members. This provision was, however, not unconditional because one
was aware that this would drive up the price for a prisoner, and would
reduce the incentive for the members to avoid capture (moral hazard).
Accordingly, ransoming was promised under three conditions only (see
Erler 1978, pp. 22–25): (1) the member must have been captured on an
official mission; (2) he must have made a clear effort to minimize the risk
of being captured; (3) he must have proven his courage in battle (or
under similar circumstances).

Hypothesis 7. Captured civilians are not treated worse than captured
soldiers provided the captor expects the same ransom.

This hypothesis stands in stark contrast to the notion that civilians
were *generally* treated badly in medieval wars. This is certainly true for
the poor part of the population, in particular the peasants, who often
were not able to raise ransom (for a mass of evidence see e.g., Vagts 1938
or Flory 1942). On the other hand, there are many accounts of rich
civilians being ransomed (e.g., Erler 1978; Schaufelberger 1952) but these
people were only a small part of the total population. Traditional historians seem to be surprised by this similar treatment of soldiers and
civilians. Thus Contamine (1981, p. 258) writes: "Certes il est frappant de
voir que les ransons des non-combattents supposés ne sont pas trop
inférieures à cettes des soudoyers."

Weakening of the Market for Prisoners

At the end of the Middle Ages independent and centralized nation-states
began to arise, the extreme case being the absolute monarchy in France
in the eighteenth century. This process was accompanied by a basic
change in philosophical thinking on war, most clearly expressed by

Rousseau in his *Contrat social* of 1762: "La guerre n'est donc point une relation d'homme à homme mais une relation d'Etat à Etat" (Rousseau 1876, p. 24). Following this view a soldier is not a criminal but is someone who follows the demands of his country.

The gradual development of independent nation-states was accompanied by the emergence of standing armies in which the soldiers became public servants paid in principle by the state (Delessert 1977, pp. 16 and 28–30). In the same period, military technology began to change. The new firearms (rifles) could be used effectively only if the firing power was concentrated. Therefore, the soldiers had to fight in line under strict discipline (see Brennan and Tullock 1982). The military commanders could no longer allow individual soldiers to fight in an uncoordinated manner or, in particular, to take prisoners on their own account.

Changes in weapon technology led to prisoners being taken at an increasingly higher level of military organization. In consequence, ransoming negotiations began to shift from the individual to a higher level of social (military) organization. The individual's property right in prisoners was gradually attenuated. This corresponds to a process of an increasing taxation of individual ransom by collective units. The war party engaging in centralized bargaining over prisoners could obtain more favourable terms of exchange over an atomistic counterpart. The opponent had an incentive to follow suit.

Towards the end of the seventeenth century, and during the eighteenth century, *ransoming cartels* became common. These treaties were based on bilateral exchange, and were concluded *before* a battle or a war took place. They stipulated exactly the exchange rates to be used. Usually, exchange proceeded on the basis of rank for rank, and the remaining prisoners were then ransomed according to the prices agreed on by paying a sum of money in a stipulated currency. The cartels also determined whether the exchanges were to take place during or after the battle, whether parole was to be granted, and the agreements usually contained provisions relating to the sick and wounded.

The first ransoming agreements of this kind were concluded between the military commanders in the field. An example is the Cartel of Sluys (Ecluse) agreed on between the French Major-General Marquis de Barail and the English Major-General Conway during the Seven Years War (1759). Prisoners had to be returned fifteen days after capture, and in order to settle the likely balances after the exchange of rank for rank, a table of ransoms for the various ranks was included. A field marshal was worth £2,500, while a private of the line cost £40; guardsmen were £70. Regimental officers were to be ransomed for the equivalent of one month's pay (Glover 1982, pp. 168–170; Gurlt 1873, p. 25). Later, ransoming cartels were concluded between states. An example is the treaty made by England with France in 1780. In this cartel, the ransom for each rank was stated and ranged from £60 for a commander in chief, £12 for a colonel, to £1 for a common sailor (Flory 1942, p. 112). The ransoming prices fixed in the cartels varied considerably depending on the relative scarcities and the expected outcome of the battle or war. While the price ratio of an officer of top rank relative to a common soldier in the above-mentioned treaty between England and France of 1780 was 60:1, it was 5,000:1 in cartels of 1673 and 1675 concluded between France and the Netherlands. The higher price of military commanders relative to soldiers in the seventeenth century compared to the eighteenth century also reflects the fact that military commanders had more decision power in the earlier period and that in this period the outcome of a battle or war depended more on them than in the following century.

Ransoming cartels were not only concluded between "civilized" nations of similar culture but also with what were then called "Barbary States", for instance between Britain and Algiers in 1664, or between the United States and Morocco in 1786.

In the earlier cartels the ransom receipts were distributed to the soldiers engaged in the particular military encounter. In the eighteenth century the ransom was increasingly put into the public treasury, the soldiers being paid by the state. War booty gradually lost its import-ance as a means of inducing men to go to war. From there it was only a small step to explicitly transferring the property rights over prisoners to the state.

Property Rights Belong to the State

The transfer of the right

The final transfer of the property right over prisoners from the individual soldier to the state was brought about by two changes in technology and society:

1. More effective, long range firing weapons became available for mobile and large scale use on the battle field. Canons are designed to kill or wound the enemy in a collective effort. If the property right had remained with the individual soldiers they would have had no incentive to use these new war technologies effectively. Indeed, throughout the eighteenth century, the artillery was stationed on the left flank of an army

to indicate that it must yield "precedence and honor to the rest of the army" (Vagts 1938, p. 44). This change in military technology led the state to ratify the definite transfer of property rights over prisoners from the individual to the state, a transfer which was initiated by the gradual shift towards ransoming cartels mentioned above.

2. The French Revolution led to the 'levée en masse" of the male population as a result of the rise of nationalism and the advent of democracy. *Conscription* was introduced; the material incentive to go to war was substituted by democratically sanctioned force. In consequence, the property right over prisoners could be taken away from the individual soldiers without impairing the pursuit of war.

Both the change in military technology and the introduction of the compulsory draft enabled, and made it efficient for, the state to hold the property rights over prisoners, and to appropriate the ransom. War became a relation between states; "soldiers were not be held responsible for the war, nor its consequences" (Delessert 1977, p. 29). Under this changed property rights structure, the individual soldier no longer had an incentive to take an interest in the enemy for material reasons. Killing an enemy in battle entailed no monetary costs for the individual soldier concerned (and could even bring rewards in the form of decorations). The restraint placed on killing an enemy when it would be possible to do so must therefore be based on ethical motives only. As it may be assumed that morality does not change with a transfer of property rights, the same *ethical motives* for not killing a defeated enemy may be taken to have existed earlier, and to a similar (or even the same) extent. A decrease in material incentives for not killing an enemy, together with a similar level of morality towards the enemy, must be expected to lead to a greater number of defeated enemies being killed. On the same grounds, the treatment of enemy soldiers who fall into captivity must be expected to worsen, because, with unchanged morality, there is no material incentive for a soldier to concern himself with the prisoners. The change in property rights is thus ceteris paribus expected to result in a lower standard of living for prisoners of war with respect to nourishment and medical care, at least as far as it hinges on the discretion of the individual soldiers.

Historical Observations

The theoretical hypothesis derived on the worsening fate of defeated enemies is well borne out by the revolutionary and Napoleonic wars at the end of the eighteenth and in the first half of the nineteenth century. In these periods, the changes in military technology and in army organization (conscription) took place and had the theoretically expected consequences.

The revolutionary and Napoleonic wars are generally observed to have been of great brutality, in many ways exceeding by far what happened on the battlefields in former times. "In the revolutionary wars there seems to have been a tendency on both sides . . . not to regard the adversary as a lawful combatant . . . but rather as a rebel or criminal fighting for an illegal cause" (Rosas 1976, p. 62). In this spirit the leaders of the French Revolution decided that enemy soldiers were not to be given quarter and they refused to exchange prisoners or to ransom them from captivity. Trade with the enemy was considered treason and was therefore strictly forbidden to the individual soldiers by two laws promulgated by the French National Assembly (of September 12, 1792 and March 25, 1793). These rules were the result not only of ideology but also of a rational calculation by war leaders: the release of prisoners "might restore fighters to the enemy more in need of them than the French" (Vagts 1938, p. 119). As these rules were disadvantageous for the troops in the field, they were repeatedly disregarded on the scene of battle, and the decree that forbade sparing a defeated enemy was repealed (Vagts 1938, p. 120; Rosas 1976, p. 65).

Despite the repeal, bilateral exchanges of prisoners which depended on state action were often difficult, or even impossible, when the prisoners on the two sides of the conflict were of *unequal value*. Thus, in 1795 France did not agree to exchange man for man and rank for rank, ". . . her not illogical argument being that every fighting man, officer or private, was of more value to Britain [who was notoriously short of soldiers] than were three times their number of Frenchmen to France" (Abell 1914, p. 30). For a similar reason an exchange proposal of Napoleon to the British did not materialize because the French wanted to exchange Spanish and Portuguese soldiers who were of little fighting value man for man for British soldiers (Abell 1914, pp. 34–36; Glover 1982, pp. 174–189). Ransom on the basis of a man-for-man exchange is unlikely to come about when the unequal military value of prisoners is not balanced by money.

Conscription (introduced in France by law on August 23, 1793) not only led to a change in the property rights over prisoners but also drastically changed the cost of war for the leaders of the army. Until then, soldiers had been valuable goods for which one had to expend large sums, and that one therefore spared as far as possible. The "democratization" of war made the whole male population (except the very young and very old) available to the army. The monetary cost of war was thereby lowered because it was difficult and inefficient to raise taxes on the income that would have been generated in civilian occupation (the first modern direct tax starts only with the British income tax of 1799; see Neumark 1986, p. 232). According to Fuller (1961, p. 35) "conscription changed the basis of warfare. Hitherto soldiers had been costly, now they were cheap . . . [Napoleon] boasted to Metternich that he could afford to expend 30,000 men a month—men were now as cheap as dirt."

The increased brutality of war observable in the revolutionary and Napoleonic was between 1792 and 1815 (see in general e.g., Best 1979, 1980) is thus due to a decrease in the value of all soldiers: Soldiers became of less worth to their own commanders, and the enemy soldiers became of less worth to the soldiers of the adversary. Accordingly, battles led to enormous loss of life and terrible suffering amongst the wounded and prisoners. In one single battle (Borodino of 1812) for instance, the French suffered 30,000 dead and wounded, the Russians more than 44,000 (Keegan, Holmes and Gau 1985, p. 147). Obviously, moral principles were not able to stem the tide of ever increasing loss of life in war, and of the mistreatment of the prisoners of war. Exchanges of prisoners during wars took place only irregularly and unpredictably. Most prisoners had to suffer long detainment under extremely bad conditions (e.g., Abell 1914) until the end of the war, provided they lived to see it. The treatment of the wounded was "lamentably falling off from the generous humanitarian conventions observed by the military of the ancien régime" (Best 1980, p. 126).

From the middle of the nineteenth century it became clear to the political leaders of the nations that a solution must be found to improve at least the situation of the wounded and the prisoners of war. Otherwise, the system of negative incentives (conscription) and positive incentives (decorations) to join up was feared to be insufficient, in the long run, to motivate men to go to war.

Property Rights Belong (partly) to International Institutions

Reasons for the (Partial) Transfer

The shift of the property rights over prisoners from the individual soldiers to the state induced the combatants to employ the newest military technology (long distance firing weapons), but this had a negative result which, in the long run, made this property right allocation inefficient. The ever increasing brutality occurring with the use of increasingly effective weapon technology resulted in military confrontations with enormous casualties. This in turn brought the problem of motivating individual soldiers to the fore. The larger the perceived cost, the more likely a soldier is to shirk military service and active fighting, (keeping the benefits constant). If there is a widespread feeling among the soldiers that military service is intolerably cruel because of the high risk of being killed and because of the dismal fate of the wounded and captured, the willingness to serve declines. The war leadership of each nation thus has an incentive to improve the situation for their own soldiers. They would like to be able to assure them that they will receive adequate medical attention if wounded, and that they will be treated well if taken prisoner.

The leaders of a particular nation cannot provide such a "guarantee" by unilateral action because the treatment of the wounded and the prisoners depends to a large extent on the behaviour of the adversary. In this situation, two possibilities arise:

1. An *ethical norm* is set up stating that, on moral grounds, a defeated enemy has to be treated well. The question is, of course, how to set up such a norm. The prospects do not look very good in view of the fact that the Christian religion has always stressed that one's fellow man has to be treated well and may not be killed. This ethical norm has not proved to be strong enough to prevent the growing brutality of war.

2. *International rules* have to be found by consensus stipulating that each nation is obliged to treat defeated enemy soldiers well. Such a consensus is possible behind the "veil of ignorance" (Rawls 1972), that is, in a situation in which the participating nations do not know whether the rules arrived at will be to their advantage or disadvantage in a particular war, in a particular battle, or with respect to a particular type of weapon used. What matters is that the rules must be considered beneficial to the leaders of each participating nation over a whole sequence of possible future military conflicts. To the extent that such international rules are arrived at, the participating nations voluntarily transfer part of their property rights over defeated enemies to an international institution. The main problem with this approach is that international rules are a public good from the point of view of each nation. Each of them has an incentive to break the contract when it is found to be advantageous to do so in a particular situation.

Four theoretical propositions may be advanced on the basis of the foregoing:

1. It is hard and time consuming to find a consensus on suitable international rules of war;

2. the enforcement is difficult and acts of killings prisoners and bad treatment of prisoners, that is, of free-riding, will often be observed;

3. interactions and agreements between the conflicting parties concerning prisoners of war tend to be of reciprocal nature (which violates the basic idea of the humanitarian conventions); and

4. the actual treatment of prisoners is largely explicable by benefit-cost considerations of the relevant decision makers.

The Rise of International Humanitarian Institutions

The dreadful experience of the battle at Solferino (1859) motivated Henry Dunant to fight actively for the establishment of international institutions to improve the lot of wounded and captured soldiers. The basis for that effort was laid by the philosophers and lawyers of the Enlightenment such as Montesquieu (1689–1755), Vattel (1714–1767), and Rousseau (1712–1778). These ideas may have contributed to the establishment of a new morality concerning the treatment of defeated enemies, but there can be little doubt that the international humanitarian *institutions* were of considerably larger practical importance.

As expected in theory, the international humanitarian institutions were slow to emerge. The basic principles of the rules became clear in the mid-nineteenth century, but it was very difficult to find a consensus among the nations concerned. The search for mutually acceptable rules for the treatment of defeated enemies took more than a century (see Armstrong 1985 or Rosas 1976, pp. 69–84, for details). In 1864, the First Geneva Convention on the treatment of wounded and sick prisoners was held. The first multinational convention about the prisoners of war came about in 1899. A major breakthrough was achieved in the Geneva Convention of 1929, which was ratified by the main powers France, Germany, Great Britain and the United States before World War II but not by the Soviet Union and Japan. The most important international rule relating to prisoners of war is the Third Geneva Convention of 1949 which has attained almost universal acceptance. In the various conventions, the following four main international rules of warfare with respect to individual participants were fixed: (1) wounded and captured soldiers are to be spared and taken care of; (2) wounded and sick soldiers are to be exchanged without compensation during the war; (3) prisoners of war are the property of the state in whose hands they are: accordingly this state also carries the burden of responsibility, and at the end of the war the prisoners must immediately be released without compensation; (4) prisoners of war, except officers, may be employed for "nonmilitary" work. Most of these rules had already been part of *bilateral* treaties and conventions with respect to *particular* wars (Best 1980, p. 149, and very extensively Gurlt 1873); the unconditional release of prisoners after the war had, for example, already been included in the Treaty of Westphalia ending the Thirty Year's War (1618–1648). The Red Cross Conventions, on the other hand, are *multilateral* and applicable in *general* for all wars. These rules in effect state that the individual nations have transferred part of their property rights to international institutions. They agree to restrict their rights over the prisoners, in particular they relinquish the right to treat them as they think fit—putting them to death, for instance.

Parallel with the conventions, international humanitarian *organisations* were founded, most notably the Red Cross. Founded in 1863 by Dunant for the care of wounded soldiers, it concerned itself only later with the situation of the prisoners of war (for the history, see e.g., Forsythe 1977; Willemin and Heacock 1984). According to its statutes, the Red Cross is neutral and stands apart from the parties in order to act efficiently in situations of military conflict. This holds in particular for the International Committee of the Red Cross (see e.g., Forsythe 1977) but not necessarily for the national Red Cross societies with (according to Best 1980, pp. 141–142) an "efficient and in many cases total integration with their respective countries' war machines. . . ." The same is true for earlier rules based not on humanitarian but on purely Christian ethics. For example, in the fourteenth and fifteenth centuries the Church established rules to save churchmen, farmers, pilgrims and travellers, and later also women and children, but "the regulations have been nullified by contrary practice." The only exceptions were religious persons, because killing or brutal treatment meant the then heavy penalty of anathema (Delessert 1977, p. 14).

The second proposition, on the widespread inhumane treatment of prisoners of war in violation of the international humanitarian conventions, is also supported by historical evidence. The general picture is summarized in the International Encyclopaedia of the Social Sciences (1968, p. 12) which states bluntly: "The history of actual prisoner treatment during the century that saw the development and acceptance of these legal doctrines showed largely a record of deviation from these theories."

In the German-French war of 1870/1871, the humanitarian conventions then existing were disregarded by the French to a large degree, partly because the soldiers in the field knew little or nothing about these rules. In several instances, the Red Cross emblems were used in order to deceive the enemy, a tactic to which the Germans in turn tended to react by violating the conventions. This is a clear instance of the breakdown of mutually advantageous rules because of free-riding. A leading Swiss scholar of international law of the period, Bluntschli (1817, pp. 328 et seq.), complained bitterly about the deviation between the war practices and the existing rules. The results of the Hague Conventions arrived at after this war (in 1899 and 1907) were "hailed as a great achievement . . . but in World War I this progress turned out to be purely on paper" (Scheidl 1943, p. 94). The many violations of the humanitarian rules occurring in 1914–1918 may be exemplified in two areas:

1. Submarine warfare. The reasons for breaking the rules were essentially cost factors. A submarine, operating on the surface, as it would have to do to carry out the practice of visit and search, was extremely vulnerable to counterattack, and it was therefore less risky to attack a ship *believed* to be acting against one's country's interests. The same was true in World War II: ". . . the fundamental reason for rejection of restraints lay in the technical change [which] had made the surfaced submarine increasingly vulnerable" (Ranft 1979, pp. 52–54).

2. Repatriation of prisoners of war after the end of hostilities. Instead of being released immediately by the Central Powers (Germany and Austria) in November 1918 as stipulated in the conventions, at least 250,000 prisoners from Russia who were "short of clothing, half-starved, and [who had] received no [medical] attention of any kind," were repatriated only in 1922 (Delessert 1977, pp. 53–54).

In World War II, ". . . the law relating to prisoners of war [. . .] was frequently violated, in some cases on a massive scale" (Rosas 1976, p. 78). The survival chances of prisoners in Germany and the Soviet Union were low because of brutal treatment and insufficient nourishment. Fourty-five percent of the Germans captured in Russia, and sixty percent of the Russians captured by the Germans did not return to their respective countries (Keegan, Holmes and Gau 1985, p. 157). Repatriation was again exceedingly slow mainly because the prisoners were used for slave labour. In December 1947, thousands of German prisoners of war were still in French and British hands. According to United Nations figures (*Yearbook* 1959, p. 565), by 1950, 1,952,609 German prisoners in Soviet custody had still to be repatriated.

In the case of Vietnam, ". . . there is an abundance of information pointing to the widespread use of torture and summary executions [of prisoners]" (Rosas 1976, p. 171). The International Committee of the Red Cross was not allowed to visit the prison camps in North Vietnam and stopped visiting those in South Vietnam because of interference from the government. There was generally no exchange of wounded and sick prisoners during the conflict (Forsythe 1977, p. 25, 157–158; Delessert 1977, p. 113).

More than a year after the end of the Gulf war in October 1988 Iran still held more than 70,000 prisoners of war, and Iraq 30,000. But both countries signed Article 118 of the Third Geneva Convention which requires all prisoners to be freed as soon as fighting comes to an end. Fewer than 2,500 of the Gulf war's prisoners were freed, and all of them were badly wounded, ill or aged. Worse, the International Committee of the Red Cross was allowed to visit and register (and thus offer limited protection to) only two-thirds of the prisoners in detention. There is evidence (*Economist*, Nov. 11, 1989, p. 19) that both Iraq and Iran intimidated and brainwashed captives.

The third proposition suggests that the treatment (and repatriation) of prisoners of war is ruled to a large extent by intense *bargaining* and *reciprocal* agreements between the states at war. It thus essentially follows the historical pattern observed, although reciprocity is completely antagonistic to the humanitarian approach: "The obligations of States resulting from the provisions of the Geneva Conventions are essentially unilateral, not reciprocal, in character" (Draper 1965, p. 63). In an agreement between American and German delegates signed in November 1918, for example, the exchange was based on a strict equality of the numbers of valid prisoners according to rank (only wounded and sick prisoners are to be released unilaterally) (Flory 1942, p. 134). Prisoners of war are part of a package deal; they are a bargaining tool to obtain political and military concessions. The application of humanitarian principles is often made conditional on terms of reciprocity. This is evidenced in particular by the agreements in the Indo-Pakistan, Vietnam and Middle East Wars (as discussed extensively by Delessert 1977, ch. IV). The strong condemnation of bargaining and reciprocity by the Red Cross has achieved little, if anything. What has been said in the interwar period by a leading authority on humanitarian law still holds: "La réciprocité, semble à être, au moins au temps de guerre, le seul principe devant lequel se plient les gouvernements" (Werner 1928, p. 5).

The actual treatment of prisoners of war is governed by benefit and cost considerations of the relevant decision makers, as suggested in the fourth proposition. In the twentieth century, as in the centuries before, defeated enemies tend to be spared and treated well when it benefits the captor, and they tend to be killed or treated harshly when the cost of doing otherwise is high.

In modern warfare, a humane treatment of defeated enemies may yield the following *benefits*:

1. The prisoners may be integrated in the captor's army. This very old procedure (see, for example Walzer 1969) is also practiced quite often in modern times. Glover (1982, p. 163) tells the story of an entire Tyrolean regiment that was captured in Napoleon's Italian campaign of 1796. The French sold it to their Spanish allies for two dollars a head. Captured in turn by the British in 1798, it then volunteered for the British army and became the Ninety-Seventh (Queen's Germans) Regiment. In the Second World War, many Russian prisoners chose, or were forced, to join the German ranks. The German 134th Infantry Division offered all its prisoners regular status as soldiers. At the end of 1942, about half of the division was composed of former Soviet soldiers (Epstein 1974, p. 61). A well known case is the so-called Vlasov Army, which was mainly composed of prisoners of war (see e.g., Huxley-Blythe 1964). In the Korean War, 50,000 South Korean prisoners of war joined the North Korean army, and in the Vietnam War a considerable number of prisoners entered the armed forces of the former enemy (Delessert 1977, pp. 189–190). The same is reported for the war in Yemen and for the Gulf war between Iraq and Iran (Rosas 1976, p. 158).

2. In the two world wars, the detaining states employed on a massive scale prisoners of war for work either benefiting them directly by its military character or indirectly by releasing nationals for the armed forces. This conflicts with humanitarian principles (Rosas 1976, ch. 8.6) but raises the value of prisoners to the detaining power. A change in the relative benefit-cost ratio changes the way in which prisoners are treated. This is well exemplified by the way the Germans dealt with Russian and Polish prisoners of war: As long as there was no manpower shortage they were treated most brutally, so that many of them died. But when the Germans began to depend on them for manning the factories and farms, the "Untermensch" became a "guest worker" and achieved a degree of equality with the German workers (see Homze 1967, in particular pp. 169–176).

3. A further benefit from taking prisoners is a higher likelihood of surrender and defection by enemy soldiers (a strategy used by Mao and Castro), and the possibility of getting information from them (Rosas 1976, pp. 134–140). While such behaviour is not prohibited by the

humanitarian conventions, it is not in their spirit, and is rather the result of the self-interest of the parties at war.

The treatment of prisoners of war in modern times is also strongly influenced by *cost* factors. When the cost of detaining prisoners is high, states may release prisoners unilaterally if they can be reasonably certain that they are not immediately put into the army again. This happened both before and after the establishment of the humanitarian conventions. In the Mexican War (1846–1848), for example, about 10,000 prisoners were unilaterally released by United States troops because they placed such a heavy burden on the supplies (Murphy 1971, p. 479). Similarly, the Republic of Vietnam released prisoners from its jails because of the lack of physical space and the cost involved in feeding them (Prugh 1975, p. 64). When, on the other hand, prisoners could not be released without peril to one's own side, high cost of imprisonment had the opposite effect. Much of the ill-treatment of prisoners during the American War of Independence was due to the unpreparedness of the Americans to receive such a large number of prisoners (Glover 1982, p. 73). The killings, atrocities and inhumanity of the Japanese in World War II were mainly due to their being wholly unprepared to look after a large number of prisoners (Best 1980, p. 219). As has been the case in earlier periods (see our hypothesis 5), costs are thus an important determinant of the treatment of prisoners, irrespective of humanitarian rules.

Two areas of modern war are practically outside the scope of humanitarian rules, namely *guerilla* and *terrorist* activities. The accommodation of this kind of warfare within the law of modern wars has been the biggest problem since World War II (Draper 1979, pp. 135–162; Best 1979, p. 31). Many states consider guerilla fighters and terrorists to be no better than criminals to whom the humanitarian principles accorded to prisoners of war do not apply, and they have in many cases been killed on the spot, or treated badly when taken prisoner (see Rosas 1976, ch. VII; Best 1979, pp. 31–36). The Red Cross (International Committee) is quite helpless in this area (e.g., Freymond 1976, p. 105) because the element of reciprocity, which is basically rejected by the humanitarian approach, is so strong. Terrorists often resort to taking prisoners (kidnapping) in order to improve their political bargaining position, or simply to raise money. In these areas the market re-emerges to a considerable extent. Ransoming kidnapped persons is often practiced, and the payers are both individuals (family members) and the state. There is even a more or less secret market for ransoming prisoners of the "cold war" between states; during the period 1964–1977, the government of the Federal Republic

of Germany ransomed approximately 13,500 people imprisoned in
the German Democratic Republic, the prices ranging from 180,000
Deutschmark for a doctor of medicine to DM 30,000 for a worker. Better
known is the practice of exchanging spies (see Meyer 1977).

Concluding Remarks

Changes in the allocation of the property rights over prisoners explain
many of the variations in the treatment of defeated enemies in the course
of history. Benefits and costs of either killing or sparing and looking
after the vanquished adversary determine the behaviour of the individual
soldiers, but these benefits and costs differ greatly depending on the
assignment of the property right. The emergence and erosion of the rules
governing the allotment of these property rights is explicable in terms of
technological and political developments. These are the main theses of
this chapter. The propositions derived from the basis of economic theory
are compatible with historical accounts. The hypotheses are not common-
place either; a leading expert in the field (Flory 1942, p. 159) states
for example: "Prior to the middle of the the seventeenth century, the
economic interest of the captor may have had a direct relation to the
treatment accorded prisoners, but there seems to be little correlation
between alterations in the law and economic advantage since that
time . . . the leading principle seems to have been humanitarianism."
However, it has been suggested here that the economic approach is able
to throw light on the development of the rules established, and that the
actual treatment of prisoners is strongly influenced by benefits and costs
of the war participants. The economic approach also makes clear that
there may be a humane treatment of (some) prisoners even without
humanitarian conventions (as was the case with ransoming) and that the
existence of humanitarian conventions does not necessarily lead to a
better treatment of prisoners, as shown by the history of war over the last
hundred years.

In the Middle Ages the individual combatant had a well-defined property right over the enemy he took prisoner. A market for the exchange
of prisoners for monetary ransom emerged which was surprisingly efficient, benefiting both captor and captive. It need not be stressed that the
outcome was not "just" in any sense; defeated adversaries who were of
value (as determined by demand for and supply of prisoners) tended to
be spared, while prisoners of little or no value risked death.

A drastic worsening of the conditions for *all* soldiers (and civilians) resulted when the state assumed control of the property rights over prisoners in the wake of the French Revolution. This transfer of rights was possible and efficient because of new weapon developments (long-range firearms) and conscription. While the goal of forcing the soldiers to apply the new military technologies was reached, it proved to be self-defeating. Wars became so brutal that, in the long run, problems arose in inducing men to actively participate in wars. The war leaders of the various nations found it in their own interest to give up part of the property rights over prisoners by agreeing to the establishment of international humanitarian rules (Geneva Conventions) and organizations (the Red Cross). Because of free-riding incentives, these arrangements have proved to be only partially successful. These developments indicate that it is very difficult to substitute moral (humanitarian) principles and rules for material incentives.

General References to the Literature

Extensive reports on the treatment of prisoners over the course of history are provided in
>Flory, William, E.S. *Prisoners of War. A Study in the Development of International War*. Washington: American Council of Public Affairs, 1942.
>Best, Geoffrey. *Humanity in Warfare. The Modern History of International Law of Armed Conflict*. London: Weidenfels and Nicholson, 1980.
>Glover, Michael. *The Velvet Glove: The Decline and Fall of Moderation in War*. London: Hodder and Stoughton, 1982.

Legal aspects are emphasized in
>Keen, Maurice H. *The Laws of War in the Late Middle Ages*. London: Routledge and Kegan Paul, 1965.
>Rosas, Allan. *The Legal Status of Prisoners of War. A Study in International Humanitarian Law Applicable in Armed Conflicts*. Helsinki: Academia Scientiarum Fennica, 1976.

The economic approach has been applied to military aspects (tactics) by
>Brennan, Geoffrey and Tullock, Gordon. "An Economic Theory of Military Tactics: Methodological Individualism at War." *Journal of Economic Behavior and Organization* 3 (1982): 225–242.
>Wenig, Alois. "Überbevölkerung eine Kriegsursache? Einige Anmerkungen zur Bevölkerungslehre von Thomas Robert Malthus." *Kyklos* 38 (1985): 365–391.

An application to a related issue is
>Anderson, Gray M. and Tollison, Robert D. "Life in the Gulag: A Property Rights Perspective." *Cato Journal* 5 (Spring/Summer 1985): 295–304.

PART C
EXTENSIONS

The final part of the book is devoted to open questions of the "economic view of the world". The emphasis shifts from the insights provided by the economic approach to its improvement. The interaction of ethical beliefs and psychological processes within various institutions are therefore the focal points.

The limits and further developments of the economic model of man is the subject of chapter 9. In addition to mistaken critique and serious warnings, shortcomings which have to be overcome are discussed. The enrichment of preferences and constraints are the most important improvements of the economic view of human behaviour.

Chapter 10 deals with the limit of the market (or price) system which also serves to point out some disregarded aspects of the economic model of behaviour. A survey demonstrates the importance of subjective ethical values and ideas about fairness in the market sphere.

Under specific conditions the rationality assumptions underlying the behavioural model of traditional economics is doubtful, as has been suggested by psychological experiments. Part of the *anomalies* to which individuals tend to fall prey are, however, eliminated at the social level by the influence of various decision-making mechanisms. Chapter 11 argues that the economic model of behaviour as presented in this book does not lose but rather gains in importance: mankind is made up of human beings able to overcome their shortcomings by imposing rules on themselves and by creating adequate institutions.

Chapter 12 distinguishes between an objectively given possibility set and one which a particular person deems relevant only for him or herself—the *ipsative possibility* set. Under certain circumstances, not all objectively attainable alternatives are taken into consideration; in other circumstances, people believe that they can obtain more than is objectively possible. The difference between these two possibility sets is mostly determined by psychological processes, but in some cases is also consciously chosen by people. This accounts for behaviour which is otherwise inexplicable.

9 THE LIMITS AND FURTHER DEVELOPMENTS OF HOMO OECONOMICUS

Limits of the Existing Economic Model of Behaviour

The concept of "homo oeconomicus"—as of any other scientific point of view—is characterized by particular strengths and weaknesses. This book has so far concentrated mainly on the advantages of applying the economic view of the world to various problem areas. This chapter now considers various limitations of the economic approach, distinguishing between (1) mistaken critique (2) warnings to be taken seriously, and (3) weaknesses to be improved upon.

Mistaken Critique

The economic approach is often attacked for wrong reasons. It is, for instance, often claimed that the model of rational behaviour used in economics cannot be applied to other areas because there "irrational" or

139

"spontaneous" behaviour is taken to prevail. By way of practical applications to six areas the second part of this book has demonstrated that the economic approach is indeed capable of providing insights going considerably beyond what has previously been known. For this reason, this general rejection is not further considered here. Neither is it useful to discuss attacks against a version of the homo oeconomicus which is no longer relevant today, namely the fiction of a completely informed automaton maximizing with enormous speed, though it must be admitted that this version still exists in some textbooks of microeconomics, as well as in some other publications (see e.g., Hargreaves-Heap and Hollis 1987, or previously, Dahrendorf 1967).

Economists sometimes argue that it is too early to extend economics beyond its traditional area of application as long as the analysis of goods and factor markets leaves so many questions open. How can economists explain divorce rates if they are not even capable of convincingly explaining the behaviour of oligopolistic firms? It may indeed be true that economics is not very successful in the study of such topics but there is no reason to assume that it is not valuable for the analysis of other questions, or that other sciences may not be able to contribute to the solution of the oligopoly problem.

It is sometimes also said that an application of economics to other areas must necessarily be amateurish or even bungling. Only if an economist has devoted him- or herself for a long time to the study of a particular area, it is argued, may it be possible to make a worthwhile contribution. This view is mistaken for various reasons:

1. Even without a deep knowledge of a particular area new insights may be gained by applying the economic approach. The unconventional point of view for example that changes in relative prices (costs) affect human behaviour may highlight previously neglected aspects and may therewith enrich our understanding.

2. The economic way of thinking need not be applied by an economist, but may also be used by a scholar educated in the traditional science devoted to the area, as has indeed been done by political scientists, sociologists and lawyers.

3. It is often useful to collaborate with a scholar of the respective traditional science when the economic approach is used by an economist. Indeed, this has been done quite often. Knowledge of the area and existing literature is, in this case, joined with an expertise of the method employed. This form of interdisciplinarity is not simple, but promises high rewards.

Serious Warnings

In one's own interest critique from outside should be acknowledged and the advice given should be heeded. Proponents of the economic view of the world should in particular consider the following aspects:

1. Specific problems posed in other scientific disciplines are sometimes disregarded or wrongly interpreted. Only when it has become clear to which questions a particular science wants to provide answers does the potential contribution of economics, but also of the limits of the traditional discipline, become apparent.

2. Easy initial successes, when applying the economic view of the world, should not be overestimated (Hirshleifer 1985). The consequent phase of relative stagnation should provide a motivation to think about the possibilities and limits of the economic approach.

3. The application of the economic way of thinking is sometimes based on random assumptions which have nothing to do with the theory. Elements are introduced ad hoc with the sole purpose of "explaining" observed behaviour ex post. This makes it impossible to test the hypotheses advanced (see e.g., Ferber and Birnbaum's 1977 and Blaug's 1980 critique of Becker's 1976 economic theory of the family). The economic approach is often immunized by introducing not directly observable concepts, such as "altruism" in the economics of the family or "citizen's duty" in voting behaviour. The application of a benefit-cost calculus provides a convincing explanation of *changes* in voting participation in an empirically testable way. However, according to the same calculus the participation *level* in general elections and referenda should be low because participation is costly to each citizen, but the influence on the voting outcome, and therewith utility derived, is extremely small. (Casting one vote rarely changes the result of the vote.) Nevertheless, as a rule, high rates of participation are recorded. This phenomenon can easily be "explained" by attributing citizens a high utility from the very act of participation (e.g., Riker and Ordeshook 1968). But this means that suddenly a typically sociological argumentation is followed which is not compatible with the economic approach (Kirchgässner 1980, 1988). As "citizen's duty" can usually not be observed independently, there is moreover the danger that *any* level of participation is explicable ex post: "citizen's duty" need only be adjusted to the varying rates of participation.

4. The economic contribution should refrain from merely translating well-known and well-explained relationships into the economist's

language or from trying to impress the reader with economic jargon (épater le bourgeois). Rather, a language should be used which is understood by other scholars and educated lay people. The example of other disciplines should not be followed in which only those appear to be competent who express themselves in as complicated a manner as possible. Indeed, complex relationships can best be captured by an exposition which is as simple as possible because this best allows us to distinguish serious analysis from mere bluffing.

5. The economic view of the world in the United States is mainly championed by politically right-wing scholars, a fact which has disturbed some people who otherwise favour the approach. In Europe the situation is quite different (see Frey, Pommerehne, Schneider and Gilbert 1984); on the Continent, the approach is used by scientists of differing political persuasions. The European Public Choice Society, for instance, includes political economists from the political right and left, and above all politically independent scholars.

6. North American academics have strongly shaped the application of economic thinking to new areas (though Europeans have lately increasingly made important contributions). This entails the danger that typically American institutions, traditions and values are introduced into the analysis as a matter of course. Living in a large country, American scholars are often unable to see that they belong to a particular culture, and that on other continents, and especially in Europe, conditions and evaluations differ. It is the task of European academics to carefully distinguish between a general economic model of behaviour and ways of behaviour varying between cultures. Above all, the particular European institutions must be considered which strongly shape behaviour through the imposition of constraints. In this respect European scholars even have an advantage because the multitude of institutions often differ strongly from country to country, or even among regions and communities, thus providing a natural laboratory to analyse the influence of different institutions on human behaviour.

Weaknesses to be Improved Upon

The economic model of behaviour has some serious shortcomings. They can be ordered in three categories: (1) In the case of an important type of behaviour (e.g., free-riding in the presence of public goods) the results of the theory only partially hold; (2) Human behaviour can be systematically biased due to cognitive problems; (3) Human behaviour can be less influenced by economic incentives than is claimed by the rational choice approach.

Free-Riding in the Presence of a Public Good.   "Homo oeconomicus" of the economic model of behaviour is a free rider: being selfish, he or she does not voluntarily contribute to the provision of a public good, which is characterized by the property that everyone can consume without paying. The missing incentive to participate in the provision of a good from whose use nonpayers cannot be excluded is usually modelled with the help of the game theoretic model of the *prisoner's dilemma* (see chapter 3).

A rational actor pursues a noncooperative strategy, that is, he or she does not help to provide the good benefiting everyone. "Individual rationality" (meaning the pursuit of self-interest) leads to the breakdown of "collective rationality" (see Sen 1977): when everyone behaves selfishly, the good is not produced though all desire to consume it.

This prediction is made, however, under restricted conditions. Free-riding is observed less, or does not appear at all, under the following circumstances:

No Pure Public Good.   A good can be provided in a package; when a public good is supplied in conjunction with a private good which can only be consumed by payers there is an incentive to contribute to the cost of providing it. Such "selective incentives" (Olson 1965) at least partially help to overcome free-riding.

Small Groups.   In direct personal interactions free-riding is punished by other persons by withdrawing love and recognition, or by verbal and even physical attacks. In small groups in which the members depend on each other—particularly in the family, among friends and colleagues—it would be disadvantageous even for a purely selfish person to act as a free rider because he or she must reckon with the ensuing social disapproval. In individual cases one does often not consider whether it pays to make a contribution; rather the social norms are internalized. A deviation from the norm may, however, take place when it becomes apparent over the course of time that observing the norm yields less net benefits than free-riding.

Repeated Events.   People can again and again experience that while it may be advantageous for the individual not to contribute to the cost, the outcome beneficial for all will not materialize. This experience, and the "higher insight" gained therefrom, may then result in individuals voluntarily contributing to the supply of a public good.

Somewhat surprisingly, with formal optimization of the repeated game theoretic prisoner's dilemma such cooperation does not constitute a solution. This analysis first considers the last period: it corresponds to a one-shot play and thus free-riding is optimal for a particular person. Considering then the period before the last, the situation is the same, and free-riding is again optimal for an individual. Proceeding in this way through all periods according to formal optimization theory it is always rational for everyone to free ride, so the public good is not provided for. If, however, the time horizon is unlimited or is determined by a random process (corresponding, for instance, to human survival probabilities), the incentive to free ride is reduced, but not eliminated, in this optimization model.

Free-riding has been the subject of many experiments, usually in the context of repeated performances of the prisoner's dilemma. In nine different experiments under varying conditions (also with respect to the number of repetitions) it has, for example, been shown (Isaac, McCue and Plott 1985) that persons are, on average, prepared to bear 53 per cent of the cost which would be optimal under *socially* optimal (Pareto efficient) behaviour. However, the readiness to contribute to the provision of the public good falls quickly. When the game is repeated five times, the contribution falls to only 16 percent of what is socially optimal. The experiments suggest that people have a tendency to cooperate until experience teaches them that they are exploited by people with whom they interact (Dawes and Thaler 1988).

Norms leading to cooperative behaviour are often only implicit and can emerge under otherwise unlikely circumstances. In World War I, for instance, soldiers, regiments and divisions lying in trenches opposite each other developed rules of behaviour facilitating life for both sides. If broken, they would have benefited one side only (Axelrod 1984). One such rule was, for example, that the mess lines of the enemy were not fired at; another was that artillery duels were arranged to take place at particular times only. (It goes without saying that the supreme commanders of both war parties—who were, of course, not subject to the dangers of the front—soon introduced measures to make such tacit cooperation impossible.)

Solution by Appropriate Collective Institutions. People who are subject to the free-riding problem and thereby experience cost, can bind themselves in order to produce the public good desired by all (see chapters 11 and 12). They can also use political arrangements by which everyone is forced to participate in the provision of the public good. On the level of social consensus (Buchanan 1977; Frey 1983) it may be decided unanimously that the government may raise general taxes to finance public goods such as defence or law and order. Moreover, the structure of the state may be organized so that situations resembling a prisoner's dilemma are circumvented as much as possible (Johansen 1977); one possibility is to shift political decisions to the regions affected within a federal state.

The four conditions discussed make it more costly to free ride or they prevent it entirely by providing appropriate incentives for cooperation. This does not contradict the economic model of behaviour, rather it is used to avoid a socially undesired outcome.

A shortcoming of economic theory with respect to explaining behaviour only appears in *large, anonymous* groups when people act cooperatively against theoretical predictions. An example is the contribution to television stations which provide superior quality of programs without advertising (so called "public television" in the United States). The criterion of a public good is fulfilled in this case because everyone can receive this station. Another example is donations to charitable and cultural organizations (in so far as they are not solely motivated by tax advantages or prestige considerations).

The tendency to contribute to the provision of a public good under anonymous and unique conditions has been supported by careful experiments (Marwell and Ames 1981; Schneider and Pommerehne 1981). Though not everyone is willing to cooperate, there is regularly a sizeable number of people prepared to participate in the cost. The average contribution lies typically in the range of 40 to 60 percent of the socially optimal contribution.

Biased Perception.   Under specific conditions people do not act according to the model of rational behaviour underlying economics; they violate logical conditions of consistency (the so-called von Neumann-Morgenstern axioms). These deviations from the classical rationality assumptions are extensively discussed in chapter 11 dealing with the relevance of decision theoretic anomalies for economics. It is shown that the economic approach need not be surrendered. When people become aware that they fall prey to anomalies they make an effort to overcome this by appropriate measures. On both the individual and the collective level institutions may be created which help to mitigate or avoid anomalies.

Humans are Difficult to Influence.   The economic model of behaviour assumes that people systematically react to changes in the constraints. In particular, it is to be expected that a price increase (relative to other prices) induces people to engage less in the more costly activity, and to consume less of the more costly good. This prediction certainly holds under most circumstances, but under specific conditions there may be a different outcome.

Ineffectiveness of Material Incentives. In large and complex organizations such as moden firms and administrations, it is impossible to institute a system of monetary incentives in the form of payments so that everyone works fully for the firm's goals and does not shirk unpleasant tasks. The explicit labour contracts between management and workers are not necessarily complete. An attempt to steer people's behaviour in a desired direction may even lead to the contrary. Moreover, attempting to evaluate employees in a strictly calculating, instrumental way may induce at least some people to relinquish their tendency to cooperate and to work against the organization (see, in general, Williamson 1975; Sen 1982).

There are various reasons why purely material incentives (prices) may sometimes fail to reach the goals set. One of the most important and empirically best founded reasons is the destruction of *intrinsic motivation.* In laboratory experiments the following effect has been found under varying conditions (see Lepper and Greene 1978): First an activity is observed which persons undertake because they enjoy it, that is, due to purely intrinsic motivation. Then a material incentive is offered for the same activity. In the third step this material compensation is withdrawn. It turns out that persons who previously undertook the task because they enjoyed it, now discontinue it, or perform it only in a restricted way. This phenomenon is known in psychology as *the hidden cost of rewards* (Deci 1975; Lepper and Greene 1978). It can be interpreted as an effect of changing prices on the preferences of the people involved—something which is excluded in the economic model of behaviour. Such hidden costs of monetary incentives have been observed with many people but it has been particularly well established with children and inmates of psychiatric institutions (McGraw 1978). If, for instance, patients of such an institution are paid for doing a certain task (such as making one's own bed in the morning)—a so called "token economy" is established—they are no longer prepared to do anything if they are not paid for it. The net effect of introducing monetary incentives is, in this instance, counterproductive: the negative effect on morality by introducing the price system must be taken into account (see also chapter 10).

The Process Itself is Valued. The economic model of behaviour assumes that people only consider the outcome of their actions (utilitarian model):

their utility is not influenced by how this outcome is reached. For various reasons this view is too narrow. The process leading to a result must also be taken into account:

> *Rules.* In many cases, and in particular with private or public services, the outcome is difficult or impossible to evaluate. For this reason professional organizations and also administrations often establish standards or *rules* which are to be observed during the production process. Such procedural obligations are also used within firms selling their product on markets. As it is impossible to quantitatively evaluate all aspects of employees' performance, many of them are paid according to whether they follow the established rules, and not for how far they contribute to market success. If only the latter is done, jobs important to the functioning of a firm which do not directly raise revenue (such as maintaining inventories or providing general information to consumers) would be disregarded (Ouchi 1977).

> *Robustness.* A performance observed can be based on chance. If there is reason to assume that the random element is substantial, it makes sense to consider the process used, providing its correct application generally leads to satisfactory results.

> *Valuing the process itself.* Persons may not particularly like certain results but pursue the activity producing them if they attach sufficient value to the procedure as such (Sen 1977). In this case a relative price change making the result of an activity more or less expensive has little or no effect. On the other hand, a change in behaviour is attained if the relative price change (or some other change of people's possibility set) refers to the method of performance.

Motives are Important. The economic approach endeavours to explain economic behaviour by using as few assumptions as possible about the underlying motives. It is usually sufficient to postulate that people are selfish (see Meyer 1979). In some areas motives play an important role, however. It may in general be assumed that "good" motives lead to acceptable results and that "bad" motives lead to undesirable outcomes. This conception underlies criminal law, which imposes a higher punishment when a crime is undertaken for "low" motives; on the other hand, there will be a small or no punishment if the crime has been undertaken with no bad will. Criminal law reflects a widely-held view which may be important for an *explanatory* theory. Thus, employees may react in a different way to improvements of working conditions if they believe that the employer was motivated by a true interest for their situation, than when they think that the same thing has only been undertaken to increase efficiency and profits (Kelman 1981).

Commercialization Destroys Values. When prices are used to influence behaviour, the people concerned may experience considerable utility losses. Many relationships between persons are valued exactly because they cannot be bought and are taken out of the market sphere. Chapter 10 is devoted to these (and other) limits of the price system.

Further Developments of the Economic Model of Behaviour

The shortcomings of the theory of human behaviour discussed can be overcome by developing the approach in various directions.

Enriching Preferences

The assumption of selfishness underlying the model can be further developed in various ways:

Psychological Motivation. It has often been argued (e.g., Kornai 1971; Albert 1985) that the motivational basis of the economic model of behaviour must be improved. For this purpose, a great many suggestions have been advanced (in particular Duesenberry 1949; Schmölders 1962; Hirschman 1977, 1982a; Schelling 1978; Simon 1957; Katona 1975; Leibenstein 1976; Scitovsky 1976; Frank 1985, 1988). Many approaches are somewhat disappointing because they fail to really integrate the psychological theories of motivation into the human model of behaviour. A particularly important shortcoming is that institutional conditions are disregarded. The motivational assumptions are too often used without adequately taking into account the human possibility set determined by institutions.

Altruism and Ethical Preferences. Within economics, but above all in the other social sciences, selfishness is often taken to be inadequate for explaining human behaviour. In traditional economics (see e.g., Phelps 1975) altruism has been taken into account by introducing the consumption or utility of one or several other persons into an individual's utility function. This procedure tends to make it difficult to empirically test the hypotheses derived because it is afterwards always possible to "explain" behaviour by an appropriate extent of altruism.

Alternatively, the economic model of behaviour can be enriched by distinguishing between two types of preferences. In addition to selfish preferences there are ethical (or social) preferences (Harsanyi 1955). The various types of preferences can be weighted by a "meta-preference function" which allows the introduction of particular kinds of moral evaluations and preferences (Sen 1977, 1982; Hirschman 1982a; Margolis 1982). This approach will be discussed in chapters 11 and 12.

Changing Preferences. The more a person has consumed a particular good in the past, the higher it is valued in the present. This assumption (e.g., Weizsäcker 1971, 1976) can be further differentiated by distinguishing between the effect on one's own consumption (the evolution of habits, e.g., Pollak 1970) and on the consumption by other persons (preference interdependence). In both cases preferences are taken to respond passively to past experiences.

Another line of research considers preference changes in the framework of econometrically estimated "individual welfare functions," the data for which is collected from surveys of a representative sample of persons (van Praag 1968; Kapteyn and Wansbeek 1985). This approach allows an empirical analysis of the extent to which people adapt to a higher consumption level. The studies reveal that the growth of consumption leads only to a transitory increase in welfare as evaluated by persons experiencing it. The rise in subjective welfare gain is gradually eroded by getting used to a given consumption level.

Enriching Constraints

In traditional economics the opportunity set available to a particular person is restricted by income, relative price and time. When the economic view is applied beyond the conventional area of the economy, additional constraints set by social institutions, in particular norms and explicit and implicit rules, are considered.

A person's opportunity set is, however, not only determined by objective constraints, it also matters how far such restrictions are perceived (subjective constraints). Yet another constraint belonging to quite another category are *ipsative restrictions* which a person takes to be relevant to him- or herself, but not to other people. As will be shown in chapter 12, the ipsative possibility set may deviate systematically in the long run and to a large extent from the subjective and objective possibility set. This has important consequences for human behaviour.

Active and Strategic Decisions

The factors determining the behaviour of persons are not only set from outside but they can to a certain extent also constitute a conscious choice. Besides (a) perceptions, it is also possible to choose (b) preferences and (c) constraints.

Choice of Perception. A person is not completely the unwilling object at which information is directed; he or she can at least partially decide how much of it to accept (Elster 1977). The media and also the content can be selected (that information is consumed which accords with one's basic views); information is selectively taken in, remembered and interpreted (as a rule the information which conforms best with one's attitudes is more heavily weighted).

Choice of Preferences. Human beings can influence and manipulate their own preferences in various ways. In the context of the economic model of behaviour the most important are:

Adaptive Preference Foundation. Wishes can be adjusted to the possibilities available. The "sour grape reaction" consists of adjusting the goals downwards because one believes or knows that one cannot reach them. The "forbidden fruit is sweet reaction" consists in raising the desire for those goods which are beyond one's reach. This second preference adaption thus occurs in an exactly opposite direction from the first one (see Sen 1982).

Conscious Character Planning. A discontented person who knows the reasons for his state of mind can deliberately change his preferences in order to fulfil a greater number of his or her wishes. This reaction is similar to adaptive preference changes but in this case it is not the reduction of desire for unreachable goods that is stressed but rather the *reachable* goods are evaluated more *highly*. To drive a Volkswagen does not mean that a Jaguar would be estimated less but one decides to derive more pleasure out of one's Volkswagen simply because one owns the

Volkswagen and not the Jaguar. This corresponds to the "endowment effect" (see chapter 11) but it is willingly produced.

Preferences can also be chosen under consideration of the effects the behaviour will produce on future preferences. Those desires are cherished which one knows will enrich the preferences one will have in the future (March 1978). People undertake an activity (e.g., listening to classical music) though they do not enjoy it at present because they expect that once their tastes have changed they will like it.

Active Choice for Dissonance Reduction.   Under some conditions people decide to believe in something even though they "know really" that it does not hold true. Workers in dangerous jobs, for instance, tend not to use the security measures available; they prefer to think that their work is safe. Such behaviour can be considered rational: Believing a job is safe yields utility because it is unpleasant to constantly be aware of danger. The costs involved with such a belief consist in the higher probability of having an accident because the beliefs collide with reality. The belief chosen is optimal when marginal utility equals marginal cost. On this basis a theory of beliefs (Hirschman 1965; Akerlof and Dickens 1982) can be introduced into the economic model of behaviour.

Conscious Choice of Constraints.   Normally, human behaviour is determined by the possibility set formed by the constraints imposed by the environment. Under certain conditions a person can also set himself or herself restrictions. This procedure is known as "strategic precommitment" and also under other names (such as "egonomics") and will be discussed in chapter 12.

Enriching preferences and constraints, and their active choice by persons, extends the economic model of behaviour in important and fruitful ways. For many—even possibly most—questions the simple model of man discussed in the first part of the book is capable of explaining behaviour in a satisfactory way. One of the advantages of the economic approach is its flexibility; when it appears necessary, various additional aspects can be introduced without running into methodological problems.

General References to the Literature

A useful methodological critique of the economic approach to the study of human behaviour may be found in

Blaug, Mark. *Methodology of Economics*. Cambridge: Cambridge University Press, 1980.

The behavioural assumptions are criticized as being too restrictive in

Sen, Amartya K. "Rational Fools: A Critique of the Behavioural Foundations of Economic Theory." In: Sen, Amartya K. *Choice, Welfare and Measurement*. Oxford: Blackwell, 1982, pp. 84–107.

Simon, Herbert A. *Reason in Human Affairs*. Oxford: Blackwell, 1983.

Hirschman, Albert O. "Against Parsimony: Three Easy Ways of Complicating Some Categories of Economic Discourse." *American Economic Review, Papers and Proceedings* 74 (May 1984): 89–96.

A critique from a quite different point of view is

Lutz, Mark A. and Lux, Kenneth. *Humanistic Economics. The New Challenge*. New York: Bootstrap Press, 1988.

Original and important developments of the economic model of behaviour and its applications are

Hirschman, Albert O. *Shifting Involvements. Private Interests and Public Action*. Oxford: Martin Robertson, 1982.

Schelling, Thomas C. *Choice and Consequence. Perspectives of an Errant Economist*. Cambridge, Mass.: Harvard University Press, 1984.

Frank, Robert H. *Passions within Reason. The Strategic Role of the Emotions*. New York: Norton, 1988.

10 THE PRICE SYSTEM AND MORALS

Economics as the Science of Prices

An economist can best be characterized as someone who favours the use of the price system over alternative decision making mechanisms. The reason for this clear preference for the market over social choices by political, administrative, bargaining or traditional procedures is due to its efficiency properties. In general equilibrium theory, the "invisible hand theorem" establishes that the ideal price system leads to Pareto-optimality. In this efficient state, the best possible situation is achieved in the sense that the welfare of no person can be improved without harming some other person. In other words, the means available to a society are used in such a way that no unused possibilities remain unexploited, and that there is no waste (so-called optimal allocation of resources). Over the last few years it has been increasingly stressed in microeconomics that the use of prices automatically produces the required incentives so that individuals behave in a socially desirable way.

This marked preference for prices and markets is reflected in the whole economics literature, and in particular in modern textbooks. The same view has been revealed in a survey recently undertaken in the United

Table 10–1. Economists' Support of the Price System. Response to the Five Propositions on which Economists in the U.S. and Selected European Countries have the Highest Degree of Consensus.

Propositions	Percentage Who "Generally Agree"	
	United States (N = 211)	United States and Selected European Countries (N = 936)
1. Tariffs and import quotas reduce general economic welfare	79	57
2. A ceiling on rents reduces the quantity and quality of housing available	77	56
3. A minimum wage increases unemployment among young and unskilled workers	67	41
4. Cash payment are superior to transfers-in-kind	65	48
5. Flexible exchange rates offer an effective international monetary arrangement	60	48

Sources: U.S. results adapted from Kearl, Pope, Whiting and Wimmer (1979). The "selected European countries" include Austria, France, the Federal Republic of Germany (the old Länder) and Switzerland. See Pommerehne, Schneider, Gilbert and Frey (1984) and Frey, Pommerehne, Schneider and Gilbert (1984).

States (Kearl, Pope, Whiting and Wimmer 1979) of the views of professional economists. Over 200 randomly selected members of the American Economic Association were asked to respond to roughly 30 propositions on economic topics. They could indicate whether they "generally agree," "agree with provisions," or "generally disagree," or they could abstain.

Table 10–1 reports the results for those five propositions on which American professional economists revealed the highest degree of consensus.

It may be seen that all these propositions deal directly with the price system, either arguing for its use ("cash payments are superior to transfers-in-kind"; "flexible exchange rates are effective") or arguing against interfering with it ("tariffs and import quotas reduce welfare"; "rent ceilings reduce the quantity and quality of housing"; "a minimum wage increases unemployment"). The first column lists the percentage of

American respondents who have indicated that they "generally agree" with the propositions. The majority thus clearly supporting the use of the price system varies between 60% and 79%. Accordingly the rejection rates ("generally disagree," not listed) is extremely small, ranging (with one exception, the proposition on minimum wages) between 2% and 3% of the respondents.

It may be objected that this overwhelming support of the price system is a typically American feature which does not apply to Europe. In order to test this conjecture, a series of surveys was undertaken for the selected European countries Austria, France, the Federal Republic of Germany (old Länder) and Switzerland. The responses relating to the whole sample including American and European economists (N = 936) are listed in the second column of table 10–1. These results indicate that the overall level of support of the price system is somewhat lower. Nevertheless, between 41% and 57% of professional western economists "generally agree" that the price system is a more desirable decision making mechanism than its alternatives, and that it is in particular superior to regulatory inter-ferences into the economy. If the respondents "agreeing with provision" are included, the majority in support of the use of prices is above 83% (the exception being the proposition on minimum wages with 67% sup-port). As may be seen by a comparison of the two columns, the rela-tive levels of support among the propositions are quite similar. It may thus be concluded that professional economists do indeed favour the price system.

To say the least, noneconomists are less convinced of the superiority of the price system than professional economists are. Indeed, they often show an open animosity to the use of prices.

This attitude is even visible among people with a training in econ-omics. As soon as they have left the halls of academia and are confronted with "real life" issues they become less enthusiastic about the price system. Table 10–2 lists those economists affirmatively responding to the same propositions as above, dividing the overall sample between full professors of economics still in academia and economists employed by government and confronted with practical issues.

In three of the five propositions the economists working in "prac-tical life" are clearly less enthusiastic about the price system than the academics of highest rank. (In the other two propositions, the level of support is similar.) The reasons why noneconomists (and economists engaged in "practical life") are sceptical about the price system, or even reject it, will be discussed under four headings. The first set of reasons (discussed in the following section) relates to lack of information. The use

Table 10-2. Differences in Views About the Price System Between Full Professors of Economics and Economists Employed in Government. (Same five propositions as in table 10-1.)

	Percentage Who "Generally Agree" (U.S. and Selected European Countries)	
Propositions	Full Professors (N = 219)	Economists Employed in government (N = 239)
Tariffs reduce economic welfare	53	55
Rent ceiling hurts housing	58	45
Minimum wage increase unemployment	45	33
Cash better than in-kind-transfers	49	49
Flexible exchange rates are effective	50	44

Sources: See table 10-1

of prices is often blocked by interest groups who otherwise expect to lose in the distributional struggle. This set of reasons refers to political economy (discussed in the third section). The price system is considered to be "unfair" under identifiable conditions which are discussed in the fourth section based on survey results and experiments. The final section argues that the economy and society can only be adequately understood if one goes beyond the price system.

Incomplete Information

A straightforward and general explanation of why the price system is not used is that noneconomists are not sufficiently aware of its excellent properties for resource allocation. Two reasons for this lack of knowledge must be distinguished, because they have quite different consequences for the economist as policy adviser.

Everyday experience shows that economic knowledge is not particularly widespread—at least not in the professional economists' sense. Above all, the basic mechanism of the "invisible hand" is not widely understood.

This lack of economic knowledge can be overcome by increasing the quantity and improving the quality of economics teaching. This is the economist's task at various levels of education, including the general public. An important role is played in this respect also by economic journalism. At present, and particularly on the European continent, the transfer of modern economic knowledge to the general readers, is not undertaken very successfully.

The second reason for the insufficient knowledge about the properties of the price system is both more important and more interesting. The lack of knowledge on economics is taken to be willingly and rationally chosen by people.

For many noneconomists an adoption of economic theory would often result in a sizeable loss of educational capital already acquired in other fields of knowledge. A lawyer, for instance, who has been trained that the essence of policy consists in detailed regulations of an area, would have to acquire a completely different stance if he or she exposed him or herself to the economic view which holds the price system in most cases to be better able to achieve a given goal. To throw away such acquired educational capital presents a loss which people seek to avoid. A lawyer usually does better to pursue his or her relative advantage, namely that of favouring and interpreting regulations.

Insofar as the lack of knowledge on economics is the result of such selfish behaviour, economists as policy advisers have a difficult task. Merely providing information of how efficient the price system is compared to its alternatives, usually has little effect on the net benefit calculus of the noneconomists tied to a different paradigm. A more effective approach is to influence the educational system at its roots, but this attempt is, of course, resisted by the adherents of other paradigms. The only way out seems to be to demonstrate to those benefiting from an efficient allocation of resources via the price system that economic knowledge is profitable, and that it is therefore worthwhile to acquire and to introduce into the educational system.

Conflict Over Income Distribution

The price system is rejected in many cases because of its distributional consequences. According to this interpretation the price system is *known* to work efficiently, but is nevertheless rejected. It is often dismissed precisely *because* it works so well. Some economists educated in the tradition of welfare theory find this argument difficult to swallow because they assume that costless compensation is possible. If this were really the case, distributional considerations would indeed be no argument against the use of prices for resource allocation. Distribution would be settled by appropriately assigning the initial bundle of resources, or by redistributing the market outcome.

Redistribution or compensation carrying no costs is *not* usually possible in reality, and therefore political aspects and government intervention prevail. In modern political economy, and in particular in the context of revenue and rent seeking (Buchanan, Tollison and Tullock 1980; Tollison 1982), it has been convincingly shown that the reason for government interventions is not "market failure" (in the sense of Bator 1958) but the struggle over income distribution. Groups threatened by the price system actively transform considerations of efficiency into those of distribution. This is well visible, for instance, when increases in public prices for transport or communication are discussed. Invariably, the subject is publicly discussed in terms of distribution, and often in terms of prospective losses which affect a very small section of the population.

The neglect of efficiency and the emphasis on distribution in economic policy discussions should not come as a surprise to economists: Efficiency, and therewith the use of the price system, is a public good for whose supply there is little incentive. On the other hand, the shares in the product appropriated by a pressure group is a private good where interests are clearly defined and well visible.

In the current politico-economic process, the economist as a policy adviser cannot hope to influence much the prevalent attitude of neglecting efficiency (and the price system) in favour of income distribution (and direct government intervention and regulation). The politico-economic equilibrium observable in reality is based on rational decisions of actors knowing their interests. They are unlikely to be impressed by economists pointing out the potential utility gains of using the price system because of its public good nature; they are concerned with the distributional issues. In such a setting, information on the consequences of using prices for allocation *may* suggest to certain groups in the population that they will be among the prospective losers, inducing them to oppose the price system. In this instance, "objective" economic advice has counterproductive effects (from the point of view of efficiency).

The situation is quite different when economic advice is proffered at the *constitutional level* (Buchanan and Tullock 1962; Buchanan 1977) or at the *level of the social consensus* (Frey 1983). With respect to income distribution, the essential difference to the current politico-economic level is that the actors find themselves in a state of uncertainty about their future position in the politico-economic process. Or, as Rawls (1972) would say, they have to make their decisions behind the "veil of ignorance." A person cannot form well-founded ideas as to which economic sector, profession, and income class he or she will belong to, and therefore what his or her distributional interests are going to be in the long run. Accordingly, no one knows whether the use of the price system improves or worsens his or her position in the income distribution. As a result, the properties of the price system are looked at in a detached, quasi-objective, way. Obviously, the efficiency characteristics of the price system will be considered with great interest by people on *this* level: potentially Pareto-efficient arrangements using the price system stand a chance of being adopted by unanimous consent. When an economy based on prices (such as the Federal Republic of Germany since its foundation in 1949) is compared to an economy based on administrative planning and control (such as the German Democratic Republic until its collapse in 1989) it becomes evident that such fundamental decisions are *conclusive* for the whole day-to-day politico-economic process, and that the economic and social well-being is much affected by how the constitutional choices with respect to decision making are taken.

Pricing is Considered Unfair

A Situation of Excess Demand

Empirical evidence has been collected to the effect that the use of prices is not welcomed by a large share of the population in circumstances where most academic economists would strongly recommend its use: many people consider pricing to be "unfair." In a representative, anonymously written survey undertaken in 1987 in Switzerland (canton of Zurich) and Germany (West Berlin) among 1,750 households (see in detail Frey and Pommerehne 1988) it was asked whether a price increase in a well-defined excess demand situation was considered to be "fair" or "unfair." The specific question posed was (in translation):

Question 1: At a sightseeing point reachable only on foot a well has been tapped. The bottled water is sold to thirsty hikers. The price is SFr/DM 1 per bottle. Daily production, and thus the stock, is 100 bottles. On a particularly hot day 200 hikers want to buy a bottle. As a consequence the supplier raises the price to SFr/DM 2 per bottle. How do you evaluate this price rise?

This question was answered by 452 persons. The respective proportions were

$$\left.\begin{array}{ll} \text{completely fair} & 5\% \\ \text{acceptable} & 17\% \end{array}\right\} \; 22\% \text{ fair}$$

$$\left.\begin{array}{lr}\text{unfair} & 44\% \\ \text{very unfair} & 34\%\end{array}\right\} \ 78\% \text{ unfair}$$

More than three-quarters of the respondents consider it unfair if excess demand for water is allocated via a price increase. One-third even consider it very unfair when the price system is used under the given conditions.

This result can hardly be dismissed as being due to chance, neither is it the result of the particular example shown. Two variations of corresponding excess demand situations result in even more strongly negative evaluations of the use of pricing by the population. In the first case excess demand was put in a different framework.

Question 2: A hardware store has been selling snow shovels for 30 Swiss francs or 30 German marks. The morning after a heavy snow storm, the store raises the price to SFr/DM 40. How do you evaluate this price rise?

The answers were (N = 215)

$$\left.\begin{array}{lr}\text{completely fair} & 2\% \\ \text{acceptable} & 15\%\end{array}\right\} \ 17\% \text{ fair}$$

$$\left.\begin{array}{lr}\text{unfair} & 14\% \\ \text{very unfair} & 69\%\end{array}\right\} \ 83\% \text{ unfair}$$

In this situation, more than four-fifths of the respondents find the application of the price system to balance supply and demand unfair. The share of persons who completely agree with this procedure falls to one in fifty.

In a second variation another set of respondents was interviewed by Kahneman, Knetsch and Thaler (1986). In a telephone survey of a representative selection of inhabitants in two Canadian cities, Toronto and Vancouver, the same question was asked again. In this country, 82% of the respondents (N = 107) considered a price rise to be unfair. The question thus has led to almost identical reactions in the Canadian, Swiss and German populations.

The responses to question 1 and 2 suggest that people are rather averse to pricing, at least to cope with a situation of excess demand. However, in order to reach more definite results, three aspects must be considered:

1. The fairness of pricing must be analysed in a *comparative perspective*. No system of decision making is completely fair, or completely unfair. What matters is how prices perform relative to their alternatives.
2. Fairness partly depends on the expected supply response when a

price is raised. The question of whether the situation depicted is unique and unexpected or a regularly occurring, predictable event is crucial. The use of prices and other means for coping with excess demand must be expected to differ between their use as a *rationing device* or as a general *decision making procedure*.

3. The evaluation of fairness is related to a *point of reference*, a notion of "just price."

These aspects will now be discussed in turn.

The Comparative Perspective. Confronted with an excess demand situation, the fairness of pricing should be judged relative to the *alternatives* which could be used in lieu of a price increase. Questions 1 and 2 presented so far have not mentioned any alternative device for solving the excess demand situation. In the following question the *relative fairness* of alternative ways of coping with a situation of excess demand was dealt with. This is in line with the Comparative Analysis of Institutions (see chapter 1). No ideal way of dealing with social problems exists—this would be a "Nirwana approach"—but we have to compare imperfect situations existing in reality. In our study, three relevant alternatives to pricing for allocation were considered (see e.g., Dahl and Lindblom 1953):

1. A *traditional* procedure where a fixed *rule* is applied irrespective of the extent to which demand exceeds supply. One of the rules commonly used is the principle of "first come, first served," which allocates solely on the basis of the point in time the good or service is demanded. While this scheme is often applied, it does not a priori seem to be particularly "fair," especially in the case of water shortage. After all, hikers who arrive at the sightseeing point later in the day may easily be more thirsty, and therefore more in "need" of water, than those arriving earlier.

2. The second device for allocating a scarce good may be a *random mechanism*. Each hiker has the same chance of getting water, but the probability is, of course, less than 100%. As abstract random mechanisms were not expected to be widely known in the population, it was suggested as an example that persons with a surname starting with A through to P, while Q to Z would have to do without.

Random allocations meet an important criterion of "fairness," namely that each person is treated equally, but it does not take any aspect of "need" into consideration, that is, some hikers might be more thirsty. In academic writings, random mechanisms have been suggested as rational procedures particularly for voting (e.g., Intriligator 1973; Mueller 1978).

3. The third allocation procedure suggested in the survey is distribution by a selected *group of people* acting according to their respective principles. The most important of such groups is *government* which is bound by democratic rules. These rules are put into effect by public officials. They follow administrative principles, that is, a special form of rationality, and possibly also of justice or "fairness." In order not to evoke any negative feelings which may be connected with the government, the survey suggested that the allocation of water is undertaken by the local authorities, which distribute it "according to their respective judgement." This vague formulation was used on purpose in order to convey the notion that allocation depends on the evaluation of a selected group of people who act according to administrative principles which are only imperfectly known by the citizens affected. However, the economic theory of bureaucracy (Breton and Wintrobe 1982) points to many different systematic biases inherent in administrative decision making; according to this theory the resulting allocation is neither expected to be efficient nor in any way "fair."

None of the four allocation devices used in the survey can, according to a priori reasoning, be expected to be "fair" when dealing with a situation of excess demand. If anything, economists may produce a number of arguments on why allocation by tradition, by a random procedure, or by administrative decision is not more just than using pricing, and many would argue that they are clearly less just than raising the price.

The wording in the questionnaire was:

Question 3: Please indicate *how fair* you evaluate the following means to distribute the water among the hikers to be:

(a) A price increase to SFr/DM 2 per bottle?
(b) Selling the water at SFr/DM 1 per bottle according to the principle "first come, first served"?
(c) Selling the water at SFr/DM 1 per bottle following a random procedure (e.g., to give to all persons whose surname starts with A to P)?
(d) The local authorities buy the water for SFr/DM 1 per bottle and distribute it according to their own judgement?

The answers are presented in table 10–3, for simplicity distinguishing only between fair and unfair.

Table 10–3. Subjective Evaluations of Alternative Allocation Procedures (in percent of all respondents).

	Allocation Procedure			
	Price	Tradition	Random	Administration
Fair	27%	76%	14%	43%
Unfair	73%	24%	86%	57%
	(N = 293)	(N = 299)	(N = 288)	(N = 289)

The theoretical proposition on which this section is based is borne out: The price system is considered *relatively* fairer when other explicit procedures are presented, and where it is therefore made even more obvious that the excess demand must somehow be cleared. When the market's fairness is evaluated in an isolated context as in question 1, 22% of the respondents find it to be fair, while when confronted with alternatives as in question 3, 27% consider it to be fair. (The difference is, however, only statistically significant at the 90% level of confidence.)

Table 10–3 reveals a clear ranking with respect to the subjective fairness of the various decision making devices. The *traditional* procedure of "first come, first served" is considered by far to be the fairest: more than three-quarters of the respondents judge it to be fair. This result is not obvious and would not be expected from the point of view of economic theory because it does not take "need" into account, except if it is assumed that late-comers to the sightseeing point are generally less thirsty (which is difficult to imagine).

A distinct second rank is attributed to an allocation by an *administration*, which more than four out of ten respondents take to be fair. This is again surprising from the point of view of the economic theory of bureaucracy which advances good reasons why the general population could be quite unfavourably inclined towards that kind of decision making institution. It would appear that the inhabitants of the canton of Zurich and the city of Berlin have considerable faith in the public administration. They tend to rely on public officials following what they consider to be the "just" rules laid down in the administrative regulations.

Pricing ranks third with respect to subjective fairness under the conditions portrayed in the survey. Only slightly more than one-quarter consider it to be fair, that is, people judge it to be by far less fair than clearing an existing excess demand via traditional or administrative rules.

Allocation by using a *random procedure* is ranked fourth; the respondents could not see any fairness properties in applying a principle they probably know best from gambling and lotteries. The low evaluation of the random mechanisms may be due to the fact that it is not widely known, and not considered suitable for "serious matters," such as the allocation of water.

Rationing Device vs. Decision Making System.   The subjective evaluation of fairness when dealing with excess demand depends on whether the situation is unique and unpredictable, or recurrent and to be expected. In the first case, supply is more or less given, and excess demand must be cleared by a *rationing device*. If, on the other hand, the situation occurs often and is to some extent a normal event, it can be expected that suppliers do adjust. The procedure envisaged is then not only applied in one instance but in many future cases, that is, there is a choice between *decision making systems*, partly behind the veil of ignorance.

It may be hypothesized that a price rise is judged to be fairer when it is part of a decision making system than when it is a pure rationing device. In a recurrent situation, a price rise gives suppliers an incentive to produce more, so that the excess demand situation will be mitigated or completely removed in the future.

The following question was asked to test the *relative fairness* of pricing as a rationing device compared to a decision making mechanism.

Question 4: How do you evaluate the price rise when a hot day was *completely unforeseeable*? Do you then consider a price rise to SFr/DM 2 per bottle of water to be more, equally or less acceptable than when hot days normally occur in the season considered?

The answers were (N = 148):

more	8%
equally acceptable	28%
less	64%

The theoretical expectation is supported (or more precisely, not rejected) by the empirical evidence. Price rises are considered particularly unfair in situations where they serve to ration demand, compared to when they serve as a decision making mechanism. This implies that there is less aversion to pricing when it may be expected that supply is therefore raised.

Just Price Re-enters.   One of the basic tenets of welfare theory is that individuals gain when their opportunity set is larger: Those whose utility increases when they choose a bundle of goods in the enlarged set are better off, while all the others do not lose. Following economic theory one would therefore expect that when the respondents are confronted with a situation in which they have more opportunities available, they would be more content. Specifically, our survey introduced two possibilities for consumers to circumvent excess demand: In the first case an *additional beverage* is introduced and only the price of this second beverage is raised in the excess demand situation (question 5); in the second case an additional supplier is introduced who offers the bottles of water at a constant price (question 6). It is hypothesized that the price increase for bottles of water by the first supplier is considered to be *fairer* because the would-be consumers can easily switch to the other beverage or to the other supplier. The questions posed were

Question 5: Consider the following situation: the supplier at the sight-seeing point offers also a *more expensive* beverage at SFr/DM 5 per bottle. On a particularly hot day the price of *this more expensive* beverage is raised to SFr/DM 8 per bottle. Do you consider this price rise
     more acceptable,
     equally acceptable,
     less acceptable,

than when *only water* is offered and its price is raised?

Question 6: We now have a situation in which another supplier located near the sightseeing point also offers water, but at a price of SFr/DM 1 per bottle. Do you consider the price increase to SFr/DM 2 by the supplier at the sightseeing point
     more acceptable,
     equally acceptable,
     less acceptable,

than if this second supplier did *not* exist? Table 10–4 lists the answers to these two questions.

Enlarging the opportunity set for the consumers leads in both questions to quite similar *adverse* reactions. The answers are inconsistent with the theoretical ideas advanced above: the price system should be judged more favourably. These responses are rather surprising because it is difficult to see why a price increase for a commodity is considered less acceptable when consumers can easily switch to another beverage (question 5) or to another supplier (question 6).

Table 10-4.   The Effect of Enlarging the Opportunity
Set on Subjectively Evaluated Fairness.

	Question 5	Question 6
More	26%	26%
Equally acceptable	19%	22%
Less	55%	52%

The unexpected result is explicable when a particular *normative* or *ethical* attitude of individuals is assumed. Consumers evaluate fairness by starting from a "fair" or "just price" which in psychology corresponds to an adaptation level (Helson 1964) or to an anchor (Kahneman, Slovic and Tversky 1982). In marketing (see e.g., Emery 1969) this concept is well known. In economics, reference points have been introduced, among others, by Duesenberry (1949) in consumption theory, and more recently by Frank (1985) in income distribution, but without much effect on orthodox economics. When a supplier raises the price for a particular commodity while keeping the prices for comparable goods constant, the price increase for this commodity is seen as proof that consumers are treated unfairly. Observing that other prices are not increased conveys the impression to consumers that the supplier has acted willfully. The price rise has not been "forced" by external factors such as a price rise in inputs (see Thaler 1985; Kahneman, Knetsch and Thaler 1986). Raising prices in order to profit from an increase in demand is considered to be illegitimate. Opportunity cost (the supplier not using the possibility to make a profit) is taken to differ sharply from a rise in "real" cost from the point of view of consumers' evaluation of fairness. In economics, no such distinction between "real" cost and opportunity cost is made. As long as one sticks to a normative or optimizing framework the two costs are identical, but the survey results discussed suggest that one should be most careful to transfer this identity to an *explanatory* framework. There are good reasons to assume that individuals have a notion of a "just" or "fair price," and of *changes* thereof, which it is important to take into account in positive analysis. If this is not done, individual behaviour may well be modelled in an inappropriate way, leading to systematical errors in explanation and prediction.

Beyond Prices

This chapter has shown that while orthodox economists give preeminence to pricing for resource allocation, the population rather dislikes the use of prices, even in well-defined situations of excess demand. The notion that pricing is "unfair" or "immoral" and may lead to undesired social consequences is shared by many unconventional social scientists.

In his book *The Social Limits to Growth* which had a great influence in the social sciences (outside economics), Hirsch (1976) argues that the price system *as a whole* debases moral values such as "truth, trust, acceptance, restraint, obligation" (p. 143). The market destroys through its "commercialization effect" its own essential basis. Similar views have been put forward by Max Weber (1920–1921), Schumpeter (1942), and the (then) New Left, for instance by Horkheimer (1952) and Marcuse (1965), but also by economists such as Arrow (1970, 1974). These are but the latest representatives of a sentiment held by both progressives such as Marx and Engels (for whom it was a cornerstone of their critique against capitalism) in the nineteenth century, and conservatives in the eighteenth century (who found the moral effect of the market to be particularly disgusting). Following this train of thought the price system has a bad effect on morality quite independent of its particular uses. Accordingly, it should be restricted.

As has been pointed out, the crucial question is whether the price system is *more* or perhaps *less* destructive of morals than alternative decision making systems. Consider a planned economy. It has often been argued that it massively worsens ethical norms. Individuals are observed to become completely cynical, maintaining a strict distinction between their personal beliefs, and what is proclaimed publicly. Similarly, an economy based on bargaining may lead individuals to use strategic behaviour where it is inappropriate, for example, in much of personal life. It is not difficult to think of further cases where non-price decision making systems destroy morals.

The price system as the villain debasing cherished values is an idea which was held in only some phases of intellectual history. As shown by Hirschman (1977, 1982b), the exact opposite view was intensively brought forward from the sixteenth to the nineteenth century. According to the "doux commerce" thesis the price system is not only more productive than its alternatives (the well-known invisible hand idea) but also

> would generate as a by-product, or external economy, a more 'polished' human type—more honest, reliable, orderly, and disciplined, as well as more friendly and helpful. (Hirschman 1982b, p. 1465)

During the eighteenth century the price system was widely seen as a civilizing agent of much power and magnitude. Leading protagonists of this view were, for instance, Montesquieu in his *l'esprit des lois* (1749), Condorcet (1795) and Kant in his *Zum ewigen Frieden* (1795). Surprisingly, the champions of the price system of the Chicago School (Friedman, Stigler) argue exclusively with the efficiency argument and disregard the possibly positive effect on morals.

This chapter has put forward various reasons (beyond classical market-failure) why most people under many circumstances resist the use of the price system, or reject it completely. The reasons adduced are only partly convincing, particularly if looked at in comparison to other decision making systems. There is little to suggest that the use of prices should be substituted by political, administrative, bargaining or tradition-based decisions.

Nevertheless, it has been shown that the use of the price system may create problems and difficulties. In general, economists, when confronted with such results not in line with established teaching, tend to be extremely cautious and conservative. They are inclined to simply disregard the undesired results or they are embraced within orthodoxy, not rarely with the consequence that what is important is silently pushed aside.

The author prefers to look at the difficulties and paradoxes as a *challenge* to existing economic theory and to search for what is valuable in a new, even though possibly disturbing, idea or result. The counterargument that economics thereby becomes more complicated is not valid (as Sen (1977) and Hirschman (1984) have made clear).

The differences in the evaluation of the price system between academic economists and nearly everyone else suggest the following conclusions:

1. It is high time for economics to go beyond showing the efficiency of the (ideal) price system for resource allocation. In many cases, efficiency is simply not the issue at stake.

2. Little is gained by considering those resisting or rejecting the price system as uninformed or fools. Rather, their worries should be taken seriously because they prevent the more extensive use of prices for resource allocation.

3. Undesirable distributional consequences are only one of the reasons why noneconomists often mistrust the price system. Other important reasons have to do with perceived unfairness and immorality.

4. The economic view must extend beyond an outcome orienta-

tion to include the valuation of processes and motives in a nonconsequentialist view.

5. Psychological aspects relating to the behaviour of individuals have to be considered in the context of existing institutional (and therewith historical) conditions when drawing conclusions for the society as a whole. This task will be taken up in the following chapter.

General References to the Literature

An extensive survey on what economists think, particularly about pricing is provided by

> Pommerehne, Werner W, Schneider, Friedrich, Gilbert, Guy and Frey, Bruno S. "Concordia Discors: Or: What Do Economists Think?" *Theory and Decision* 16 (1984): 251–308.

Politico-economic aspects of the conflict over income distribution are discussed in

> Buchanan, James M., Tollison, Robert D. and Tullock, Gordon (eds). *Toward a Theory of the Rent-Seeking Society*. College Station: Texas A&M University Press, 1980.

Important contributions to ethical economics are

> Sen, Amartya K., *On Ethics and Economics*. Oxford: Blackwell, 1987.
> Kolm, Serge-Christophe. *Justice et équité*. Paris: Centre National de la Recherche Scientifique, 1972.

Among the few existing empirical studies of ethics in economics are

> Kahneman, Daniel, Knetsch, Jack and Thaler, Richard. "Fairness as a Constraint on Profit Seeking: Entitlements in the Market." *American Economic Review* 76 (September 1986): 728–741.

Many issues touched upon in this chapter are discussed in a different perspective by

> Hirsch, Fred. *The Social Limits to Growth*. Cambridge, Mass.: Harvard University Press, 1976.
> Etzioni, Amitai. *The Moral Dimension. Towards a New Economics*. New York: Free Press, 1988.

The evaluation of the market in the course of history, as well as a wealth of original ideas on pricing, are discussed in

> Hirschman, Albert O. *The Passions and the Interests: Political Arguments for Capitalism before its Triumph*. Princeton: Princeton University Press, 1977.

11 BEHAVIOURAL ANOMALIES AND ECONOMICS

Anomalies in Human Behaviour

Over the last few years the findings by experimental psychologists that individual behaviour systematically violates rationality have caught the attention of many social scientists, among them some economists. A key experience for economists was the presentation of major anomalies by Kahneman and Tversky (1979) in *Econometrica*. A large number of anomalies of individual behaviour are now known.

In order to intuitively convey what is meant by "anomalies in individual behaviour" the following examples may be helpful.

Example I

Problem 1. Choose between alternatives A and B. In alternative A the payoff of 4,000 is received with a probability of 80% and nothing with a probability of 20%. This will be abbreviated by writing A (4,000, 0.8). In alternative B the sum of 3,000 is received with a probability of 100%, or with certainty, that is, B (3,000, 1.0). In an experiment (Kahneman and

171

Tversky, 1979, p. 266) it turns out that 20% of the respondents prefer alternative A, and 80% prefer alternative B.

Problem 2. In the same experiment, the participants had to choose between C (4,000, 0.2) and D (3,000, 0.25). In this case 65% of the respondents preferred alternative C, and 35% alternative D.

Alternative B being preferred to alternative A (B > A) implies u(3,000) > 4/5 u(4,000), or u(3,000)/u(4,000) > 4/5. On the other hand C > D implies 1/5 u(4,000) > 1/4 u(3,000), or u(3,000)/u(4,000) < 4/5. There is a contradiction.

As it may be thought that such an inconsistency in choosing between alternatives is due to the abstract formulation, the following example 2 (due to Tversky and Kahneman, 1987, p. 76) provides a similar decision situation using a realistic context.

Example 2

Imagine that the US is preparing for the outbreak of a rare Asian disease which is expected to kill 600 people. Two alternative programmes to control the disease have been proposed. Assume that the exact scientific estimates of the consequences of the programmes are as follows:

Problem 1.

	Preferred by
If programme A is adopted, 200 people will be saved	(72%)
If programme B is adopted, there is a 1/3 probability that 600 will be saved, and a 2/3 probability that no people will be saved	(28%)

Problem 2.

If programme C is adopted, 400 people will die	(22%)
If programme D is adopted, there is a 1/3 probability that nobody will die, and a 2/3 probability that 600 will die	(78%)

Programmes A and C, and programmes B and D are logically identical. In programmes A and B the outcomes are stated in positive terms (lives saved), whereas in programmes C and D outcomes are stated in negative terms (lives lost). The framing and wording of problems has an influence on judgement and choice.

As it may be thought that this behavioural inconsistency is only due to the fact that the decision situation is in a probabilistic context, example 3 (due to Quattrone and Tversky 1988, p. 727) provides a situation in which there is no uncertainty.

Example 3

Imagine you are faced with the decision of adopting one of two economic policies.

Problem 1.

	Work Force Unemployed (%)	Rate of Inflation (%)	Preferred by
Programme J	10	12	(36%)
Programme K	5	17	(64%)

Problem 2.

	Work Force Employed (%)	Rate of Inflation (%)	Preferred by
Programme L	90	12	(54%)
Programme M	95	17	(46%)

People react differently to identical economic programmes when labour market conditions are formulated in terms of unemployment than when they are formulated in terms of employment, a type of behaviour inconsistent with rational decision theory. The framing effect also obtains in this situation of certainty.

Rapidly growing empirical evidence has been gained through experiments and field studies both by economists (e.g., Allais 1953; Ellsberg 1961; Thaler 1987a, 1987b) and by cognitive psychologists (see e.g., Kahneman, Slovic and Tversky 1982; Arkes and Hammond 1986; Bell, Raiffa and Tversky 1988) that under certain conditions people *systematically deviate from rationality* as this concept is understood in economics. Instances of such anomalies in individual behaviour have been attributed names such as:

Reference Point Effect. Alternatives are evaluated by people not in terms of total wealth but relative to a reference point, often the status quo.

Sunk Cost Effect. People tend to take foregone costs into account in their decisions.

Endowment Effect. Goods in a person's endowment are valued more highly than those not held in the endowment.

Framing Effects. The way a decision problem is formulated and the way the information is presented has a marked effect on individual decisions.

Availability Bias. Recent, spectacular and personally experienced events are systematically overweighted when people make decisions.

Representativeness Bias. People systematically misconceive prior probabilities, and are insensitive to sample size.

Opportunity Cost Effect. Out-of-pocket monetary costs are given greater weight in the decision calculus than opportunity costs of the same size.

Certainty Effect. Outcomes obtained with certainty are attributed greater weight in people's decisions than those which are uncertain even when the known expected utilities are the same.

These and other anomalies of individual behaviour can be interpreted as violations of the von Neumann-Morgenstern axioms, and therefore of the model of classical subjective expected utility maximization (Schoemaker 1982; Machina 1987). The economic model of behaviour is directly affected in so far as expected utility maximization is applied for analyzing behaviour under uncertainty (which is often the case).

Anomalies result also in violations of the assumptions of stable preferences (see chapter 1). Anomalies intervene between what may be termed "basic" preferences (which can still be taken to be constant) and "effective" preferences which shift over time, and differ between individuals due to the working of anomalies. For example, the reference point effect leads "effective" preferences to differ according to which particular reference point is chosen. As a consequence, if it is not known and taken into account in explaining behaviour that different reference points are chosen under different conditions, the preferences which effectively determine behaviour exhibit unexplained shifts. The sunk cost effect and the endowment effect are two other anomalies which intervene between the "basic" and "effective" preferences and which therefore lead to violations of the assumption of stable preferences. Anomalies moreover destroy the systematic relationship postulated between changes in constraints and changes in behaviour. When persons are subject to biases with respect to the framing of decisions, the use of information (availability bias, representativeness bias, etc.), and opportunity cost, distorting intervening factors enter. If the individual anomalies are indeed as important as suggested by experimental research, it is no longer possible to rely on a systematic, and therefore predictable, effect of the constraints on behaviour. If, for example, the relative price of an activity increases due to a rise in opportunity cost, the "law of demand" would predict a relative reduction in that activity. That prediction would, however, not hold if the opportunity cost effect (stating that such costs are fully or largely disregarded) applies. Conversely, people subject to the sunk cost effect perceive an additional constraint, and therefore act differently than they would according to existing economic theory which disregards this type of "irrational" cost.

Reaction by Economists

Economists have reacted in three different ways to these findings on paradoxical behaviour of people: (1) by taking them seriously, (2) by disregarding them and (3) by explicitly rejecting them. These reactions will now be discussed in turn.

Anomalies are Taken Seriously

The most prominent economist in this group is Arrow (1982) who shows that deviations from individual rational behaviour which he observes in intertemporal economic markets are consonant with the evidence found on the anomalies by psychologists. Arrow (1987, p. 213) explicitly considers Simon's (1957, ch. 14, 15) bounded rationality concept (compared to simple utility maximization) as a reaction to the paradoxes found.

   Other economists have (often implicitly) paid tribute to the findings on anomalies by introducing psychological concepts into economics. The best known are Scitovsky's (1976, 1981) application of Wundt's law of the optimal degree of excitement, Akerlof and Dickens' (1982) and Gilad's et al. (1987) use of cognitive dissonance, or Schelling's (1978, 1980), Hirschman's (1982a) and Thaler and Shefrin's (1981) self-commitment.

Anomalies are Disregarded

The "business as usual" attitude more often found in verbal than in written form is nourished by the fear that economic analysis breaks down when orthodox rational choice models are given up or even if they are weakened. Thus Russell and Thaler (1985, p. 1073) state that ". . . with few exceptions, economists have tended to ignore the work of the cognitive psychologists and have continued to investigate markets with only rational agents." An important example is provided by neoclassical analysis in public finance, that is, in public economics (see e.g., Atkinson and Stiglitz 1980). In particular, it is absolutely standard procedure to apply expected utility maximization to derive the theorems on optimal taxation (e.g., Allingham and Sandmo 1972; Sandmo 1976) or on optimal public prices (e.g., Boes 1981). The evidence collected on systematic violations of this theory by persons is not even mentioned despite the fact that a careful evaluator (Schoemaker 1982, p. 552) concludes that ". . . it is doubtful that the expected utility theory should or could serve as a general descriptive model."

Anomalies are Rejected

The following seven arguments of why the paradoxes found are irrelevant for economists are brought forward most often.

1. Exclusion by definition. "Should behavior in certain salient areas be found to violate rationality, it will be treated as beyond economics" (Zeckhauser 1987, p. 252). Such a narrow view (not shared by Zeckhauser) would have to be rejected by the economic approach to human behaviour championed by Becker (1976) which explicitly claims (pp. 9–10) that the rational choice model is applicable to all areas where humans act, including for example, the family (marriage, childbearing, divorce), crime or suicide. Indeed, one can argue that such a restriction of the area of economic analysis does not make sense, as it is possible to develop an economic theory not based on the classical or orthodox notions of rationality (Arrow 1987, p. 202). Simon's satisficing model, or Kahneman and Tversky's prospect model provide possible alternatives.

2. Irrelevance of laboratory evidence. It is maintained that the effects found under laboratory conditions are not applicable to the "real world." However, if economic theory is indeed a general model of resource allocation it should also be valid in a laboratory setting (Smith 1976). The burden of the proof thus lies on those who want to exclude laboratory behaviour.

A stronger rebuttal of this argument lies in the considerable amount of empirical evidence that such anomalies *do* exist in real life. The best-known case is provided by the irrational behaviour of people in the context of government subsidized flood insurance, behaviour which is not explicable in terms of maximizing subjective expected utility (Kunreuther et al. 1978; Kleindorfer and Kunreuther 1982). Arrow (1982, p. 7) provides a dramatic example of the effect of framing for the choice of medical therapy, and other examples may be found in Robertson (1974), Schelling (1978), Pratt, Wise and Zeckhauser (1979) and Samuelson and Zeckhauser (1988). In the psychological literature there are examples of overconfidence of military intelligence analysts and of systematic biases in behaviour by gamblers in casinos or by scientific investigators (see Slovic, Fischhoff and Lichtenstein 1977, pp. 15–17).

3. Insufficient incentives to respond seriously to experiments. It has often been argued that the paradoxes would disappear if irrational behaviour had sizeable negative consequences. This proposition has been extensively tested in the context of the preference reversal phenomenon (Grether and Plott 1979; Pommerehne, Schneider and Zweifel 1982; Segal 1988). It has been concluded that irrational behaviour does not vanish even when the persons have a strong monetary incentive for rational decisions. Hypothetical gamblers show the same result as with Las Vegas replications (Lichtenstein and Slovic 1971). According to Schoemaker (1982, pp. 553–554) there is *"no evidence* that suboptimal laboratory behavior improves when committing subjects financially to their decisions," a view which is intuitively supported by the argument "... it would require far more effort on the part of subjects to falsify responses deliberately than to respond truthfully" (Hogarth and Reder 1987, p. 12).

4. People learn. While anomalies may occur in isolated instances, it can be argued that they are not prevalent because people learn to avoid errors. But why, then, can paradoxes still be observed today, at a time when people have had a very long period to learn to choose according to the subjective expected utility model (going back to Bernoulli 1738), which has been taught to be "optimal"?

A more important rebuttal stresses the difficulties of learning (see Payne 1982, pp. 397–398). As it has been discussed in chapter 9, learning is not simple or automatic; uncertainty, environmental instability, and improper assessment frameworks represent serious obstacles. Learning is only possile in a well-structured feedback situation which often does not obtain, and even then it tends to be slow and at times incorrect or even perverse.

5. Experts as marginal actors suffice to produce the classical results. The fact that many, and even the majority, of people are subject to

anomalies in behaviour does not lead to anomalies at the aggregate level provided that there are a few actors who behave rationally. The empirical evidence collected suggests, however, that even "experts" fall prey to at least some of the paradoxes. For example, it has been found that "bankers and stock market experts predicting closing prices for selected stocks showed substantial over-confidence . . . ," (Slovic, Fischhoff and Lichtenstein 1977, p. 15). Machina (1987, p. 128) notes that even professional decision theorists of high class, among them Savage, have acted irrationally (according to their own definition), and that pointing out the errors had little effect on future behaviour. The paradoxes do not stem from lack of intelligence or knowledge but are the product of deeper-lying characteristics of human nature.

6. Anomalies are randomly distributed and average out in the aggregate. This argument has been put forward forcefully by Becker (1962, 1976): People do err, but the errors occur in all directions, and are therefore irrelevant for the aggregate level in which economists are interested.

7. Competitive markets eliminate anomalies. This is the "standard counterargument" within economics (Arrow 1982, p. 7). If most agents' behaviour is subject to anomalies, rational persons can make a lot of money and will eventually take over all wealth. Therefore, rational behaviour dominates the overall market. The tendency of only efficient actors to survive in the market—in the case of firms only those that maximize profits—was suggested long ago by Alchian (1950) and Friedman (1953).

Arguments 1 to 4 relate to the individual level which is of limited relevance; some economists even consider it to be of no importance *per se*. Also, theoretical and empirical evidence against the first four arguments has already been adduced. Arguments 5 to 7 relate to the social or aggregate level and are therefore crucial from the economic point of view. The subsequent discussion will concentrate on arguments 5, 6 and 7.

This chapter asks the question: How relevant for economics which is interested in social *phenomena* are the anomalies found at the level of *individual* decision makers? This problem has scarcely been treated in the literature. In the case of psychologists this is not surprising, as this discipline deals with individual-level phenomena. In economics, the stated irrelevance of the individual-level paradoxes often tends to be more the result of an underlying faith or ideology in "rationality" than the result of a careful theoretical and empirical investigation. It may be noted that the question has so far also been disregarded in the newly arising area of economic psychology as witnessed, for example, by two modern textbooks (Furnham and Lewis 1986; Lea, Tarpy and Webley 1987) where the problem is not even mentioned.

When the question of the relevance or irrelevance of the individual-level paradoxes is treated in economics, it is done in a too narrow and unrealistic way: the subject has been how much the *market* is able to eliminate the anomalies (see the many contributions in Hogarth and Reder 1987).

A broader view is taken here in two respects:

1. A *multitude of decision making systems* is considered. The economic market is only one such system; others are democracy, bargaining and administration (following Dahl and Lindblom 1953).

2. The processes or institutions intervening between individual-level decisions and aggregate outcomes may work in all directions. They may not only *eliminate* or *weaken* individual-level anomalies but may also be *neutral* or even *strengthen* them. In the last two cases the anomalies are transferred to the aggregate level and are therefore relevant for economics.

Our analysis leads to four main general conclusions:

1. The *market* system eliminates individual anomalies only under very limited conditions, though there is a tendency to weaken them.

2. Another *competitive* process exists—namely democracy—which, under appropriate conditions, eliminates anomalies.

3. Institutions *other than competitive processes* exist which are capable of weakening anomalies.

4. Under some conditions nonmarket decision making institutions may *strengthen* individual-level anomalies.

The following section distinguishes between the individual-level and social-level of analysis, and the fourth section analyses how anomalies are transformed in the aggregation process.

The fifth section discusses under what conditions anomalies lead to cost, provoking people to react and the sixth section analyses how anomalies may lead to the emergence or conscious creation of institutions in order to overcome or mitigate their costly effects. The final section deals with the interaction between anomalies and institutions.

Table 11-1.

		Social level	
		Anomalies do not exist	Anomalies exist
Individual level	Anomalies do not exist	No problem A	Creation B
	Anomalies exist	Elimination C	Maintenance D

Individual and Social Levels

A 2 × 2 matrix serves well to illustrate the logically possible relationships between the level of individual decision making and social outcomes (table 11-1).

Cell A comprises the normal case dealt within economics: there are no anomalies (i.e., violations of rationality in the sense of the von Neumann-Morgenstern axioms) either at the individual or at the social level. Cell B includes cases where only the *process* of aggregation produces social-level anomalies. Well known and important examples are the preference aggregation paradox (Arrow 1963; Sen 1970), problems connected with public goods, and Schelling-type problems (Schelling 1978, 1984b). Cell C comprises cases where the institutions involved in the aggregation process are able to produce "normal" social results. The best known (and so far unique) institution considered as working to this effect is the perfectly competitive economic market. In cell D are cases presenting a problem and challenge to economics, where individual-level paradoxes are transferred to the social level. The aggregating institutions are either neutral or strengthen the paradoxes, or they are not able to sufficiently weaken them to make them irrelevant for practical purposes. Cells C and D are the subject of this chapter. In view of the fact that economists tend to take cell C to be the only applicable one, it is sufficient to provide *relevant examples* for processes and institutions falling into cell D in order to show that the individual-level paradoxes found should be taken seriously.

On the basis of table 11-1 it is possible to discuss argument 6 of the preceding section which states that anomalies are randomly distributed and are therefore eliminated in the aggregate by the law of large numbers. Russell and Thaler (1985, p. 1074) reject this argument: "Since the errors that have been identified are systematic (i.e., in a predictable direction) this statement is simply wrong." The argument is, however, not far-reaching enough. Irrespective of whether the individual anomalies are randomly distributed or have a systematic bias, there may be institutions which either eliminate or maintain them at the aggregate level. Thus, systematic anomalies *may*, but need not, be eliminated through appropriate institutions. As will be argued in the following sections, institutions exist which block the effect of the law of large numbers. Argument 6 therefore is not relevant once the importance of the aggregating processes and institutions is accepted.

Anomalies are Transformed

Aggregation Through the Market

A fully efficient, perfectly competitive market working under ideal conditions eliminates anomalies existing at the individual level. Put positively: ". . . rationality . . . is most plausible under very ideal conditions" (Arrow 1987, p. 201). This conclusion leads to two questions: (1) do such markets exist in reality, and (2) what happens in a less than fully competitive market?

Considerable theoretical and empirical evidence has been collected up to now suggesting that the markets that exist, including financial markets, which are often thought to correspond most closely to an ideal competitive market, are not able to eliminate individual-level anomalies. According to Arrow (1982, pp. 7–8), even if everyone else is irrational, it does not follow that a rational actor is able to exploit the existing arbitrage possibilities. If a firm invests in research and development (R&D), the depressed current profits may be the only information irrational investors consider (this is a case of the biased availability heuristic). A rational investor who correctly takes the current stock market price to be below the expected value of future higher profits produced by the R&D investment may not realize any part of this gain during the gestation period. If the rational investor's discount rate is sufficiently high, there is no possibility of exploiting the irrational behaviour of others even in the long run, and the aggregate effect of a depressed stock market price remains despite good profit prospects.

In a later paper, Arrow (1987, pp. 209 et seq.) reminds his fellow economists that the fully competitive market of general equilibrium theory, which is required for the elimination of anomalies, must include markets for *all* future goods, but "... we certainly know that many—in fact most—markets do not exist." This being the case, the information gap must be filled up by some kind of conjecture, and through this process there is a wide enough gap for anomalies to enter. With respect to this particular problem, incomplete markets have closely analogous consequences to the existence of market power.

Other well-known attacks against the elimination thesis have been brought forward by Russell and Thaler (1985) for consumer goods markets, and by Miller (1987) for financial markets. They argue that the notion that "competition will render irrationality irrelevant is apt only in very special cases, probably rarely observed in reality" (Russell and Thaler 1985, p. 1071). A sizeable number of empirical studies for financial markets claim to find aggregate anomalies even here. When people are risk averse—the normal assumption in economics—risk taking has to be compensated, and risk and return should be positively correlated. According to Banz (1981) small companies attain a higher rate of return than larger companies with a similar degree of risk; Basu (1977) finds a higher rate of return for firms with a lower price/earnings ratio; Bacharach and Galai (1979) find that the estimated risk of companies is affected by the actual stock prices; Bowman (1982) calculates a negative relation between the traditional risk measure (simple variance) and average return across industries; Shiller (1981, 1984, 1987a) shows that the volatility of stock prices is too high relative to the discounted value of dividends; De Bondt and Thaler (1985, 1987) find that stocks which are losers at first systematically tend to become winners, and vice versa; and Thaler (1987b, 1987c) shows that seasonalities (there are January, weekend, holiday, Monday and intraday effects) have systematic consequences for financial markets, results which in part are corroborated by evidence gained in experimental markets (Coursey and Dyl 1986; Forsythe et al. 1984).

Akerlof and Yellen (1985a, 1985b, 1987) explore the degree to which rational actors eliminate profits by speculation in nonperfect markets. They find that "near-rational actors" who are not at, but only in the neighbourhood of, the profit maximizing equilibrium experience small losses. The incentive to behave "fully-rationally," and to therewith compete away all profits and to eliminate individual-level anomalies is small. Similar conclusions are reached by Haltiwanger and Waldmann (1985) and for a more competitive surrounding, Jones and Stock (1987).

To summarize, serious theoretical reasons and empirical observations have accumulated to support the belief that in economic markets as they exist in reality—and this includes financial markets—individual-level anomalies are not eliminated at the aggregate level. It follows that if elimination is claimed it must be proved for the specific market and time period in question. At best there may be a general tendency for individual-level anomalies to *weaken* in well-functioning markets. This conjecture is supported by market model experiments which suggest that "market models based on rational choice principles (including the sub-species of satisficing) do a pretty good job of capturing the essence of very complicated phenomena" (Plott 1987, p. 141). Another piece of evidence supporting the notion that anomalies are weakened by well-functioning markets relates to Brookshire and Coursey's (1987) and Coursey, Hovis and Schulze's (1987) findings that anomalies in the form of the endowment effect, the reluctance to trade, the buying-selling discrepancy, or the curse of knowledge (Camerer, Loewenstein and Weber 1989), decrease, but do not disappear, when an appropriately specified market for the elicitation of the value of a given public good exists (see also Knetsch and Sinden 1987).

Democracy and the State

A fully competitive two-party democratic system with continuous elections and logrolling to allow arbitrage leads, under appropriate conditions, to a Pareto-efficient outcome and eliminates anomalies at the aggregate level (see e.g., Hinich and Ordeshook 1971 and Riker and Ordeshook 1973). The forces of political competition thus lead to the same result as in the case of a fully efficient market, but this particular institutional setting is even more unlikely to obtain in reality.

Democracy has a crucial effect on the transfer process, apart from its efficiency property through political competition. Democracy can be considered to be *the* institutional setting which allows, and encourages, diversity of opinions: the same problem is looked at from many different angles or in terms of many different *frames*. The diversity of frames brought about by the democratic process helps to overcome one-sided views and a number of individual-level anomalies. In a constitutional democratic system, the institution of checks and balances, as well as the freedom of opinion and of the press, further strengthen this tendency. The force of this elimination process becomes even more vivid if one looks at the opposite institutional setting. In an authoritarian system the political leadership *imposes* one particular frame, and the people are forced to follow and use this frame when social questions are discussed.

The constitution and the law in a democratic society are important institutions that weaken individual-level anomalies, a function that seems to have been overlooked in scientific discourse. Whether these institutions have spontaneously arisen or have been designed, they are a reaction to the people's interest in reducing the cost produced by individual-level anomalies at the social level. A legal provision to this effect is more likely to emerge if the cost of establishing and maintaining it is lower than the cost of anomalies (see, in general, North 1986; Coleman 1988; Ullmann-Margalit 1977; Schotter 1981).

Four types of legal provisions designed to weaken individual anomalies may be distinguished:

1. Actors who may be particularly prone to anomalies are not allowed to make certain types of decisions. For example, children and the insane do not have voting rights and are not allowed to form contracts.

2. Social inconsistencies can be eliminated by appropriate legal norms. Constitutions typically include formal procedures to solve such cases; the judges of the highest court, who are independent of the democratic process, are often given the authority to do so.

3. The law reduces the number of alternatives between which a particular person has to choose, therewith (see Payne 1982, pp. 386–387) facilitating decisions and reducing the occurrence of individual-level anomalies. There are a great many cases of such agenda restrictions. In many areas contracts have to follow a rigidly set structure imposed by law. Insurance contracts are an example. In the case of marriage contracts, only a very limited set of alternatives is available. Democratic systems also tend to restrict the number of types of basic education and to limit the entry of private schools. Another instance is money, where the (national) alternatives are generally reduced to the type issued by the central bank. In both cases the reduction of alternatives between which a person may decide may be interpreted as an effort to reduce individual-level anomalies. (Of course other, not necessarily competing, interpretations of these phenomena are possible.)

4. The law opens the possibility for people to retract a decision, thus supporting the possibility of learning through repetition. It is possible to revoke some contracts. For example, goods purchased at the door may be returned within a certain time period, or, in the case of an important life decision, divorce is allowed. There are also institutional provisions designed to directly support people in their decision, for example, consumer education and information provided by the government. Thus, the legal system helps to establish stable conditions with a well-identifiable feedback mechanism necessary for successful learning.

While there are legal institutions in democracies that serve to weaken the effects of individual-level anomalies, there is no reason to assume that they completely eliminate them. Indeed, in the current politico-economic process of a democracy, as opposed to the constitutional or rules level, strong forces tend to *strengthen* individual anomalies. A democratic government punishes successful persons and firms by taxation and supports unsuccessful people and firms based on the solidarity principle or because they have the stronger political arguments. If persons and firms prone to anomalies or irrational behaviour have a higher probability of being poor and making losses, and the rational ones of being successful—an assumption which is basic to the idea of the survival of the fittest in the market—then this intervention by democratic governments blocks the anomaly-reducing process of the competitive market. The effects produced by anomalous actors are strengthened and those by rational actors weakened. As this redistribution process through taxation and subsidies is of considerable magnitude in modern societies, this strengthening of anomalies by the intervening effect of democratic institutions should not be disregarded.

To summarize, in a democracy a broad set of institutions weakens anomalies in people's actions. On the other hand, current interventions by governments tend to strengthen already existing individual-level anomalies at the social level. As a result, it may be concluded that a consideration of democratic institutions provides no reason to neglect individual-level paradoxes but rather reasons to take them seriously.

Bargaining and Interest Groups

Incentives to form stable interest groups to engage in bargaining processes are unequally distributed in a society. Producers (including the suppliers of labour) are represented by strong interest groups, while consumers and taxpayers are only weakly active in the bargaining process (Olson 1965; Moe 1980). Anomalies among producers, also reflected within the corresponding interest group, are strengthened at the aggregate level by the intervening bargaining process. At the same time, rational behaviour on the part of producers receives a higher weight at the aggregate level. In contrast, both types of behaviour are scaled down at the aggregate level in the case of individual anomalies among consumers and tax payers. The net outcome at the aggregate level is open. There is no reason to believe that bargaining processes eliminate the anomalies existing at the individual-level. More can be said about the endowment effect (Thaler 1980; Samuelson and Zeckhauser 1988). As long-established interests tend to be better organized than newer ones (Olson 1982) the endowment effect and its interpretation as a "status quo bias" is strengthened, which gives this particular phenomenon greater aggregate weight.

Administration and Bureaucracy

This particular aggregation process works by formal rules that represent a special type of "rationality" (quite different from that based on the von Neumann-Morgenstern axioms). Administrative rationality functions with formal chains of command, but there is also considerable mutual inter-dependence between the various hierarchical levels due predominantly to informational requirements (Breton and Wintrobe 1982).

Administrative processes tend to impose one (legalistic) "frame" (in the sense of Kahneman and Tversky 1982) on all problems, and thus achieve the opposite effect of democracy: individual-level anomalies tend to be strengthened. This may be exemplified by the treatment of opportunity cost. Thaler (1980) found that people systematically undervalue the opportunity cost compared to out-of-pocket cost. This tendency is strengthened by the administrative process. Public (as well as private) bureaucracies are steered by budgets that only record monetary receipts and outlays. Opportunity costs do not normally appear in budgets and are therefore of little interest to bureaucrats, as long as they fall on people other than themselves. It may be observed that a valuable plot of land or building in public property remains unused for long periods of time because the costs are not directly visible in the budget.

Administrative procedures are capable of eliminating *some* individual paradoxes because they are, at least in principle, based on the idea of formal consistency. But members of the public bureaucracy pursue goals of their own (Tullock 1965; Downs 1957; Niskanen 1971), and are well able to distort formal rules for that purpose. To reach their own goals they actively exploit individual-level anomalies. A case in point is the endowment effect. Public administrators may find it advantageous to keep property in their hands even if it would be profitable to sell it. They then appeal to the bias in persons, strengthened by means of propaganda, not to part with their possessions (even though they would never have bought them at the price they could reach). This applies, for instance, to cultural property with which the administrators of public museums are unwilling to part (see Frey and Pommerehne 1989a, ch. 8).

On the basis of these considerations it would be difficult to argue that the administrative process effectively eliminates individual-level anomalies. Rather, the opposite is true.

Accepting the existence of irrationalities in individual behaviour does not mean that the rational choice approach has to be given up. On the contrary, the analysis pursued here remains within the rational choice framework. However, the analysis approaches the subject from a more general point of view. It is accepted that human beings are fallible and due to cognitive limitations are unable to always act rationally (see Sen 1977), but the social process spontaneously creates, or people consciously design, institutions which correct (part of) these individual irrationalities which burden people with costs. The analysis relies even more strongly on rational choice than conventional theory because rationality is seen as a means to overcome irrationalities.

Anomalies and their Cost

Irrational behaviour in the sense of deviations from the von Neumann-Morgenstern axioms leads to cost for the people concerned. These costs may be the cost of missed opportunities, or outright monetary cost. They provoke various kinds of consequences which may be arranged in three hierarchical steps.

Awareness of Cost

For various reasons, the cost created by anomalous behaviour is not always taken into account by the person acting. The alternatives offering better opportunities may simply be outside the considerations of the individual (they are outside the "ipsative" possibility set, see chapter 12) and therefore they are not aware that an opportunity has been missed. Alternatively, a person may know that superior alternatives are available, but he or she chooses not to evaluate the consequent cost. Empirical evidence exists (Thaler 1980) which shows that people indeed tend to disregard opportunity cost compared to out-of-pocket cost (opportunity cost effect). In both cases, people are not concerned with the cost of their anomalous behaviour. No reaction is, therefore, to be expected, and the persons concerned will pursue their irrational kind of behaviour.

Normally, however, persons falling prey to anomalies become aware of the costs entailed, at least in time. This may happen either by the anomalously acting persons *themselves* noting the cost, or being made aware of it by *other* people. It is useful to distinguish between two different kinds of anomalies in this context:

1. There are anomalies to which (almost) everyone falls prey. Examples are the tendency to misevaluate small probabilities or the certainty effect (Kahneman and Tversky 1979). Another instance is framing effects, whereby people are influenced by the way in which alternatives are formulated. As has been pointed out, even experts fall prey to such anomalies.

2. Other anomalies are *only* relevant for those persons acting, while outsiders are immune. This applies to two important anomalies often observed in daily life: The sunk cost effect (Thaler 1980)—people take past cost into account though they should not—is obviously irrelevant to other people because they did not have to carry these costs. The endowment effect (Thaler 1980)—people attach a higher value to what they own than they would do if they did not own the object—is also specific to the person acting and outsiders are not affected.

In the second type of anomaly people standing outside are equipped to inform the person falling prey to the anomaly about his or her irrationality. It remains open, however, whether the person concerned accepts the information offered.

Reaction to Cost

Even when a person behaving in an anomalous way is aware of the cost entailed by his or her action, he or she may still not react but continue to act as before. The cost of reacting (transaction cost) may be too high compared to the possible cost reduction or the potential gain. This applies, for instance, to some of the stock market anomalies noted above, where the buying and selling fees may be higher than the profit one can make. The reluctance to act though one is aware that one's position is not "optimal" has been stressed as an important feature of procedural rationality in Simon's (1957, 1978) concept of "satisficing," or "bounded rationality," and in Leibenstein's (1976) concept of "inert areas." It follows that the anomalies and their concomitant cost remain and can be empirically observed.

In many cases, however, the transaction costs are not so high as to prevent action. People then consider and compare alternative possibilities for action, depending on a cost-benefit calculus. Such action may be undertaken by the person falling prey to the anomalies. Often, other decision makers who see the chance of reaping profits from the irrationality of others take action. Examples are subjectively undervalued or overvalued stocks, or public lotteries, where it is known that some numbers are more unpopular than others (see Thaler and Ziemba 1988), hence one may make a profit by betting on such numbers because when they win, the lottery sum is divided among fewer participants than in the case of more popular numbers. Another example is the disregard of small probabilities with respect to natural disasters (Kunreuther 1976; Kunreuther et al., 1978). Irrational people are prepared to pay a higher price for the land than what it is actually worth when natural disasters are taken into account. This may happen because they wrongly believe that no disaster is going to occur. Rational people may reap a profit by offering such land at a higher price than it is worth if the correct disaster probabilities were taken into account. As a result of this supply of land, the price moves in the direction consistent with a rational evaluation, and the anomaly is no longer visible.

Level of Reaction

The reactions to the cost of anomalies may take place at two different levels.

1. On the *individual level* people may resort to self-commitment, that is, they may impose rules upon themselves designed to help them to avoid anomalies. The individual may be regarded as a "multiple self" (Elster 1986) consisting of a planner who knows that there is a risk of irrational behaviour, and of a doer (Margolis 1982) who tends to fall prey to the anomalies. This concept has been discussed as a solution to "akrasia," or weakness of will (Sen 1977) but is perfectly applicable to the case of anomalies. For instance, a professor may be well aware of a tendency to accept too many tasks which he or she will later regret, and, knowing this, may make it a rule never to accept immediately but to wait a few days before coming to a decision.

2. Reactions to the cost of anomalies may also occur at the *collective level*. People acting irrationally may look for help from the outside. Such help may come from other persons, in particular the family, or from friends or colleagues (e.g., a male professor may ask his wife to restrain him when he tries to undertake too much). Another possibility is to resort

to institutions: The endeavour to deal with individual anomalies thus constitutes a reason for the existence of institutions.

How Institutions Emerge

Institutions do not necessarily emerge even if people are willing to pay for their establishment and functioning. The veil of ignorance may help to overcome the free riding problem involved; at least one of Olson's (1965) conditions for collective action—small groups, selective incentives, or coercion—must be fulfilled in order for institutions to emerge. If an institution already exists which takes over the additional function of dealing with anomalies, only marginal costs (which are often small) matter. Institutions may come about by *spontaneous* action of which the *market* is the most prominent case. Entrepreneurs offer devices that help people willing to pay the price demanded to overcome the anomalies they are subject to. It has already been mentioned that irrational behaviour of others may be exploited provided competitive markets exist.

On the market, suppliers may offer counselling services designed to overcome the anomalies. With respect to business and financial affairs many different forms of consulting firms exist or rapidly emerge when an opportunity arises. Tax consultants, for instance, help people (and firms) to deal with the tendency to disregard opportunity cost. Financial consultants help to deal with the many anomalies observed on the stock market. Counselling is also found in more private spheres; private management seminars teach the participants how to organize their activities efficiently and consistently, and the many forms of psychotherapy help people avoid irrationalities, or, more often, to reduce the cost once they have occurred.

Other kinds of institutions which may spontaneously emerge are *social norms* and *traditions*. The most important ones are in the context of the family or other small social groups. The family may prevent irrationalities by inducing people to make decisions in the context of a larger set of persons and a longer time horizon (more than one generation). For instance, anomalies often arise when two people in love intend to marry. The parents and other relatives may point out the many other conditions which are necessary in a well-functioning partnership. In more traditional settings, which still prevail in many parts of the world (and which were also dominant in Europe in earlier times), parents arrange marriages. The family setting is also important to reduce the costs of anomalies, be they monetary or psychic. Because the altruism among family members prohibits the exploitation of anomalous family members, the family provides a safe haven which is available under all circumstances even if it is needed as a consequence of foolish behaviour. Thus, alcoholics or drug addicts may turn to their families, as may those who go "bankrupt" in their marriage and business affairs.

Other institutions designed to deal with anomalies are *consciously designed* by human action. An example of these are *clubs* such as college fraternities (at German universities the "Verbindungen," "Burschenschaften" and "Korps"), freemasons, or the Rotary and Lyons clubs. One important function, but of course not their only one, is to help members who have fallen prey to anomalies to avoid them in the future and to reduce the cost once they have occurred. There are a great number of other institutions, such as churches, which may be seen in this light.

Nowadays the *government* is one of the most important institutions for dealing with individual anomalies. Laws serve to regulate those activities wherein people are especially prone to act anomalously. Examples are tight regulations with respect to credits and insurance. In many countries, for example in some parts of Switzerland, people are forced to insure their houses against elementary risk, and health and old age insurances are compulsory. (Obviously, other, and supplementary, explanations can be given for the existence of such laws, such as moral hazard or adverse selection.)

While institutions serve several purposes, three major types may be distinguished with respect to dealing with anomalies of individuals' behaviour:

1. Prevention of anomalies. People are guided by institutions so that they behave in a rational manner.
2. Reduction of cost. Institutions serve to mitigate the consequent cost for people who have fallen prey to anomalies.
3. Redistribution of cost. Institutions shift the cost of an irrational behaviour among people and/or between time periods. Thus, consumption may be reduced in one period in order to compensate the same person when becoming the victim of an irrational action brought about by him or herself.

These three "ideal" types of institutions dealing with individual anomalies may be illustrated for the case of elementary risk insurance. In this area, (1) anomalies may be prevented by enforcing insurance or by providing additional incentives for insurance; (2) cost may be reduced by inducing people by force or incentives to build safer houses which are more resistant to fire and floods, or by prohibiting building in risky areas; (3) cost may be redistributed by compensating home owners through public funds or charitable organization when they are insufficiently insured and suffer damages.

Interactions Between Anomalies and Institutions

The relevance of the paradoxes in individual behaviour found by psychologists and economists depends on the social processes intervening between the individual and aggregate levels. These processes are guided and formed by decision making institutions of which the market is only one among several.

We can draw the following conclusions with respect to specific decision making systems:

1. The *market* fully eliminates individual-level anomalies under only very restricted conditions, unlikely to obtain in reality. There is, however, a tendency for the market to weaken individual-level anomalies at the aggregate level.

2. *Democracy* and *state* activity in the current politico-economic process strengthens individual anomalies through taxing rational and economically successful actors, and through subsidizing irrational and unsuccessful actors. At the constitutional level, on the other hand, the legal system tends to weaken individual-level anomalies by excluding actors prone to irrationality, directly eliminating aggregate-level inconsistencies by reducing the number of alternatives in uncertain and difficult decision areas, and by facilitating repetitive decisions. More important, democracy as the decision system encouraging diversity of opinions constantly produces many "frames" for a particular problem, thereby helping to avoid individual anomalies. In a dictatorship only one frame is allowed which more often leads to aggregate-level anomalies.

3. A *bargaining* system leads to countervailing predictions because of the unequal intensity to which interest groups are organized. In so far as the well-organized groups are particularly prone to fall prey to paradoxes, social bargaining strengthens aggregate-level anomalies.

4. An *administrative* social decision making system tends to weaken aggregate level anomalies because it is based on principles of formal

consistency. However, one frame imposed by bureaucracy, the budget, strengthens anomalies at the individual level.

Moreover, public bureaucrats have an incentive to exploit such anomalies for their own purposes, thus strengthening them in the aggregate.

With respect to economic theory, a solution to the difficulties posed by the traditional model of subjective expected utility maximization may be sought in two quite different directions:

Firstly, an effort may be made to *reformulate the expected utility model* so as to embody the paradoxical effects found at the individual level. This approach has been undertaken by a number of different scholars (see e.g., Loomes and Sugden 1982; Machina 1987). This attempt to come to grips with the anomalies found poses two problems:

1. Do the reformulations do justice to the anomalies found, that is, are they really able to capture the essence of the particular kinds of irrationality found? The views of the scholars engaged in this endeavour conflict on this point and it may be well to remember March's (1978, p. 597) caution that "By suitably manipulating . . . one can save classical theories of choice as 'explanations' of behaviour in a formal sense but probably only at the cost of stretching a good idea into a doubtful ideology." However, despite these dangers, such reformulations are sometimes useful.

2. The second problem in this approach is directly connected with the aggregation process discussed. As has been argued (see table 11–1), institutions may eliminate, weaken or even create anomalies appearing at the aggregate level. This means that even if the reformulation of the expected utility maximization model is able to embody the individual-level anomalies, the task remains of determining in what way the institutions shaping the aggregation process deal with those anomalies. Finding a "satisfactory" individual level-formulation is thus only part of the task.

A second, and quite different way of coping with the individual level anomalies is to endeavour to find a formulation of the decision process of actors that is as immune as possible to these irrationalities. One way (following Stigler and Becker 1977) is to push back the emphasis on individual preferences and to concentrate instead on the *constraints*, that is, on the person's possibility set. The relevant constraints do not only consist of restraints imposed by income, prices and time, but also include subjective or cognitive constraints (see chapter 12). This approach may be useful to embody the cognitive limitations emphasized by psychologists as well as by some economists. A careful analysis of the various types of constraints may allow the person's possibility set to be narrowed down so much that it is of little importance which particular point in this set is chosen, as the consequences on the aggregate are minor.

This chapter proposes that individual decision making theory should be closely integrated with new institutional economics—by means of the analysis provided by the comparative theory of institutions, public choice, transaction costs and law and economics. Our analysis suggests a new role for institutions which seems to have received little attention so far. Institutions may emerge as a result of the benefits and costs produced by the individual-level anomalies and may serve to weaken such anomalies at the aggregate level. However, under some identifiable conditions, existing institutions bring about the opposing effect of strengthening or creating such anomalies at the aggregate level.

General References to the Literature

Laboratory evidence on anomalies may be found in the following collections of articles

> Kahneman, Daniel, Slovic, Paul and Tversky, Amos (eds). *Judgement Under Uncertainty: Heuristics and Biases.* Cambridge: Cambridge University Press, 1982.
>
> Arkes, Hal R. and Hammond, Kenneth R. (eds). *Judgement and Decision Making: An Interdisciplinary Reader.* Cambridge: Cambridge University Press, 1986.
>
> Bell, David E., Raiffa, Howard and Tversky, Amos (eds). *Decision Making. Descriptive, Normative, and Prescriptive Interactions.* Cambridge: Cambridge University Press, 1988.

A broad and enjoyable account of the irrationalities in individual behaviour is provided in

> Dawes, Robyn M. *Rational Choice in an Uncertain World.* San Diego and New York: Harcourt, Brace, Yovanovich, 1988.

Various points of view on anomalies by economists are collected in

> Hogarth, Robin M. and Reder, Melvin W. (eds). *Rational Choice.* Chicago: University of Chicago Press, 1987.

Surveys from the economic point of view are

> Schoemaker, Paul J. "The Expected Utility Model: Its Variants, Purposes, Evidence and Limitations." *Journal of Economic Literature* 20 (June 1982): 529–63.
>
> Machina, Mark J. "Choice Under Uncertainty: Problems Solved and

Unsolved." *Journal of Economic Perspectives* 1 (1987): 121–54.
A more applied discussion with many examples is provided by
Thaler, Richard H. "The Psychology of Choice and the Assumptions of
Economics." In: Roth, Alvin E. (ed.). *Laboratory Experimentation in
Economics*. Cambridge: Cambridge University Press, 1987, pp. 99–130.

12 AN IPSATIVE THEORY OF HUMAN BEHAVIOUR

Orthodox Economics Challenged

Human beings sometimes act in surprising ways, which, for an outside observer, are sometimes difficult to understand or to make sense of. This chapter focuses on such a behavioural anomaly so far neglected, but of great importance to economics: the systematic overestimation of positively valued events, and the systematic underestimation of negatively valued events. These biases have been empirically shown to hold, for example, in the following areas:

1. Even if people are well aware of the probability of getting a disease such as cancer, they still tend to assume that it afflicts others, but not themselves. More generally, most people believe that they are more likely than average to live past eighty years of age (Weinstein 1979). That this is objectively impossible does not induce people to think otherwise.

2. The great majority of people consider themselves to be better-than-average drivers and more or less immune to accidents (Svenson 1978). Each one of them experiences having made trip after trip without accident, and then tends to interpret this as evidence of an exceptional

197

driving skill. They also believe that they are less likely than the average person to be injured by the working tools they operate (Rethans 1979), and they conceive hazardous occupations to be low-risk.

3. People are aware of the fact that natural disasters such as floods and earthquakes may happen, but assume that they will be less affected than others.

4. Even if people are aware of the substantial risk of divorce, they tend to believe that the given risk applies to others, not to their own marriage. This may be called the Elizabeth Taylor effect: whenever she got married, and this was often the case, she proclaimed in good faith that this time it was for life—only to be divorced a year or two later.

5. People may know the statistical incidence of crime but still think that only other people will become victims.

These examples suggest that people do not take the alternatives available to them as binding: some objectively impossible alternatives are considered, other alternatives that are possible are disregarded (Frey and Foppa 1986; Foppa 1987). The possibility set which a *particular* person takes to be relevant *for himself or herself*—it will be called the *ipsative possibility set* (IPS)—differs from the objective possibility set (OPS). The difference does not lie in the fact that people have limited information or intelligence: these factors account for the difference between the objective and the subjective possibility set (a difference which is well known in economic theory and will therefore not be further discussed here). An important feature of the difference between the ipsative and the objective possibility sets is that there is no tendency over time for the difference to narrow down; rather, the difference can be maintained over long periods of time, and there are circumstances in which it even increases.

The systematic overextension or underextension of one's possibility set is difficult or impossible to reconcile with the "spirit" of orthodox economic theory, and in particular with its central tenet, the relative price effect. This chapter endeavours to provide a simple and straightforward explanation of these paradoxes by differentiating between an *objective* possibility set and an *ipsative* possibility set, which is defined by the *personal* view about the possibilities. An effort is made to formulate testable propositions and to provide empirical evidence incompatible with the orthodox economic model of behaviour as expounded, for example, by Stigler and Becker (1977). It is argued that the differences are relevant for attempts to influence human behaviour through economic policy. There are even identifiable instances in which an orthodox economic policy via the control of relative prices yields a counterproductive outcome.

The approach used here stays within the rational choice framework (and even within utility maximization), that is, the results are not gained by assuming any kind of irrationality, or by an arbitrary or unexplained shift of preferences. Rather, the economic approach to explaining human behaviour is exploited more fully by differentiating between the two basically different kinds of possibility sets indicated.

In both the case of an overextension and an underextension of the ipsative possibility set two situations will be distinguished. A deviation between the two possibility sets may be due to (1) effects due to human nature or psychological traits, and (2) conscious strategic design.

The ipsative limits to human behaviour are discussed in the following section. The third section treats the case of an overextension of the ipsative possibility set beyond what is objectively possible. The final section puts the theory into a wider perspective.

Ipsative Limits to Human Behaviour

Under many circumstances people's actions are not constrained effectively by the objective conditions (objective possibility set OPS) but rather by the set of possibilities which they consider relevant for themselves, that is, by the ipsative possibility set (IPS).

In the simplified case of the two activities or goods X and Y, an underextension is graphically shown in figure 12–1.

The person considered is objectively able to reach utility U* at point P* on the boundary of the objective possibility set OPS but does not consider the shaded area B. His or her ipsative possibility set IPS encompasses only area OEF so that utility maximization leads to the choice of point P_0 with utility U_0. To an outside observer, the person has a utility opportunity loss of $(U^* - U_o)$. However, the person considered does *not* experience this loss because the larger objective possibility set ODC is beyond his or her own consideration. Empirical evidence exists (Thaler 1980) that opportunity costs are indeed treated by people quite differently than actual cost.

The underextension of the ipsative set is not restricted to mentally disturbed people but is a common phenomenon among perfectly rational actors. It seems that most people consider only a rather small part of what is objectively possible. To an outside observer, the life of these people appears to be rather narrow and moving along a trodden path, and that obvious possibilities for improving the situation are disregarded.

An underestimation of the ipsative set may happen (1) due to human nature, and (2) due to design.

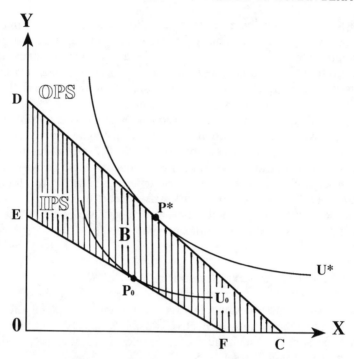

Figure 12–1.   The Ipsative is Smaller than the Objective Possibility Set.

Underextension Due to Human Nature

The observation that people sometimes disregard obvious possibilities
for improving their situation is empirically well founded. An important
example is provided by large investment decisions of firms. The general
observation that "individuals look at only a few possible outcomes rather
than the whole distribution . . ." (March and Shapira 1987, p. 1405; see
also Alderfer and Bierman 1970) also applies to managers considering
investment and divestment in multinational corporations: "The search for
solutions is "simple minded," with the first acceptable alternative being
adopted" (Boddewyn 1979, p. 94). Schmölders (1978, p. 21) found that
only half of industrial corporations in Northrhine-Westphalia took more
than one location into consideration, one quarter made a choice between
two locations. A similar result appeared in an extensive survey of
managerial perspectives on risk and risk taking by March and Shapira
(1987, p. 1412): managers focus on very few aspects, and sequentially

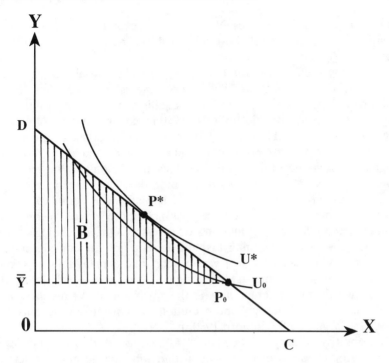

Figure 12–2.   A Position of Higher Utility (U*) is Beyond Consideration.

consider a relatively small number of alternatives (i.e., there is satisficing, Simon 1955; March and Simon 1958), and sometimes only one single critical focal value commands all attention. Even managers acting under more or less competitive conditions consider only part of the whole objective possibility set, and may therefore stay at a point judged by outside observers to be suboptimal (see, more extensively, Frey and Heggli 1989).

Another example relates to the amount of information people gather: ". . . present research and examples drawn from everyday life show that some kinds of information that the scientists regard highly pertinent and logically compelling are habitually ignored by people" (Nisbett, Borgida, Crandall and Reed 1982, p. 116).

Why is there not a movement from the position of lower utility to a feasible one of higher utility, that is, an extension of the ipsative set towards the objective possibility set? Consider figure 12–2 where it is assumed that the quantity $O\overline{Y}$ of activity or good Y is under consideration, but all quantities $Y > \bar{Y}$ are beyond consideration. An example may be a person who does not drink more than one bottle of wine each evening.

An author such as Becker (1962, in particular) would argue that a person, by experiencing marginal improvements in his or her utility, would be induced to move from the disequilibrium boundary solution P_0 (where the highest possible utility U_0 within the ipsative set $O\bar{Y}P_0C$ is reached) towards P^*. However, it is argued here that such a possibility is simply beyond consideration: the person concerned does not even imagine a move beyond $\bar{Y}$; area B does not belong to his personal choice set. It is an instance where learning does not take place. While psychologists have indeed stressed that learning is a complicated and uncertain process (e.g., Brehmer 1980; Einhorn 1980), economists normally simply assert that learning takes place. One psychologist even sees "... the area of learning [as] the focal point for considering the relative merits of psychological versus economic explanations of choice behaviour. Some economists have argued that ... one will learn the optimal rule through interaction with the environment. Vague assertions about equilibrium, efficiency and evolutionary concepts are advanced to bolster this argument" (Einhorn 1980, p. 269).

The ipsative theory of behaviour allows us to derive empirically testable propositions which are not in line with the normal predictions of orthodox economic theory, or which, at least, point out the great importance of limiting cases:

1. The relative price effect or the law of demand does not work. When the relative price of activities or goods X are Y is changed (as in figure 12-3, when the relative price changes from OD/OC to OD'/OC' and to OD"/OC"), the individuals maintain their consumption at P_0 (while P^* changes to P^{**} and to P^{***}). The reason for this "inert area" (see, for this related concept, Leibenstein 1976, 1978) is, of course, that P_0 is a corner solution. The fact that behaviour is immune to changes in relative prices is not incompatible, but it is certainly not in the "spirit" of neo-classical theory; the idea that changing relative prices do affect demand is a *major* element of orthodox economic thinking.

Attending cultural events such as the opera, concerts of classical music, or visiting museums are examples. Some people do not even consider such an activity, and therefore changing the price of such cultural events has no effect on their attendance. An analysis of four Rotterdam museums reveals, for example, that the rate of *first* visits is unaffected by price variations, while other visitors show the expected negative

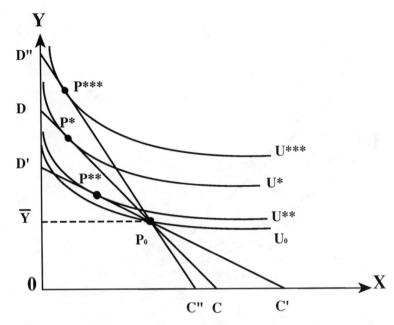

Figure 12–3.   Relative Price Changes Do Not Affect Behaviour.

price elasticity of demand (Goudriaan and van 't Eind 1985, p. 106). If pricing is used as an instrument for opening up museums and other cultural institutions to new groups of visitors, one would have to expect little success.

Another example is provided by tax morality which does seem to be an issue not open to marginal evaluation but rather an issue of principle among taxpayers. Some of them do not even think of actively finding ways and means to cheat on taxes, while others with a low tax morality go as far as possible, taking into account the punishment to be expected when detected. In Switzerland, most citizens seem to belong to the first, in Germany to the second group. A change in the relative cost of cheating on taxes versus being honest only affects the behaviour of the second groups. Indeed, such a relative price change may result in a perverse effect: when the government threatens citizens of high tax morality with increased punishments, this may be taken by them as an indication that the government distrusts them, which leads them to do likewise. The "game" of mutual trust between citizens and government is then changed into one of opposition, with negative results for all (see also Weck-

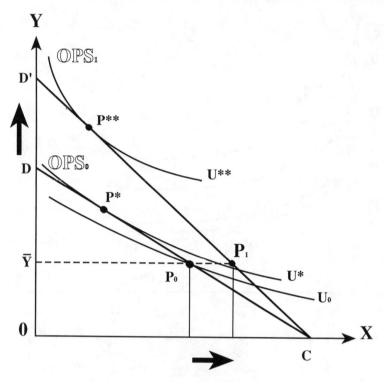

Figure 12-4.   A "Perverse" Effect of a Relative Price Change.

Hannemann, Pommerehne and Frey 1984). This is an illustration of the second proposition:

   2. A relative price change may result in an unexpected change in behaviour. Consider figure 12-4.

   The price of activity or good Y is lowered so that the objective possibility set enlarges from ODC to OD'C, and the (irrelevant) equilibrium shifts from P* to P**. Actual consumption moves from P_0 along $\bar{Y}$ to P_1, that is, the savings due to a lower price of Y are used exclusively to increase the consumption of X. In this case, a decrease in the relative price of good Y leads to an increase in the relative quantity consumed of good X which, strictly speaking, is not incompatible with neoclassics because the increased demand for the good or activity which becomes relatively more expensive is due to the income effect. However, this constellation is certainly not in the "spirit" of what traditional neo-classics would assume when a relative price change occurs.

Underextension Due to Design

A large number of processes exist which a person knows to be beyond his or her control. Such *self-coercive processes* are an example of the weakness of will or *akrasia* (Sen 1974, 1977). Coercive processes or compulsory consumption (Winston 1980) where no marginal choice is possible may be of three kinds:

1. Psychic. Love ("l'amour fou") and hate (à la Michael Kolhaas or Ahab) may go so far as to lead to self-destruction. Equally, friendship and often family bonds (at least in the European sense) are of an absolute nature with complete trust, at least in principle.
2. Physical. Addiction on this level ranges from watching television to smoking, drinking, gambling and drug taking, and it is characterized by the fact that many, or most, people find it impossible to exercise control at the margin.
3. Social. Many professions or careers once entered into do not allow "free choice" to the persons involved. The same is true for prostitution and crime where an exit is difficult, and sometimes not even possible. Coercive processes cannot be directly controlled by the person in question; they are beyond his or her power. They can indirectly be controlled only by moving to another decision making level where a person sets for himself or herself *rules* or *constraints*, as discussed in the previous chapter.

In the framework of ipsative theory, coercive pressures are analysed within the two possibility sets distinguished. Consider figure 12–5, with Y a coercive good if its consumption exceeds $\bar{Y}$.

The person knows that a choice of the utility maximizing point P* with utility U* cannot be maintained, but that he or she moves along the budget line to the maximum possible consumption of Y at P^c (the movement is indicated by an arrow). In this setting it is rational for such a knowledgeable person not to cross $\bar{Y}$ (though P* yields higher utility than U_0), because the final consumption at P^c yields a lower utility U^c than at P_0. The choice of an ipsative possibility space with $Y \leqslant \bar{Y}$ is preferable to the objectively possible set even though at P_0 there is marginal disequilibrium. The analysis thus differs from Stigler and Becker's (1977) treatment of addiction because they assume that a person

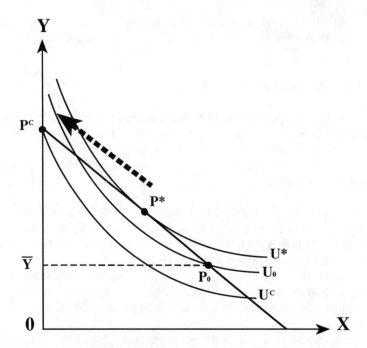

Figure 12–5.   Choice of an Ipsative Set in Order to Evade a Coercive Process.

may always make a marginal choice. They model the coercive process by resorting to human capital accumulated by addictive consumption.

The section has considered those circumstances where people do not fully use the objective possibilities they have but are effectively constrained by ipsative limits relevant only to themselves. The following section looks at the opposite case where people think that the opportunities open to them (i.e., their ipsative possibility set) are greater than objectively possible.

Overextending the Ipsative Limits

In the simplified case of two activities or goods X and Y, an overextension of what people consider to be possible for themselves over what objective conditions permit is graphically shown in figure 12–6.

The objective possibility set is given by ODC, and the larger ipsative possibility set by OEF. The maximum achievable utility level U_0 is

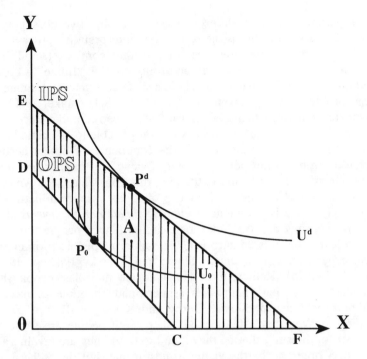

Figure 12–6.   The Ipsative is Larger than the Objective Possibility Set.

reached at P_0, but the person concerned believes that utility U^d can be reached at P^d. The shaded area A indicates the overextension area.

Again, the two instances of overextension due to human nature (1), and due to design (2) are discussed.

Overextension Due to Human Nature

There is a tension or conflict between point P^d which is desired but not objectively feasible, and P_0 which is feasible but not the most desirable. If such an incompatibility were typical for mentally ill persons only, or the result of an error soon to disappear, the incompatibility would not be of much relevance for economics. However, it is argued here that such an overextension happens in many situations for perfectly normal, rational people, and that there is no tendency for the ipsative possibility set to converge to the objective set. Nonadjustment holds because "reality" can be "constructed" in many different ways. The objective possibility set OPS is not given but rather is the result of an interpretative process of an actor. The interpretation varies according to the "context" (see Tversky and Kahneman 1981) as well as according to the "frame" (Tversky and Kahneman 1974), that is, psychological factors may determine the relevant problem space (Newell and Simon 1972; Schoemaker 1980).

Overextension is particularly relevant when considerable uncertainty exists. In this setting, a person always finds it possible to associate him or herself with another domain so that the experience of others becomes irrelevant from his or her personal point of view. This *ipsative probability* may deviate systematically and in the long run from what is known in the literature as objective and subjective probability (see de Finetti 1968; Savage 1954): there is a tendency to *underestimate negative events* and to *overestimate positive events*. Under some circumstances, people stubbornly refuse to learn, there is "a surprising . . . failure of people to infer from lifelong experience" (Kahneman, Slovic and Tversky 1982, p. 18; see also Hogarth 1975). Rather, there is a "judgemental bias: people [have a] predilection to view themselves as personally immune to hazards" (Fischhoff, Lichtenstein, Slovic, Derby and Keeney 1981, pp. 29–30). According to Weinstein's findings (1980, p. 806) people are subject to "unrealistic optimism", that is, they "tend to think they are invulnerable. They expect others to be the victim of misfortune, not themselves" (see also Kirscht, Haefner, Kagelas and Rosenstock 1966).

The following table reproduces empirical evidence of unrealistic optimism for future life events. It shows that overextension of the ipsative set is a common feature in the areas discussed in the introduction.

Most of the events refer to diseases where people obviously have a very strong tendency to exclude themselves from the base of the population as a whole, and to put themselves in another category. In all cases the underestimation of negative, and the overestimation of positive events (in table 12–1 "living past 80") means that the ipsative is larger than the objective possibility set: the constraints in terms of monetary and nonmonetary resources are discounted by people when they consider their *own* situation. Such an overextension of the ipsative possibility set would be of little consequence for economics if it were only found in the sphere of evaluation. But it also has an important influence on *behaviour*. For this purpose, the behavioural consequences in the areas discussed above will be sketched and empirical evidence quoted:

1. Diseases. Individuals tend to have too few cancer tests (American Cancer Society 1966), and generally tend to behave as if they were going

Table 12–1.   Unrealistic Optimism for Future Life Events.

Event	Mean Comparative Judgement of Own Chances vs. Others' Chances (percent)[1]
1. Having a drinking problem	−58.3
2. Attempting suicide	−55.9
3. Divorced a few years after married	−48.7
4. Heart attack before age 40	−38.4
5. Contracting venereal disease	−37.4
6. Getting lung cancer	−31.5
7. Being sterile	−31.2
8. Having a heart attack	−23.3
9. Living past 80	12.5
10. Tripping and breaking bone	−8.3
11. Having your car stolen	−7.3
12. Victim of mugging	−5.8

[1] In making a comparative judgement, students estimated the difference in percent between the chances that an event would happen to them and the average chances for other students (of the same sex) at their college. For positive events, the response that one's own chances are greater than average is considered optimistic, and the response that one's own chances are less than average is considered pessimistic. For negative events, the definitions of optimistic and pessimistic responses are reversed.
N = 123 to 130, depending on rating form and missing data. Student's t was used to test whether the mean is significantly different from zero. Events 1 to 8 are significant at the 99.9% , event 9 at the 99%, and events 10 to 12 at the 95% level.
Source: Weinstein (1980), p. 810.

to live forever, for example, a large number of people do not write a last will.

2. Accidents. As may easily be tested by asking someone who takes part in a hazardous type of sport whether he or she considers it to be dangerous, there is a standard reply: accidents are attributed to insufficient training, to recklessness or to bad equipment. As a consequence, people tend to be careless, for example, they are generally reluctant to wear seatbelts in cars even when they admit that they are useful in the case of an accident (Robertson 1974), and they tend to insure too little (Robertson 1977). Those in hazardous occupations systematically act as if their work were not risky and tend not to voluntarily use the safety equipment available (Akerlof and Dickens 1982). People are under an "illusion of control": while they sometimes pay lip service to the concept of chance, they *behave* as if chance events could be controlled (Langer 1982; van Raaij 1985). The same illusion

applies to managers. They do not accept the idea that the risks they face are inherent in their situation (Strickland, Lewicki and Katz 1966); rather, they make an effort to use their skills to control the risks (Adler 1980; Keyes 1985; March and Shapira 1987; Shapira 1986).

3. Natural disasters. There is convincing empirical evidence (Kunreuther 1976; Kunreuther, Ginsberg, Miller et al., 1978) that even if extremely attractive flood and earthquake insurance is available (the federal government subsidizes it up to 90 percent), the large majority does not make use of it (not even those who do not speculate on the help by government in the case of a disaster). The fundamental bias discussed thus induces behaviour which an outside observer would have to evaluate as contrary to subjective utility maximization.

4. Divorce. Today, more than ever, people enter into marriage almost unprepared. Few make an appropriate marriage contract or make early preparations for a possible divorce (because such acts are interpreted as evidence of lack of love). When somebody experiences a divorce he or she often remarries, with the result that divorced persons remarrying are likely to divorce again. No learning effect takes place but rather the contrary: While divorce rates in first marriages show a steady decline, divorce rates for remarriages have climbed (Bianchi and Spain 1986, pp. 38–39).

5. Crime. People living in high crime areas (and not emigrating) tend to disregard the prevalence of crime, probably in order to decrease their psychic cost or cognitive dissonance (see Akerlof and Dickens 1982). As a consequence, they tend to become less careful than a benevolent outside observer would advise them to be.

This discussion suggests that the extension of the ipsative set beyond the objective possibility set affects human behaviour in a significant way.

It should be noted that only a subset of the effects is revealed in individual behaviour. Another part is evidenced by institutions created in response to the behavioural consequences of overextending the ipsative set. In all western countries, for example, the law stipulates a marriage contract because people tend to refrain from making one themselves.

According to the view here proposed, Becker's (1976, p. 167) statement, "Even irrational decision units must accept reality and could not, for example, maintain a choice that was no longer within their opportunity set" turns out to be only partly true. While the second part of the sentence is obviously true (almost by definition), the first part is not. Even rational individuals do not simply "accept reality" but—especially when uncertainty is involved—may maintain a cognition of reality which outside observers consider mistaken, with important consequences for behaviour.

Overextension Due to Design

The ipsative may also be extended beyond the objective possibility set as a purposeful device to *induce motivation* and *work effort* which would otherwise not come forth. Similar to Leibenstein (1976, 1978) or Hirschman (1958), but contrary to orthodox neoclassics, work intensity is not given but can be influenced by appropriate personal strategies.

Towards a Broader Perspective

It is high time that economic theory accepts that human beings are not perfectly functioning automatons who maximize utility as seen and predicted by an outside observer. Humans are weak and fallible. This does not mean that they just act "irrationally"; rather they take into account that they are not perfect and grope for ways to mitigate the damaging effects which may result from their weakness and fallibility. A similar reaction has also been discussed in chapter 11 for the case of anomalous behaviour in the sense of deviating from the von Neumann-Morgenstern axioms of rationality.

   In this chapter an attempt has been made to explicitly model one important aspect of the imperfections of human beings. Traditional neoclassical microtheory has been extended by differentiating two possibility sets for human action. In addition to the objective (and subjective) possibility sets (which tend to merge over time) there is quite another set of possibilities which the person considers relevant for his or her person only. This set has been called "ipsative" in order to emphasize that it is relevant only for a particular person from his or her own point of view.

   The ipsative and the objective possibility sets differ in four major respects:

   1. The objective possibility set OPS is *marginal*. Small changes can meaningfully be evaluated in terms of benefits and costs. The ipsative possibility set IPS is nonmarginal or *absolute*; alternatives are either considered in full or not at all.
   2. OPS is *symmetric*. An increase or a decrease in relative prices have in principle the same effect (with a negative sign). IPS is *asymmetric*,

alternatives which are outside the ipsative set are beyond consideration irrespective of how relative prices change. Once alternatives are inside the ipsative set, the "normal" relative price effects obtain.

3. OPS is *transpersonal*: A benevolent outside observer who is well informed about a person's marginal utility and marginal costs would suggest exactly those actions which the informed person would choose himself or herself. IPS is *personal*: the environment is looked at from a point of view only relevant for the looker. Consequently a benevolent outside observer would often suggest different actions from the ones undertaken by the person concerned.

4. OPS assumes that a *choice* between alternatives can be made, guided by expected utility maximization. Accordingly, a change in relative prices has a systematic effect on behaviour according to the fundamental law of demand. IPS assumes that there are cases where no direct choice between alternatives is possible as autonomous processes prevent a choice being made. People have *limited control* between alternatives, and a real choice can be made only by moving to the (constitutional) level where rules may be adopted.

The developed ipsative theory of human behaviour relies strongly on psychological evidence. An effort has been made towards an integration of economics and psychology, similar to those which have been made by such writers as Herbert Simon, Harvey Leibenstein, George Akerlof or Tibor Scitovsky, but psychological effects have been analysed here within the context of utility maximization. Unexpected results have been reached by carefully constructing a person's set of possibilities. It has become clear that the explanations offered do not, in a strict sense, contradict existing economic theory. Standard neoclassics is flexible enough to describe "all observed human behaviour as optimal, provided it is modelled in the appropriate manner" (Schoemaker 1982, p. 539). In a "postdictive" sense orthodox theory and ipsative theory are thus not mutually exclusive. The critical criteria for the differential evaluation of theories is whether one of them is more parsimonious, conforms better to common sense, and can more easily be reconciled with empirical observations (without having to add auxiliary assumptions).

The ipsative model developed is only a first step; many aspects are only tentative and have to be explored further. In particular, the conditions under which people do not undertake all which is objectively possible (the ipsative is a subset of the objective possibility set), and under which the ipsative set is extended beyond the objective set have to be more fully analysed. For the case of an under- or overextension by design these conditions have (at least partly) been identified here, but the conditions for an under- or overextension due to human nature have still to be explored. Are they solely dependent on personality traits, or are they also context dependent? Structural conditions must be identified in which human beings systematically underextend, and other structural conditions in which they systematically overextend, their ipsative set. Once these structural conditions are known it will be possible to empirically test the ipsative model by direct observation.

General References to the Literature

Challenges to orthodox economics (beyond those mentioned after chapters 2, 9 and 10) come from

> Sen, Amartya K. and Williams, Bernhard (eds). *Utilitarianism and Beyond.* Cambridge: Cambridge University Press, 1982.
> Margolis, Howard. *Selfishness, Altruism and Rationality. A Theory of Social Choice.* Cambridge: Cambridge University Press, 1982.
> Elster, Jon (ed.). *The Multiple Self.* Cambridge: Cambridge University Press, 1986.

Empirical evidence for the under- and overestimation of the ipsative possibility space are provided for insurance markets by

> Kunreuther, Howard, Ginsberg, Ralph, Miller, Louis et al. *Disaster Insurance Protection: Public Policy Lessons.* New York: Wiley, 1978.

For management behaviour see

> March, James G. and Shapira, Zur. "Managerial Perspectives on Risk and Risk Taking." *Management Science* 33 (November 1987): 1404–1418.

and more generally

> Weinstein, Neil D. "Unrealistic Optimism about Future Life Events." *Journal of Personality and Social Psychology* 39 (1980): 806–820.

An important contribution to a descriptive theory of consumer behaviour is

> Thaler, Richard H. "Toward a Positive Theory of Consumer Choice." *Journal of Economic Behavior and Organization* 1 (March 1980): 39–60.

REFERENCES

Abell, Francis (1914). *Prisoners of War in Britain* 1756–1815. London: Oxford University Press.

Achenbaum, A.A. (1966). "Knowledge is a Thing Called Measurement." In: Adler, L. and Crespi, I. (eds). *Attitude Research at Sea*. Chicago: American Marketing Association, pp. 111–126.

Adler, Stanley (1980). "Risk Making Management." *Business Horizons* 23: 11–14.

Ainslie, George (1975). "Specious Reward: A Behavioural Theory of Impulsiveness and Control." *Psychological Bulletin* 82 (July): 463–496.

Ajzen, Icek (1988). *Attitudes, Personality and Behavior*. Milton Keynes: Open University Press.

Ajzen, Icek and Fishbein, Martin (1973). "Attitudinal and Normative Variables as Predictors of Specific Behaviors." *Journal of Personality and Social Psychology* 27: 41–57.

Akerlof, George A. (1984). *An Economic Theorist's Book of Tales*. Cambridge: Cambridge University Press.

Akerlof, George A. and Dickens, William, T. (1982). "The Economic Consequences of Cognitive Dissonance." *American Economic Review* 72 (June): 307–319.

Akerlof, George A. and Yellen, Janet L. (1985a). "Can Small Deviations from

215

Rationality Make Significant Differences to Economic Equilibria?" *American Economic Review* 75 (Sept.): 708–720.

Akerlof, George A. and Yellen, Janet L. (1985b). "A Near-Rational Model of the Business Cycle, with Wage and Price Inertia." *Quarterly Journal of Economics* 100 (Supplement): 821–838.

Akerlof, George A. and Yellen, Janet L. (1987). "Rational Models of Irrational Behavior." *American Economic Review* 77 (May): 137–142.

Albert, Hans (1985). "Anmerkungen zum Ökonomischen Denken." *Konstanzer Blätter für Hochschulfragen* 23 (Dec.): 6–17.

Alchian, Armen A. (1950). "Uncertainty, Evolution, and Economic Theory." *Journal of Political Economy* 58 (June): 211–221.

Alchian, Armen A. (1977). *Economic Forces at Work*. Indianapolis: Liberty Press.

Alchian, Armen A. and Demsetz, Harold (1972). "Production, Information Costs, and Economic Organization." *American Economic Review* 62 (Dec.): 777–795.

Alderfer, Clayton P. and Bierman, Harold (1970). "Choices with Risk: Beyond the Mean and Variance." *Journal of Business* 43: 341–353.

Allais, Maurice (1953). "Le comportement de l'homme rationnel devant le risque: Critique des postulats et axiomes de l'école américaine." *Econometrica* 21 (Oct.): 503–546.

Allingham, Michael G. and Sandmo, Agnar (1972). "Income Tax Evasion: A Theoretical Analysis." *Journal of Public Economics* 1: 323–338.

American Cancer Society (1966). *A Study of Motivational and Environmental Deterrents to the Taking of Physical Examinations that Include Cancer Tests*. New York.

American Legal Foundation (1990). *Terrorism and the Media*. Washington, D.C.

Anderson, Gary M. (1988). "Mr. Smith and the Preachers: The Economics of Religion in the Wealth of Nation." *Journal of Political Economy* 96: 1066–1088.

Anderson, Gary M. and Tollison, Robert D. (1985). "Life in the Gulag: A Property Rights Perspective." *Cato Journal* 5 (Spring/Summer): 295–304.

Anderson, Robert C. (1974). "Paintings as an Investment." *Economic Inquiry* 12 (March): 13–26.

Arkes, Hal R. and Hammond, Kenneth R. (eds) (1986). *Judgement and Decision Making: An Interdisciplinary Reader*. Cambridge: Cambridge University Press.

Armstrong, J.D. (1985). "The International Committee of the Red Cross and Political Prisoners." *International Organization* 39: 615–642.

Aronson, Elliot and Carlsmith, J. Merrill (1968). "Experimentation in Social Psychology." In: Lindsey, Gardner and Aronson, Elliot (eds). *The Handbook of Social Psychology Vol. 2*. Reading, Mass.: Addison-Wesley.

Arrow, Kenneth J. (1963). *Social Choice and Individual Values*. New York: Wiley, 2nd ed.

Arrow, Kenneth J. (1970). "Political and Economic Evaluation of Social Effects and Externalities." In: Margolis, Julius (ed.). *The Analysis of Public Output*.

New York: Columbia University Press, pp. 1–23.

Arrow, Kenneth J. (1974). *Limits of Organizations*. New York: Norton.

Arrow, Kenneth J. (1975). "Gifts and Exchanges." In: Edmund Phelps (ed.). *Altruism, Morality and Economic Theory*. New York: Sage, pp. 13–28.

Arrow, Kenneth J. ('982). "Risk Perception in Psychology and Economics." *Economic Inquiry* 20 (Jan.): 1–9.

Arrow, Kenneth J. (1986). "Economic Theory and the Hypothesis of Rationality." In: Eatwell, John et al. (eds). *The New Palgrave, A Dictionary of Economics*. Vol. 2. London: Macmillan, pp. 69–75.

Arrow, Kenneth J. (1987). "Rationality of Self and Others in an Economic System." In: Hogarth, Robin M. and Reder, Melvin W. (eds). *Rational Choice*. Chicago: University of Chicago Press, pp. 201–215.

Ashenfelter, Orley (1989). "How Auctions Work for Wine and Art." *Journal of Economic Perspectives 3* (Summer): 23–36.

Assmann, Heinz-Dieter (1978). "Die Transformationsprobleme des Privatrechts und die ökonomische Analyse des Rechts." In: Assmann, Heinz-Dieter; Kirchner, Christian and Schanze, Erich (eds). *Ökonomische Analyse des Rechtes*. Kronberg: Athenäum, pp. 21–74.

Atkinson, Anthony B. and Stiglitz, Joseph E. (1980). *Lectures on Public Economics*. New York and London: McGraw Hill.

Atkinson, Scott E., Sandler, Todd and Tschirhart, John (1987). "Terrorism in a Bargaining Framework." *Journal of Law and Economics* 30 (April): 1–22.

Axelrod, Robert (1984). *The Evolution of Cooperation*. New York: Basic Books.

Bacharach, B. and Galai, D. (1979). "The Risk-Return Relationship and Stock Prices." *Journal of Financial and Quantitative Analysis* 14: 421–441.

Baldwin, Robert E. (1985). *The Political Economy of U.S. Import Policy*. Cambridge, Mass.: MIT Press.

Bandura, A. (1969). *Principles of behavior modification*. New York: Holt, Rinehart and Winston.

Bandura, A. (1973). *Social Learning Theory*. Englewood Cliffs, N.J.: Prentice-Hall.

Banz, Rolf W. (1981). "The Relationship between Return and Market Value of a Common Stock." *Journal of Financial Economics* 9: 3–18.

Basu, Sanjoy (1977). "The Investment Performance of Common Stocks in Relation to their Price-Earning Ratio: A Test of the Efficient Market Hypothesis." *Journal of Finance* 32: 663–682.

Bator, Francis M. (1958). "The Anatomy of Market Failure." *Quarterly Journal of Economics* 72 (Aug.): 351–379.

Battalio, Raymond C. et al. (1973). "A Test of Consumer Demand Theory Using Observations of Individual Consumer Purchasing." *Western Economic Journal* 11: 411–428.

Baumol, William J. (1965). *Welfare Economics and the Theory of the State*. Cambridge, Mass.: Harvard University Press.

Baumol, William J. (1986). "Unnatural Value: or Art Investment as Floating Crap Game." *American Economic Review* 76 (May): 10–14.

Baumol, William J. and Bowen, William G. (1966). *Performing Arts—The Economic Dilemma*. Cambridge, Mass.: Twentieth Century Fund.

Baumol, William J. and Oates, Wallace E. (1979). *Economics, Environmental Policy, and the Quality of Life*. Englewood Cliffs, N.J.: Prentice-Hall.

Becker, Gary S. (1962). "Irrational Behavior and Economic Theory." *Journal of Political Economy* 70 (Jan./Feb.): 1–13.

Becker, Gary S. (1968). "Crime and Punishment: An Economic Approach." *Journal of Political Economy* 76 (2): 169–217.

Becker, Gary S. (1971). *The Economics of Discrimination*. Chicago: University of Chicago Press, 2nd ed.

Becker, Gary S. (1973). "A Theory of Marriage: Part I." *Journal of Political Economy* 81 (July/Aug.): 813–846.

Becker, Gary S. (1974). "A Theory of Marriage, Part II." *Journal of Political Economy* 82 (2): 11–26.

Becker, Gary S. (1976). *The Economic Approach to Human Behavior*. Chicago: Chicago University Press.

Becker, Gary S. (1981). *A Treatise on the Family*. Cambridge, Mass.: Harvard University Press.

Becker, Gary S. (1988). "Family Economics and Macro Behaviour." *American Economic Review* 78 (No. 1, March): 1–13.

Becker, Gary S. and Murphy, Kevin M. (1988). "A Theory of Rational Addiction." *Journal of Political Economy* 96 (Aug.): 675–700.

Bell, David E. (1982). "Regret in Decision Making under Uncertainty." *Operations Research* 30 (Sept./Oct.): 961–981.

Bell, David, E., Raiffa, Howard and Tversky, Amos (eds). (1988). *Decision Making. Descriptive, Normative and Prescriptive Interactions*. Cambridge: Cambridge University Press.

Bendix, Reinhard (1952). "Social Stratification and Political Power." *American Political Science Review* 46: 357–375.

Bergman, Barbara R. (1986). *The Economic Emergence of Women*. New York: Basic Books.

Bernberg, R.E. (1952). "Socio-Psychological Factors in Industrial Morale: I. The Prediction of Specific Indicators." *Journal of Social Psychology* 36: 73–82.

Bernoulli, August (1921). "Basels Kriegsführung im Mittelalter." *Basler Zeitschrift für Geschichte und Altertumskunde* 19: 106–129.

Bernoulli, Daniel (1738). "Specimen Theoriae Novae de Mensura Sortis." *Commentarii Academiae Scientarum Imperialis Petropolitanae* 5: 175–192.

Best, Geoffrey (1979). "Restraints on War by Land before 1842." In: Howard, Michael (ed.). *Restraints on War: Studies in the Limitation of Armed Conflict*. Oxford: Oxford University Press.

Best, Geoffrey (1980). *Humanity in Warfare. The Modern History of International Law of Armed Conflict*. London: Weidenfels and Nicholson.

Best, Geoffrey (1982). *War and Society in Revolutionary Europe, 1770–1870*. Leicester: Leicester University Press.

Bianchi, Suzanne M. and Spain, Daphne (1986). *American Women in Transition*.

New York: Sage.

Black, Duncan (1958). *The Theory of Committees and Elections*. Cambridge: Cambridge University Press.

Blau, Francine D. and Ferber, Marianne A. (1986). *The Economics of Women, Men, and Work*. Englewood Cliffs, N.J.: Prentice-Hall.

Blaug, Mark (1980). *Methodology of Economics*. Cambridge: Cambridge University Press.

Blaug, Mark (ed.). (1968/69). *Economics of Education*, Vol. 1 and 2. Harmondsworth: Penguin.

Blaug, Mark (ed.). (1976). *The Economics of the Arts*. London: Martin Robertson.

Boddewyn, Jean J. (1979). "The Managerial Dimensions." In: Van den Bulcke, Daniel, Boddewyn, Jean J., Martens, Bernard and Klemmer, Paul. *Investment and Divestment Policies of Multinational Corporations in Europe*. Westmead: Saxon House, pp. 61–158.

Boes, Dieter (1981). *Economic Theory of Public Enterprise*. Berlin: Springer.

Boettcher, Erik (1983). "Einleitung: Der Neue Institutionalismus als Teil der Lehre der Neuen Politischen Ökonomie." In: Boettcher, Erik, Herder-Dorneich, Philipp and Schenk, Karl-Ernst (eds). *Jahrbuch für Neue Politische Ökonomie* Vol. 2. Tübingen: Mohr (Siebeck), pp. 1–15.

Bombach, Gottfried (1977/78). "Neue Politische Ökonomie." *List Forum* 9: 65–77 and 132–144.

Borchardt, Knut (1979). "Zwangslagen und Handlungsspielräume in der grossen Wirtschaftskrise der frühen dreissiger Jahre: Zur Revision des überlieferten Geschichtsbildes." *Bayerische Akademie der Wissenschaften*: Jahrbuch 1979. Munich: Beck, pp. 1–47.

Boulding, Kenneth (1962). *Conflict and Defense, A General Theory*. Ann Arbor: University of Michigan Press.

Boulding, Kenneth (1968). *Beyond Economics*. Ann Arbor: University of Michigan Press.

Boulding, Kenneth E. (1977). "Peace Research." *International Social Science Journal* 29: 601–614.

Boulding, Kenneth E. (1986). "The Economics and Noneconomics of the World War Industry." *Contemporary Policy Issues* 4 (Oct.): 12–21.

Bowman, E. (1982). "Risk Seeking by Troubled Firms." *Sloan Management Review* 23: 33–42.

Bracher, Karl Dietrich (1964). *Die Auflösung der Weimarer Republik. Eine Studie zum Problem des Machtverfalls in der Demokratie*. Villingen: Ring, 4th ed.

Bracher, Karl Dietrich, Sauer, Wolfgang and Schulz, Gerhard (1962). *Die Nationalsozialistische Machtergreifung*. Cologne and Opladen: Westdeutscher Verlag.

Bradford, David F. and Rosen, Harvey S. (1976). "The Optimal Taxation of Commodities and Income." *American Economic Review, Papers and Proceedings* 66 (2): 94–102.

Brehmer, B. (1980). "In One Word: Not from Experience." *Acta Psychologica*

45: 33–42, 223–241.

Brennan, Geoffrey and Buchanan, James M. (1980). *The Power to Tax. Analytical Foundations of a Fiscal Constitution.* Cambridge: Cambridge University Press.

Brennan, Geoffrey and Buchanan, James M. (1983). "Predictive Power and the Choice among Regimes." *Economic Journal* 93 (March): 89–105.

Brennan, Geoffrey and Buchanan, James M. (1985). *The Reason of Rules—Constitutional Political Economy.* Cambridge: Cambridge University Press.

Brennan, Geoffrey and Tullock, Gordon (1982). "An Economic Theory of Military Tactics: Methodological Individualism at War." *Journal of Economic Behaviour and Organization* 3: 225–242.

Breton, Albert and Wintrobe, Ronald (1982). *The Logic of Bureaucratic Conduct.* Cambridge: Cambridge University Press.

Brookshire, David S. and Coursey, Don L. (1987). "Measuring the Value of a Public Good: An Empirical Comparison of Elicitation Procedures." *American Economic Review* 77 (Sept.): 554–566.

Brown, Courtney (1982). "The Nazi Vote: A National Ecological Study." *American Political Science Review* 76: 285–302.

Brunner, Karl (1987). "The Perception of Man and the Conception of Society: Two Approaches to Understanding Society." *Economic Inquiry* 25 (July): 367–388.

Brunner, Karl (ed.). (1982). *Economics and Social Institutions. Insights from the Conference Series on Public Policy.* Amsterdam: North-Holland.

Buchanan, James M. (1965). "Ethical Rules, Expected Values and Large Numbers." *Ethics* 76 (Oct.): 1–13.

Buchanan, James M. (1969). *Cost and Choice: An Inquiry on Economic Theory.* Chicago: Markham.

Buchanan, James M. (1977). *Freedom in Constitutional Contract. Perspective of a Political Economist.* College Station: Texas A&M University Press.

Buchanan, James M. (1987). *Economics. Between Predictive Science and Moral Philosophy.* College Station: Texas A&M University Press.

Buchanan, James M. and Tullock, Gordon (1962). *The Calculus of Consent. Logical Foundations of Constitutional Democracy.* Ann Arbor: University of Michigan Press.

Buchanan, James M., Tollison, Robert D. and Tullock, Gordon (eds). (1980). *Toward a Theory of the Rent-Seeking Society.* College Station, Texas: Texas A&M University Press.

Buck, J.L. (1937). *Land Utilization in China.* Chicago: University of Chicago Press.

Bumke, Joachim (1986). *Höfische Kultur: Literatur und Gesellschaft im hohen Mittelalter.* Munich: dtb.

Bundeszentrale für politische Bildung (1978). *Der Nationalsozialismus.* Information zur Politischen Bildung 123/126/127, Bonn.

Butler, David J. and Hey, John D. (1987). "Experimental Economics: An Introduction." *Empirica* 14: 157–186.

Camerer, Colin F. (1987). "Do Biases in Probability Judgement Matter in

Markets? Experimental Evidence." *American Economic Review* 77 (Dec.): 981–997.

Camerer, Colin , Loewenstein, George and Weber, Martin (1989). "The Curse of Knowledge in Economic Settings: An Experimental Analysis." *Journal of Political Economy* 97 (No. 5, Oct.): 1232–1254.

Cameron, Samuel (1988). "The Economics of Crime Deterrence: A Survey of Theory and Evidence." *Kyklos* 41: 301–323.

Coase, Ronald H. (1960). "The Problem of Social Cost." *Journal of Law and Economics* 3 (Oct.): 1–45.

Coase, Ronald H. (1984). "The New Institutional Economics." *Journal of Institutional and Theoretical Economics* 140 (March): 229–231.

Cole, Sonia M. (1955). *Counterfeit*. London: John Murray.

Coleman, James S. (1987). "Norms as Social Capital." In: Radnitzky, Gerhard and Bernholz, Peter (eds). *Economic Imperialism—The Economic Approach Applied Outside the Field of Economics*. New York: Paragon House, 135–155.

Coleman, James S. (1990a). *Foundations of Social Theory*. Cambridge, Mass.: Harvard University Press.

Coleman, James S. (1990b). "The Emergence of Norms." In: Michael Hechter, Karl-Dieter Opp und Reinhard Wippler (eds). *Social Institutions. Their Emergence, Maintainance and Effects*. New York: Gruyter.

Collard, David (1978). *Altruism and the Economy. A Study of Non-Selfish Economics*. Oxford: Martin Robertson.

Condorcet, Marquis de (1795). *Esquisse d'un tableau historique du progrès de l'esprit humain*. Paris: Diannyaere.

Contamine, Philippe (1981). *La France au XIVe et XVe siècle. Hommes, mentalités, guerre et paix*. London: Variorum Reprints.

Cooper, Michael H. and Culyer, Anthony J. (eds). (1973). *Health Economics*. Harmondsworth: Penguin.

Cooter, Robert and Helpman, E. (1974). "Optimal Income Taxation for Transfer Payments and Different Welfare Criteria." *Quarterly Journal of Economics* 88 (Nov.): 656–670.

Cooter, Robert and Ulen, Thomas (1988). *Law and Economics*. Glenview: Scott, Foresman.

Corsi, Jerome R. (1981). "Terrorism as a 'Desperate' Game." *Journal of Conflict Resolution* 25 (March): 47–86.

Coursey, Don L. and Dyl, Edward A. (1986). *Price Effects of Trading Interruptions in an Experimental Market*. University of Wyoming working papers (March).

Coursey, Don L., Hovis, John L. and Schulze, William D. (1987). "The Disparity between Willingness to Accept and Willingness to Pay Measures of Value." *Quarterly Journal of Economics* 3 (Aug.): 679–690.

Crelinston, Ronald and Szabo, Denis (1980). *Hostage Taking*. Lexington, Mass.: Lexington Books.

Croll, Elisabeth (1983). *Chinese Women since Mao*. New York: Sharpe.

Dahl, Robert A. and Lindblom, Charles L. (1953). *Politics, Economics and*

222   REFERENCES

Welfare. New York: Harper.
Dahrendorf, Ralph (1958). "Homo Sociologicus: Versuch zur Geschichte, Bedeutung und Kritik der sozialen Rolle." *Kölner Zeitschrift für Soziologie und Sozialpsychologie* 10: 178–208.
Dahrendorf, Ralph (1967). *Pfade aus Utopia, Arbeiten zur Theorie und Methode der Soziologie*. Munich: Piper.
Dasgupta, Parta (1982). *The Control of Resources*. Oxford: Blackwell.
Dawes, Robyn M. (1988). *Rational Choice in an Uncertain World*. San Diego and New York: Harcourt, Brace, Jovanovich.
Dawes, Robyn M. and Thaler, Richard H. (1988). "Anomalies: Cooperation." *Journal of Economic Perspectives* 2 (Summer): 187–197.
DeAlessi, Louis (1983). "Property Rights, Transaction Costs and X-Efficiency: An Essay in Economic Theory." *American Economic Review* 73 (March): 64–81.
DeAlessi, Louis (1990). "Form, Substance and Welfare Comparisons in the Analysis of Institutions." *Journal of Institutional and Theoretical Economics* 146 (March): 5–23.
De Bondt, Werner F.M. and Makhija, Anil K. (1988). "Throwing Good Money after Bad? Nuclear Power Plant Investment Decisions and the Relevance of Sunk Costs." *Journal of Economic Behavior and Organization* 10 (1988): 173–199.
De Bondt, Werner F.M. and Thaler, Richard H. (1985). "Does the Stock Market Overreact?" *Journal of Finance* 40 (July): 793–805.
De Bondt, Werner F.M. and Thaler, Richard H. (1987). "Further Evidence on Investor Overreaction and Stock Market Seasonality." *Journal of Finance* 42 (July): 557–581.
Deci, Edward L. (1971). "Effects of Externally Mediated Rewards on Intrinsic Motivation." *Journal of Personality and Social Psychology* 18: 105–115.
Deci, Edward L. (1975). *Intrinsic Motivation*. New York: Plenum Press.
Delessert, Christiane S. (1977). *Release and Repatriation of Prisoners of War at the End of Active Hostilities*. Thesis No. 291. Geneva: Institut Universitaire de Hautes Etudes Internationales.
Demsetz, Harold (1964). "The Exchange and Enforcement of Property Rights." *Journal of Law and Economics* 7 (Oct.): 11–26.
Demsetz, Harold (1967). "Toward a Theory of Property Rights." In: Furubotn, Erik G. and Pejovich, Steve (eds). *The Economics of Property Rights*. Cambridge, Mass.: Ballinger, pp. 31–42.
Downs, Anthony (1957). *An Economic Theory of Democracy*. New York: Harper and Row.
Draper, Gerald I.A.D. (1965). "The Geneva Conventions of 1949." *Recueil des Cours de l'Academie de Droit International* 114: 59–163.
Draper, Gerald I.A.D. (1979). "Wars of National Liberation and War Criminality." In: Howard, Michael (ed.). *Restraints on War: Studies in the Limitation of Armed Conflicts*. Oxford: Oxford University Press.
Duesenberry, James S. (1949). *Income, Saving and the Theory of Consumer*

Behavior. Cambridge, Mass.: Harvard University Press.

Durkheim, Emile (1885). *Les règles de la méthode sociologique.* Paris.

Earl, Peter E. (ed.). (1988). *Psychological Economics.* Boston, Dordrecht and Lancaster: Kluwer.

Earl, Peter E. (1990). "Economics and Psychology: A Survey." *The Economic Journal* 100: 718–755.

Eberhard, Wolfram (1962). *Social Mobility in Traditional China.* Leiden: Brill.

Eckstein, Alexander (1968). "The Economic Heritage." In: Eckstein, A., Galenson, W., Liu Ta-chung (eds). *Economic Trends in Communist China.* Chicago: Aldine.

Eckstein, Alexander (1976). *China's Economic Development. The Interplay of Scarcity and Ideology.* Ann Arbor: University of Michigan Press.

Eggertsson, Thrainn (1990). *Economic Behaviour and Institutions: Principles of Neoinstitutional Economics.* Cambridge: Cambridge University Press.

Ehrenberg, Ronald G. (1977). "Household Allocation of Time and Religiosity: Replication and Extension." *Journal of Political Economy* 85: 415–423.

Ehrlich, Isaac (1973). "Participation in Illegitimate Activities: A Theoretical and Empirical Investigation." *Journal of Political Economy* 81 (May/June): 521–565.

Ehrlich, Isaac (1975). "The Deterrent Effect of Capital Punishment: A Question of Life and Death." *American Economic Review* 65 (June): 397–417.

Einhorn, Hillel J. (1980). "Learning from Experience and Suboptimal Rules in Decision Making." In: Wallsten, Thomas S. (ed). *Cognitive Processes in Choice and Decision Behavior.* Hillsdale, N.J.: Erlbaum, pp. 1–20.

Einhorn, Hillel J. and Hogarth, Robin M. (1978). "Confidence in Judgement: Persistence of the Illusion of Validity." *Psychological Review* 85: 395–416.

Einhorn, Hillel J. and Hogarth, Robin M. (1981). "Behavioral Decision Theory: Processes of Judgement and Choice." *Annual Review of Psychology* 32: 53–88.

Einhorn, Hillel J. and Hogarth, Robin M. (1986). "Decision Making Under Ambiguity." *Journal of Business* 59 (Oct.): 225–250.

Eisenstadt, S.N. (1973). *Tradition, Change, Modernity.* New York and London: Wiley.

Ellsberg, Daniel (1961). "Risk, Ambiguity and the Savage Axioms." *Quarterly Journal of Economics* 75 (Nov.): 643–669.

Elster, Jon (1977). "Ulysses and the Sirens: A Theory of Imperfect Rationality." *Social Science Information* 16: 469–526.

Elster, Jon (1989). *Ulysses and the Sirens.* Cambridge: Cambridge University Press.

Elster, Jon (1982). "Sour Grapes—Utilitarianism and the Genesis of Wants." In: Sen, Amartya K. and Williams, Bernard (eds). *Utilitarianism and Beyond.* Cambridge: Cambridge University Press, pp. 219–238.

Elster, Jon (ed.). (1986). *The Multiple Self.* Cambridge: Cambridge University Press.

Emery, Fred (1969). "Some Psychological Aspects of Price." In: Taylor, Bernard and Wills, Gordon (eds). *Pricing Strategy.* London: Staples, pp. 98–111.

Epstein, Max (1974). *Theater und Volkswirtschaft.* Berlin: Leonard Simon.

Erler, Adalbert (1978). *Der Loskauf Gefangener. Ein Rechtsproblem seit drei Jahrtausenden.* Berlin: Erich Schmidt.

Etzioni, Amitai (1988). *The Moral Dimension. Towards a New Economics.* New York: The Free Press.

Fair, Ray C. (1987). "The Effect of Economic Events on Votes for President." 1984. Updated Discussion Paper, Yale University.

Fei, Hsiao-tung (1939). *Peasant Life in China: A Field Study of Country Life in the Yangtze Valley.* New York: Dutton.

Ferber, Marianne A. and Birnbaum, Bonnie G. (1977). "The New Home Economics: Retrospect and Prospects." *Journal of Consumer Research* 4 (June): 19–29.

Ferber, Robert and Hirsch, Werner Z. (1982). *Social Experimentation and Economic Policy.* Cambridge: Cambridge University Press.

Finetti de, Bruno (1968). "Probability: Interpretations." In: Sills, D.E. (ed.). *International Encyclopedia of the Social Sciences* (Vol. 12). New York: Macmillan, pp. 496–504.

Fischhoff, Baruch, Lichtenstein, Sarah, Slovic, Paul, Derby, Stephen L. and Keeney, Ralph (1981). *Acceptable Risk.* Cambridge: Cambridge University Press.

Fischhoff, Baruch, Slovic, Paul and Lichtenstein, Sarah (1977). "Knowing with Certainty: The Appropriateness of Extreme Confidence." *Journal of Experimental Psychology: Human Perceptions and Performance* 3: 552–564.

Flory, William E.S. (1942). *Prisoners of War. A Study in the Development of International War.* Washington: American Council of Public Affairs.

Fogel, Robert W. (1965). "The Reunification of Economic History with Economic Theory." *American Economic Review* 55 (May): 92–98.

Foppa, Klaus (1987). "Individual Resources, Objective Constraints, and the Ipsative Theory of Behavior." *Mimeo.* Berne: University of Berne, Institute of Psychology.

Forsythe, David P. (1977). *Humanitarian Politics: The International Committee of the Red Cross.* Baltimore and London: John Hopkins University Press.

Forsythe, Robert, Delfrey, Thomas R. and Plott, Charles R. (1984). "Futures Markets and Informational Efficiency: A Laboratory Examination." *Journal of Finance* 39 (Sept.): 55–69.

Frank, Robert H. (1985). *Choosing the Right Pond.* Oxford: Oxford University Press.

Frank, Robert H. (1987). "If Homo Economicus Could Choose His Own Utility Function, Would He Want One with a Conscience?" *American Economic Review* 77 (Sept.): 593–604.

Frank, Robert H. (1988). *Passions within Reason. The Strategic Role of the Emotions.* New York: Norton.

Frey, Bruno S. (1978). *Modern Political Economics.* London: Martin Robertson.

Frey, Bruno S. (1983). *Democratic Economic Policy.* Oxford: Blackwell.

Frey, Bruno S. (1984). *International Political Economics*. Oxford: Blackwell.

Frey, Bruno S. (1985). *Umweltökonomie*. Göttingen: Vandenhoeck & Ruprecht, 2nd ed.

Frey, Bruno S. (1990). "Institutions Matter—The Comparative Analysis of Institutions." *European Economic Review* 34 (May): 443–449.

Frey, Bruno S. and Eichenberger, Reiner (1989). "Should Social Scientists Care About Choice Anomalies?" *Rationality and Society* 1 (July): 101–122.

Frey, Bruno S. and Foppa, Klaus (1986). "Human Behaviour: Possibilities Explain Action." *Journal of Economic Psychology* 7: 137–160.

Frey, Bruno S. and Heggli, Beat (1989). "An Ipsative Model of Business Behaviour." *Journal of Economic Psychology* 10: 1–20.

Frey, Bruno S. and Pommerehne, Werner W. (1987). "International Trade in Art: Attitudes and Behaviour." *Rivista Internazionale di Scienze Economiche e Commerciali* 34 (6): 465–486.

Frey, Bruno S. and Pommerehne, Werner W. (1988). "Für wie fair gilt der Markt?—Eine empirische Untersuchung zur Einschätzung in der Bevölkerung." *Hamburger Jahrbuch für Wirtschafts-und Gesellschaftspolitik* 33: 223–237.

Frey, Bruno S. and Pommerehne, Werner W. (1989a). *Muses and Markets. Explorations in the Economics of the Arts*. Oxford: Blackwell.

Frey, Bruno S. and Pommerehne, Werner W. (1989b). "Art: An Empirical Inquiry." *Southern Economic Journal* 56 (Oct.): 396–409.

Frey, Bruno S. and Weck, Hannelore (1981). "Hat Arbeitslosigkeit den Aufstieg des Nationalsozialismus bewirkt?" *Jahrbücher für Nationalökonomie und Statistik* 196: 1–31.

Frey, Bruno S. and Weck, Hannelore (1983). "A Statistical Study of the Effect of the Great Depression on Elections: The Weimar Republic, 1930–1933." *Political Behavior* 5: 403–420.

Frey, Bruno S., Pommerehne, Werner W., Schneider, Friedrich and Gilbert, Guy (1984). "Consensus and Dissension Among Economists: An Empirical Inquiry." *American Economic Review* 74 (Dec.): 986–994.

Freymond, Jacques (1976). *Guerres, Révolutions, Croix-Rouge*. Geneva: Hautes Etudes Internationales Presse.

Friedman, Debra and Hechter, Michael (1988). "The Contribution of Rational Choice Theory to Macrosociological Research." *Sociological Theory* 6 (Autumn): 201–218.

Friedman, Milton (1953). *Essays in Positive Economics*. Chicago: University of Chicago Press.

Fuller, John F.C. (1961). *The Conduct of War 1789–1961: A Study of the Impact of the French Industrial and Russian Revolutions on War and Its Conduct*. New Brunswick, N.J.: Rutgers University Press.

Furubotn, Eirik and Pejovich, Steven (eds). (1974). *The Economics of Property Rights*. Cambridge, Mass.: Ballinger.

Furubotn, Eirik and Richter, Rudolf (eds). (1984). "The New Institutional Economics—A Symposium." *Journal of Insitutional and Theoretical*

Economics 140 (March): 1–6.

Gäfgen, Gérard and Monissen, Hans-Georg (1978). "Zur Eignung soziologischer Paradigmen, Betrachtungen aus der Sicht des Ökonomen." *Jahrbuch für Sozialwissenschaft* 29: 113–144.

Gilad, Benjamin, Kaish, Stanley and Loeb, Peter D. (1987). "Cognitive Dissonance and Utility Maximization." *Journal of Economic Behavior and Organization* 8: 61–73.

Glover, Michael (1982). *The Velvet Glove. The Decline and Fall of Moderation in War.* London: Hodder and Stoughton.

Goff, Brian and Tollison, Robert D. (eds). (1990). *Sportometrics.* College Station: Texas A&M University Press.

Goudriaan, René and van 't Eind, Gerrit Jan (1985). "To Fee or Not to Fee: Some Effects of Introducing Admission Fees in Four Museums in Rotterdam." In: Owen, Virginia Lee and Hendon, William S. (eds). *Managerial Economics of the Arts.* Akron, Ohio: Association for Cultural Economics, pp. 103–109.

Graner, Walter (1976). *Antiquitäten als Kapitalanlage.* Munich: Heyne.

Granet, M. (1976). *Die chinesische Zivilisation.* Munich: Piper.

Grether, David M. and Plott, Charles R. (1979). "Economic Theory of Choice and the Preference Reversal Phenomenon." *American Economic Review* 69 (Sept.): 623–638.

Griffin, J.M. (1974). "An Econometric Evaluation of Sulfur Taxes." *Journal of Political Economy* 82 (July/Aug.): 661–688.

Gurlt, E. (1873). *Zur Geschichte der internationalen und freiwilligen Krankenpflege im Kriege.* Leipzig: Vogel.

Gurr, T.R. (1979). "Some Characteristics of Political Terrorism in the 1960s'." In: Stohl, Michael (ed.). *The Politics of Terrorism.* New York: Dekker.

Güth, Werner, Schmittberger, R. and Schwarz, B. (1982). "An Experimental Analysis of Ultimatum Bargaining." *Journal of Economic Behaviour and Organization* 3: 367–388.

Guttman, L. (1944). "A Basis for Scaling Qualitative Data." *American Sociological Review* 9: 139–150.

Halperin, William S. (1946). *Germany Tried Democracy.* New York: Crowell.

Haltiwanger, John and Waldmann, Michael (1985). "Rational Expectations and the Limits of Rationality: An Analysis of Heterogeneity." *American Economic Review* 75 (June): 326–340.

Hannan, Michael T. (1982). "Families, Markets, and Social Structures: An Essay on Becker's A Treatise on the Family." *Journal of Economic Literature* 20 (March): 65–72.

Hargreaves-Heap, Shaun and Hollis, Martin (1987). "Economic Man." In: Eatwell, John et al. (eds). *The New Palgrave, A Dictionary in Economics*, vol. 2. London: Macmillan, pp. 54–55.

Harris, Richard (1961). "The Forgery of Art." *New Yorker* 37: 112–145.

Harsanyi, John (1955). "Cardinal Welfare, Individualistic Ethics, and Intertemporal Comparisons of Utility." *Journal of Political Economy* 63 (June): 309–321.

Heberle, Rudolf (1945). *From Democracy to Nazism.* Baton Rouge: Louisiana State University Press.

Heinemann, Klaus (ed.). (1984). *Texte zur Ökonomie des Sports.* Schorndorf: Hofmann.

Heiner, Ronald A. (1983). "The Origin of Predictable Behavior." *American Economic Review* 73 (Sept.): 560–595.

Helbich, Wolfgang (1968). "Die Bedeutung der Reparationsfrage für die Wirtschaftspolitik der Regierung Brüning." In: Jasper, Gotthard (ed.). *Von Weimar zu Hitler, 1930–1933.* Cologne/Berlin: Kiepenheuer/Witsch, pp. 72–98.

Helson, Harry (1964). *Adaption Level Theory.* New York: Harper & Row.

Hentschel, Volker (1978). *Weimars letzte Monate. Hitler und der Untergang der Republik.* Düsseldorf: Droste.

Hetzel, H. (1889). *Die Humanisierung des Krieges in den letzten hundert Jahren, von der französischen Revolution bis zur Gegenwart, 1789–1889: Die Tatsachen und die Literatur.* Frankfurt: Königliche Hofbuchdruckerei Trowitsch & Sohn.

Hewstone, Miles, Stroebe, Wolfgang, Codol, Jean-Paul and Stephenson, Geoffrey M. (eds). (1988). *Introduction to Social Psychology. A European Perspective.* Oxford: Blackwell.

Hibbs, Douglas C. (1987). *The Political Economy of Industrial Democracies.* Cambridge, Mass.: Harvard University Press.

Himmelstein, P. and Moore, J.C. (1963). "Racial Attitudes and the Action of Negro- and White-background Figures as Factors in Petition Signing." *Journal of Social Psychology* 61: 267–272.

Hinich, Melvin J. and Ordeshook, Peter C. (1971). "Social Welfare and Electoral Competition." *Public Choice* 11: 73–88.

Hirsch, Fred (1976). *The Social Limits to Growth.* Cambridge, Mass.: Harvard University Press.

Hirsch, Werner Z. (1988). *Law and Economics. An Introductory Analysis.* New York: Academic Press, 2nd ed.

Hirschman, Albert O. (1958). *The Strategy of Economic Development.* New Haven: Yale University Press.

Hirschman, Albert O. (1965). "Obstacles to Development: A Classification and a Quasi-Vanishing Act." *Economic Development and Cultural Change* 13 (July): 385–393.

Hirschman, Albert O. (1970). *Exit, Voice and Loyalty.* Cambridge, Mass.: Harvard University Press.

Hirschman, Albert O. (1977). *The Passions and the Interests: Political Arguments for Capitalism before its Triumph.* Princeton: Princeton University Press.

Hirschman, Albert O. (1982a). *Shifting Involvements. Private Interests and Public Action.* Oxford: Martin Robertson.

Hirschman, Albert O. (1982b). "Rival Interpretations of Market Society: Civilizing, Destructive, or Feeble?" *Journal of Economic Literature* 20 (Dec.): 1463–1484.

Hirschman, Albert O. (1984). "Against Parsimony: Three Easy Ways of Complicating Some Categories of Economic Discourse." *American Economic Review, Papers and Proceedings* 74 (May): 89–96.

Hirshleifer, Jack (1984). *Price Theory and Applications.* Englewood Cliffs, N.J.: Prentice-Hall.

Hirshleifer, Jack (1985). "The Expanding Domain of Economics." *American Economic Review* 75 (6) (Dec.): 53–68.

Hirshleifer, Jack (1987). *Economic Behaviour in Adversity.* Brighton: Wheatsheaf.

Hitch, Charles J. and McKean, Ronald N. (1961). *Economics of Defense in the Nuclear Age.* Cambridge, Mass.: Harvard University Press.

Hochheimer, Albert (1967). *Verraten und Verkauft. Die Geschichte der europäischen Söldner.* Stuttgart: Henry Goverts.

Hogarth, Robin M. (1975). "Cognitive Processes and the Assessment of Subjective Probability Distributions." *Journal of the American Statistical Association* 70 (June): 271–294.

Hogarth, Robin M. and Reder, Melvin W. (eds). (1987). *Rational Choice.* Chicago: University of Chicago Press.

Hoggatt, A.C., Friedman, J.W. and Gill, S. (1976). "Price Signaling in Experimental Oligopoly." *American Economic Review, Papers and Proceedings* 66 (May): 261–266.

Homze, Edward L. (1967). *Foreign Labor in Nazi Germany.* Princeton, N.J.: Princeton University Press.

Horkheimer, Max (1952). *Zum Begriff der Vernunft.* Frankfurt: Klostermann.

Huxley-Blythe, Peter (1964). *The East Came West.* Caldwell: Caxton.

Iannaccone, Lawrence R. (1988). "A Formal Model of Church and Sect." *American Journal of Sociology* 94: 241–268.

Iannaccone, Lawrence R. (1991). "The Consequences of Religions Market Structure: Adam Smith and the Economics of Religion." *Rationality and Society* 2 (April): 156–177.

Im, Eric I., Cauley, Jon and Sandler, Todd (1987). "Cycles and Substitutions in Terrorist Activities: A Spectral Approach." *Kyklos* 40: 238–255.

Intriligator, Michael P. (1973). "A Probabilistic Model of Social Choice." *Review of Economic Studies* 40 (4): 553–560.

Isaac, R. Mark, McCue, Kenneth F. and Plott, Charles (1985). "Public Goods Provision in an Experimental Environment." *Journal of Public Economics* 26: 51–74.

Isard, Walter (1988). *Arms Races, Arms Control, and Conflict Analysis. Contributions From Peace Science and Peace Economics.* Cambridge: Cambridge University Press.

Jasper, Gotthard (ed.). (1968). *Von Weimar zu Hitler, 1930–1933.* Cologne and Berlin: Neue Wissenschaftliche Bibliothek, Kiepenheuer & Witsch.

Jenkins, Brian M. (1982). *Terrorism and Beyond: An International Conference on Terrorism and Low-Level Conflict.* Santa Monica: Rand.

Jenkins, Brian M. and Ronfeldt, D. (1977). *Numbered Lives: Some Statistical*

Observations from 77 International Hostage Episodes. Santa Monica: Rand.
Johansen, Leif (1977). "The Theory of Public Goods: Misplaced Emphasis?" *Journal of Public Economics* 7: 147–152.
Jöhr, Walter A. (1972). "Zur Rolle des psychologischen Faktors in der Konjunkturtheorie." *Ifo-Studien* 18: 157–184.
Jones, Stephen R.G. and Stock, James H. (1987). "Demand Disturbance and Aggregate Fluctuations: The Implications of Near Rationality." *Economic Journal* 97 (March): 49–64.
Kahneman, Daniel and Tversky, Amos (1973). "On the Psychology of Prediction." *Psychological Review* 80: 237–251.
Kahneman, Daniel and Tversky, Amos (1979). "Prospect Theory: An Analysis of Decision Under Risk." *Econometrica* 47 (March): 263–291.
Kahneman, Daniel and Tversky, Amos (1984). "Choices, Values, and Frames." *American Psychologist* 39 (April): 341–350.
Kahneman, Daniel, Knetsch, Jack and Thaler, Richard (1985). "Perceptions of Unfairness: Constraints on Wealth Seeking." Paper presented at the conference on the Behavioral Foundations of Economic Theory, Graduate School of Business, University of Chicago, October.
Kahneman, Daniel, Knetsch, Jack and Thaler, Richard (1986). "Fairness as a Constraint on Profit Seeking: Entitlements in the Market." *American Economic Review* 76 (Sept.): 728–741.
Kahneman, Daniel, Slovic, Paul and Tversky, Amos (eds). (1982). *Judgement Under Uncertainty: Heuristics and Biases*. Cambridge: Cambridge University Press.
Kaltefleiter, Werner (1966). *Wirtschaft und Politik in Deutschland: Konjunktur als Bestimmungsfaktor des Parteiensystems*. Cologne, Opladen: Westdeutscher Verlag.
Kant, Immanuel (1795). *Zum Ewigen Frieden, Kants gesammelte Schriften*. Königliche Preussische Akademie der Wissenschaft (ed.), Vol. 8, Berlin and Leipzig 1923. Photomechanical reproduction 1969.
Kapteyn, Arie and Wansbeek, Tom (1985). "The Individual Welfare Function: A Review." *Journal of Economic Psychology* 6: 333–363.
Katona, George (1975). *Psychological Economics*. Amsterdam: Elsevier.
Katz, Irwin and Benjamin L. (1960). "Effects of White Authoritarianism in Biracial Work Groups." *Journal of Abnormal and Social Psychology* 61: 448–456.
Kearl, James R., Pope, Clayne L., Whiting, Gordon L. and Wimmer, Larry T. (1979). "A Confusion of Economists?" *American Economic Review, Papers and Proceedings* 69 (May): 28–37.
Keegan, John, Holmes, Richard and Gau, John (1985). *Soldiers: A History of Men in Battle*. London: Hamish Hamilton.
Keen, Maurice H. (1965). *The Laws of War in the Late Middle Ages*. London: Routledge and Kegan Paul.
Kelman, Steven (1981). *What Price Incentives? Economists and the Environment*. Boston: Auburn House.

Kelman, Steven (1983). "Economic Incentives and Environmental Policy: Politics, Ideology, and Philosophy." In: Thomas C. Schelling (ed.). *Incentives for Environmental Protection*. Cambridge Mass.: MIT Press, pp. 291–331.

Kennedy, Gavin (1975). *The Economics of Defence*. London: Faber and Faber.

Keyes, Ralph (1985). *Changing It*. Boston: Little, Brown.

Kirchgässner, Gebhard (1980). "Können Ökonomie und Soziologie voneinander lernen?" *Kyklos* 33: 420–448.

Kirchgässner, Gebhard (1988). "Die neue Welt der Ökonomie." *Analyse und Kritik* 10: 107–137.

Kirchgässner, Gebhard (1991). "Homo Oeconomicus. Das Ökonomische Modell individuellen Verhaltens und seine Anwendung in den Wirtschafts—und Sozialwissenschaften." Tübingen: Mohr (Siebeck).

Kirscht, J.P., Haefner, D.P., Kagelas, S.S. and Rosenstock, I.M. (1966). "A National Study of Health Beliefs." *Journal of Health and Human Behavior* 7: 248–254.

Kirzner, Israel M. (1979). *Perception, Opportunity and Profit. Studies in the Theory of Enterpreneurship*. Chicago and London: University of Chicago Press.

Kleindorfer, Paul R. and Kunreuther, Howard (1982). "Misinformation and Equilibrium in Insurance Markets." In: Finsinger, Jörg (ed.). *Issues in Pricing and Regulation*. Lexington MA: Lexington Books.

Kliemt, Hartmut (1985). *Moralische Institutionen: Empirische Theorien ihrer Evolution*. Freiburg (Breisgau): Alber.

Knetsch, Jack L. (1985). "Experimental Evidence of Non-Reversibility of Indifference Curves: The Reluctance to Trade." *Mimeo*. Burnaby: Simon Fraser University, Dept. of Economics.

Knetsch, Jack L. and Sinden John A. (1987). "The Persistence of Evaluation Disparities." *Quarterly Journal of Economics* 102 (Aug.): 691–695.

Knetsch, Jack L. and Sinden, John A. (1984). "Willingness to Pay and Compensation Demanded: Experimental Evidence of an Unexpected Disparity in Measures of Value." *Quarterly Journal of Economics* 99 (Aug.): 507–521.

Kolm, Serge-Christophe (1972). *Justice et Equité*. Paris: Centre National de la Recherche Scientifique.

Kornai, Janos (1971). *Anti-Equilibrium*. Amsterdam: North Holland.

Kunreuther, Howard (1976). "Limited Knowledge and Insurance Protection." *Public Policy* 24 (2): 227–261.

Kunreuther, Howard and Slovic, Paul (1978). "Economic Psychology and Protective Behavior." *American Economic Review* 68 (May): 64–69.

Kunreuther, Howard, Ginsberg, Ralph, Miller, Louis, et al. (1978). *Disaster Insurance Protection: Public Policy Lessons*. New York: Wiley.

Kutner, B., Wilkins, C. and Yarrow, P.R. (1952). "Verbal Attitudes and Overt Behavior Involving Racial Prejudice." *Journal of Abnormal and Social Psychology* 47: 649–652.

La Piere, Richard T. (1934). "Attitudes vs. Actions." *Social Forces* 13: 230–237.

Landes, William M. (1978). "An Economic Study of U.S. Aircraft Hijackings, 1961–1976." *Journal of Law and Economics* 21 (April): 1–32.

Lang, Olga (1968). *Chinese Family and Society.* New Haven: Yale University Press, 2nd ed.

Langer, Ellen J. (1982). "The Illusion of Control." In: Kahneman, Daniel, Slovic, Paul and Tversky, Amos (eds). *Judgement under Uncertainty: Heuristics and Biases.* Cambridge: Cambridge University Press, pp. 231–238.

Laqueur, Walter (1978). *Zeugnisse Politischer Gewalt. Dokumente zur Geschichte des Terrorismus.* Kronberg/Ts.: Athenäum.

Laqueur, Walter (1987). *The Age of Terrorism.* Boston: Little, Brown.

Laqueur, Walter (ed.). (1977). *Terrorismus.* Kronberg/Ts.: Athenäum.

Lea, Stephen E.G., Tarpy, Roger M. and Webley, Paul (1987). *The Individual in the Economy. A Survey of Economic Psychology.* Cambridge: Cambridge University Press.

Leibenstein, Harvey (1976). *Beyond Economic Man: A New Foundation for Microeconomics.* Cambridge, Mass.: Harvard University Press.

Leibenstein, Harvey (1978). "On the Basic Proposition of X-Efficiency Theory." *American Economic Review* 68 (May): 328–332.

Lepper, Mark R. and Greene, David (eds). (1978). *The Hidden Costs of Reward: New Perspectives on the Psychology of Human Motivation.* New York: Erlbaum.

Lewis, Alan (1982). *The Psychology of Taxation.* Oxford: Blackwell.

Lichtenstein, Sarah and Slovic, Paul (1971). "Reversals of Preference between Bids and Choices in Gambling Decisions." *Journal of Experimental Psychology* 89 (1): 46–55.

Lichtenstein, Sarah and Slovic, Paul (1973). "Response-Induced Reversals of Preference in Gambling: An Extended Replication in Las Vegas." *Journal of Experimental Psychology* 101: 16–20.

Likert, Rensis (1932). "A Technique for the Measurement of Attitudes." *Archives of Psychology* 140: 44–53.

Lindenberg, Siegwart (1983). "Utility and Morality." *Kyklos* 36: 450–468.

Lindenberg, Siegwart (1985a). "An Assessment of the New Political Economy: Its Potential for the Social Sciences and for Sociology in Particular." *Sociological Theories in Progress* (Spring): 99–113.

Lindenberg, Siegwart (1985b). "Rational Choice and Sociological Theory: New Pressures on Economics as a Social Science." *Journal of Institutional and Theoretical Economics* 141: 244–255.

Lipset, Seymour M. (1960). *Political Man.* New York: Doubleday.

Lipset, Seymour M. (1968). "Nationalsozialismus—ein Faschismus der Mitte." In: Jasper, Gotthard (ed.). *Von Weimar zu Hitler, 1930–1933.* Cologne and Berlin: Kiepenheuer & Witsch, pp. 101–123.

Loewe, M. (1965). *Imperial China. The Historical Background to Modern Age.* Cambridge: Cambridge University Press.

Loomes, Graham and Sugden, Robert (1982). "Regret Theory: An Alternative Theory of Rational Choice under Uncertainty." *Economic Journal* 92 (Dec.): 805–824.

Loomes, Graham and Sugden, Robert (1987). "Some Implications of a More General Form of Regret Theory." *Journal of Economic Theory* 41: 270–287.

Lucas, Robert E. (1976). "Econometric Policy Evaluation. A Critique." In: Brunner, Karl and Meltzer, Alan H. (eds). *The Phillips Curve and Labour Markets.* Carnegie Rochester Conference Series on Public Policy, Vol. 1. Amsterdam.

Lutz, Mark A. and Lux, Kenneth (1988). *Humanistic Economics. The New Challenge.* New York: Bootstrap Press.

MacFadyen, Alan J. and MacFadyen, Heather W. (eds). (1986). *Economic Psychology: Intersections in Theory and Application.* Amsterdam and New York: North-Holland.

Machina, Mark J. (1987). "Choice Under Uncertainty: Problems Solved and Unsolved." *Journal of Economic Perspectives* 1: 121–154.

Magee, Stephen P., Brock, William A. and Young, Leslie (1989). *Black Hole Tariffs and Endogenous Policy Theory. Political Economy in General Equilibrium.* Cambridge: Cambridge University Press.

Maital, Shlomo (1982). *Minds, Markets and Money.* New York: Basic Books.

Maital, Shlomo (1986). "Prometheus Rebound: On Welfare-Improving Constraints." *Eastern Economic Journal* 12 (July-Sept.): 337–343.

March, James G. (1978). "Bounded Rationality, Ambiguity, and the Engineering of Choice." *Bell Journal of Economics* 9 (Autumn): 587–608.

March, James G. and Shapira, Zur (1987). "Managerial Perspectives on Risk and Risk Taking." *Management Science* 33 (Nov.): 1404–1418.

March, James G. and Simon, Herbert A. (1958). *Organizations.* New York: Wiley.

Marcuse, Herbert (1965). "Industrialization and Capitalism." *New Left Review* (March/April): 3–17.

Margolis, Howard (1982). *Selfishness, Altruism, and Rationality. A Theory of Social Choice.* Cambridge: Cambridge University Press.

Marsh, R.M. (1961). *The Mandarins, The Circulation of Elites in China. 1600–1900.* New York: Crowell-Collier.

Marshall, James D., Knetsch, Jack L. and Sinden, John A. (1986). "Agents' Evaluations and the Disparity in Measures of Economic Loss." *Journal of Economic Behavior and Organization* 7: 115–127.

Marwell, Gerald and Ames, Ruth (1981). "Economists Free Ride; Does Anybody Else?" *Journal of Public Economics* 15: 295–310.

Maynard Smith, John (1982). *Evolution and the Theory of Games.* Cambridge: Cambridge University Press.

McGraw, Kenneth O. (1978). "The Detrimental Effects of Reward on Performance: A Literature Review and a Prediction Model." In: Lepper, Mark R. and Greene, David (eds). *The Hidden Costs of Reward: New Perspectives of Human Behavior.* New York: Erlbaum, pp. 33–60.

McKenzie, Richard B. and Tullock, Gordon (1975). *The New World of Economics*, 2nd ed., Homewood, Ill.: Irwin.

Meckling, William H. (1976). "Values and the Choice of the Model of the Individual in the Social Sciences." *Schweizerische Zeitschrift für Volkswirtschaft und Statistik* 112: 545–560.

Medoff, Marshall H. (1988). "Constituencies, Ideology, and the Demand for Abortion Legalisation." *Public Choice* 60: 185–191.

Mellen, Sidney L.W. (1943). "The German People and the Postwar World. A Study Based on Election Statistics, 1871–1933." *American Political Science Review* 37: 601–625.

Meyer, Michael (1977). *Des Hommes contre des Marks*. Paris: Edition Stock.

Meyer, Willi (1979). "Ökonomische Theorien und menschliches Verhalten. Zwischen theoretischen Fiktionen und empirischen Illusionen." In: Albert, Hans and Stapf, Kurt (eds). *Theorie und Erfahrung. Beiträge zur Grundlagenproblematik der Sozialwissenschaften*. Cotta: Klett.

Meyer, Willi (1987). "Was leistet die Ökonomische Theorie der Familie?" In: Todt, Horst (ed.). *Die Familie als Gegenstand sozialwissenschaftlicher Forschung*. Berlin: Duncker & Humblot, pp. 11–45.

Mickolus, Edward F. (1980). *Transnational Terrorism: A Chronology of Events*. Westport, Conn.: Greenwood Press.

Mikula, Gerold and Stroebe, Wolfgang (1977). *Sympathie, Freundschaft, Ehe: Psychologische Grundlagen zwischenmenschlicher Beziehungen*. Bern, Stuttgart and Vienna: Hans Huber.

Miller, Edward M. (1987), "Bounded Efficient Markets: A New Wrinkle to the EMH." *Journal of Portfolio Management* 13 (4): 4–13.

Mitchell, Robert E. (1969). "Family Life in Urban Hongkong." Hongkong: Urban Family Life Survey.

Moe, Terry M. (1980), *The Organization of Interests: Incentives and the Internal Dynamics of Interest Groups*. Chicago: Chicago University Press.

Montesquieu, Charles Louis (1749), *De l'esprit des lois*. Paris: Garnier.

Mueller, Dennis C. (1978). "Voting by Veto." *Journal of Public Economics* 10 (1): 57–76.

Mueller, Dennis C. (1989). *Public Choice II*. Cambridge: Cambridge University Press, 2nd ed.

Murphy, Charles H. (1971). "Prisoners of War: Repatriation or Internment in Wartime; American and Allied Experience, 1775 to Present." Prepared for the U.S. Congress, Committee on Foreign Affairs, *U.S. POWs in South East Asia*. Washington, D.C.: U.S. Government Printing Office.

Musgrave, Richard A. and Musgrave, Peggy B. (1973). *Public Finance in Theory and Practice*. New York: McGraw Hill.

Muth, J. (1961). "Rational Expectations and the Theory of Price Movements." *Econometrica* 29: 315–335.

Myers, R.H. (1970). *The Chinese Peasant Economy*. Cambridge, Mass.: Harvard University Press.

Myrdal, Gunnar (1964). *Das Wertproblem in der Sozialwissenschaft*. Hannover:

Verlag für Literatur und Zeitgeschehen.
Nelson, Richard R. and Winter, Sidney G. (1982). *An Evolutionary Theory of Economic Change*. Cambridge, Mass.: Harvard University Press.
Neumark, Fritz (1986). "Der Aufstieg der Einkommensteuer." In: Schultz, Uwe (ed.). *Mit dem Zehntel fing es an: Eine Kulturgeschichte der Steuer*. Munich: Beck.
Newell, A. and Simon, Herbert E. (1972). *Human Problem Solving*. Englewood Cliffs, N.J.: Prentice-Hall.
Nisbett, Richard E., Borgida, Eugene, Crandall, Rick and Reed, Harvey (1982). "Popular Induction: Information is Not necessarily Informative." In: Kahneman, Daniel, Slovic, Paul and Tversky, Amos (eds). *Judgement under Uncertainty: Heuristics and Biases*. Cambridge: Cambridge University Press, pp. 101–116.
Niskanen, William A. (1971). *Bureaucracy and Representative Government*. Chicago: Aldine.
North, Douglass C. (1981). *Structure and Change in Economic History*. New York: Norton.
North, Douglass C. (1986). "The New Institutional Economics." *Journal of Institutional and Theoretical Economics* 142: 230–237.
O'Lessker, Karl (1968). "Who Voted for Hitler? A New Look at the Class Basis of Nazism." *American Journal of Sociology* 74: 63–69.
Olson, Mancur (1965). *The Logic of Collective Action*. Cambridge, Mass.: Harvard University Press.
Olson, Mancur (1982). *The Rise and Decline of Nations*. New Haven, CT: Yale University Press.
Opp, Karl-Dieter (1979a). *Individualistische Sozialwissenschaft*. Stuttgart: Enke.
Opp, Karl-Dieter (1979b). "The Emergence and Effects of Social Norms. A Confrontation of Some Hypotheses of Sociology and Economics." *Kyklos* 32: 775–801.
Opp, Karl-Dieter (1985). "Sociology and Economic Man." *Journal of Institutional and Theoretical Economics* 141: 213–243.
Opp, Karl-Dieter (1986). "Das Modell des Homo Sociologicus." *Analyse und Kritik* 8: 1–27.
Opp, Karl-Dieter (1989). *The Rationality of Political Roles*. Boulder: Westview Press.
Ouchi, William G. (1977). "The Relationship between Organizational Structure and Organizational Control." *Administrative Science Quarterly* 22 (March): 95–113.
Parish, W.L. and Whyte, M.K. (1978). *Village and Family in Contemporary China*. Chicago and London: University of Chicago Press.
Parsons, Talcott (1949). *The Structure of Social Action*. New York: Free Press of Glencoe.
Parsons, Talcott (1951). *The Social System*. London: Routledge & Kegan Paul.
Parsons, Talcott (1966). "Some Considerations on the Theory of Social Change." In: Eisenstadt, S.N. (ed.). *Readings in Social Evolution and Development*.

Oxford: Pergamon Press.
Payne, John W. (1982). "Contingent Decision Behavior." *Psychological Bulletin* 92: 382–402.
Pesando, James E. (1990). "Art as an Investment: the Market for Modern Prints." *Mimeo*. Toronto: University of Toronto, Institute for Policy Analysis.
Phelps, Edmund S. (1975). *Altruism, Morality and Economic Theory*. New York: Sage.
Platte, E. (1984). "China's Fertility Transition: The One-Child Campaign." *Pacific Affairs* 57 (4): 646–671.
Plott, Charles R. (1987). "Rational Choice in Experimental Markets." In: Hogarth, Robin M. and Reder, Melvin W. (eds). *Rational Choice*. Chicago: University of Chicago Press, pp. 117–193.
Pollak, Robert A. (1970). "Habit Formation and Dynamic Demand Functions." *Journal of Political Economy* 78 (July/Aug.): 745–763.
Pollak, Robert A. (1985). "A Transaction Cost Approach to Families and Households." *Journal of Economic Literature* 23 (June): 581–608.
Pollock, James K. (1944). "An Areal Study of the German Electorate, 1930–1933." *American Political Science Review* 38 (Feb.): 89–95.
Pommerehne, Werner W. (1987). *Präferenzen für öffentliche Güter. Ansätze zu ihrer Erfassung*. Tübingen: Mohr (Siebeck).
Pommerehne, Werner W. and Frey, Bruno S. (eds). (1979). *Ökonomische Theorie der Politik*. Berlin: Springer.
Pommerehne, Werner W., Schneider, Friedrich, Gilbert, Guy and Frey, Bruno S. (1984). "Concordia Discors: Or: What Do Economists Think?" *Theory and Decision* 16: 251–308.
Pommerehne, Werner W., Schneider, Friedrich and Zweifel, Peter (1982). "Economic Theory of Choice and the Preference Reversal Phenomenon: A Reexamination." *American Economic Review* 72 (June): 569–574.
Posner, Richard A. (1986). *The Economic Analysis of Law*. Boston: Little, Brown, 3rd ed.
Pratt, John U., Wise, David and Zeckhauser, Richard (1979). "Price Differences in Almost Competitive Markets." *Quarterly Journal of Economics* 93 (May): 189–211.
Prugh, George (1975). *Vietnam Studies, Law at War: Vietnam 1964–1973*. Washington, D.C.: Department of the Army.
Quattrone, George A. and Tversky, Amos (1988). "Contrasting Rational and Psychological Analysis of Political Choice." *American Political Science Review* 82: 719–736.
Radnitzky, Gerard (1987). "The 'Economic' Approach to the Philosophy of Science." *The British Journal for the Philosophy of Science* 38 (June): 159–179.
Radnitzky, Gerard and Bernholz, Peter (eds). (1987). *Economic Imperialism. The Economic Method Applied Outside the Field of Economics*. New York: Paragon.
Ramsey, Frank P. (1927). "A Contribution to the Theory of Taxation."

Economic Journal 37: 47–61.
Ranft, Bryan (1979). "Restraints on War at Sea before 1949." In: Howard, Michael (ed.). *Restraints on War: Studies in the Limitation of Armed Conflict.* Oxford: Oxford University Press.
Rawls, John (1972). *A Theory of Justice.* Oxford: Oxford University Press.
Reitlinger, Gerald (1961). *The Economics of Taste, Vol. I. The Rise and Fall of Picture Prices 1760–1960.* London: Barrie and Rockliff.
Reitlinger, Gerald (1970). *The Economics of Taste, Vol. III: The Art Market in the 1960s.* London: Barrie and Rockliff.
Rethans, A. (1979). *An Investigation of Consumer Perceptions of Product Hazards.* Ph.D. Dissertation, University of Oregon.
Riker, William H. and Ordeshook, Peter C. (1968). "A Theory of the Calculus of Voting." *American Political Science Review* 62: 25–42.
Riker, William H. and Ordeshook, Peter C. (1973). *An Introduction to Positive Political Theory.* Englewood Cliffs, N.J.: Prentice-Hall.
Robertson, L.S. (1974). "Urban Safety Belt Use in Automobiles with Starter Interlock Belt Systems: A Preliminary Report." Washington, D.C.: Insurance Institute for Highway Safety.
Robertson, L.S. (1977). "Car Crashes: Perceived Vulnerability and Willingness to Pay for Crash Protection." *Journal of Community Health* 3: 136–141.
Rosas, Allan (1976). *The Legal Status of Prisoners of War. A Study in International Humanitarian Law Applicable in Armed Conflicts.* Helsinki: Academia Scientiarum Fennica.
Rosenberg, M.J. and Hovland, C.J. (1960). *Cognitive, Affective, and Behavioral Components of Attitudes.* New Haven, Conn.: Yale University Press.
Ross, Myron H. and Zonderman, Scott (1989). "Capital Gains and the Rate of Return on a Stradivarius." *Economic Inquiry* 27 (July): 529–540.
Roth, Alvin E. (1988). "Laboratory Experimentation in Economics: A Methodological Overview." *Economic Journal* 98 (Dec.): 157–186.
Rousseau, Jean-Jacques (1876). *Du contrat social.* Paris: Alcan.
Rozman, G. (1981). *The Modernization of China.* New York and London: Macmillan.
Runciman, Steven (1955). *History of the Crusades.* Reprint, 3 vols. Cambridge: Cambridge University Press.
Russell, Thomas and Thaler, Richard (1985). "The Relevance of Quasi-Rationality in Competitive Markets." *American Economic Review* 75 (Dec.): 1071–1082.
Sample, J. and Warland, R. (1973). "Attitudes and Prediction and Behavior." *Social Forces* 51: 292–303.
Sampson, P. (1971). "Attitude Measurement and Behaviour. Predictions in Market Research Using apriori Psychological Models of Consumer Behaviour." In: European Society for Opinion and Market Research (ed.). *From Experience to Innovation.* Helsinki, pp. 45–75.
Samuelson, Paul A. (1954). "The Pure Theory of Public Expenditures." *Review of Economics and Statistics* 36 (Nov.): 1–25.

Samuelson, Paul A. (1956). "Social Indifference Curves." *Quarterly Journal of Economics* 70 (Feb.): 1–22.

Samuelson, William and Zeckhauser, Richard (1988). "Status Quo Bias in Decision Making." *Journal of Risk and Uncertainty* 1: 7–60.

Sandler, Todd and Scott John L. (1987). "Terrorist Success in Hostage Taking: An Empirical Study." *Journal of Conflict Resolution* (March): 35–53.

Sandler, Todd, Tschirhart, John and Cauley, Jon (1983). "A Theoretical Analysis of Transnational Terrorism." *American Political Science Review* 77 (March): 35–53.

Sandmo, Agar (1976). "Optimal Taxation—An Introduction to the Literature." *Journal of Public Economics* 5: 37–54.

Sauermann, Heinz (ed.). (1967–1972). *Beiträge zur experimentellen Wirtschaftsforschung*, 3 vols. Tübingen: Mohr (Siebeck).

Sauermann, Heinz and Selten, Reinhard (1962). "Ein Oligopolexperiment." *Zeitschrift für die gesamte Staatswissenschaft/Journal of Institutional and Theoretical Economics* 115: 427–471.

Savage, Leonard J. (1954). *The Foundations of Statistics*. New York: Wiley.

Schaufelberger, Walter (1952). *Der Alte Schweizer und sein Krieg*. Zurich: Europa Verlag.

Scheidl, Franz Josef (1943). *Die Kriegsgefangenschaft: Von den ältesten Zeiten bis zur Gegenwart, eine völkerrechtliche Monographie*. Berlin: Ebering.

Schelling, Thomas C. (1960). *The Strategy of Conflict*. New York: Oxford University Press.

Schelling, Thomas C. (1978). "Egonomics, or the Art of Self-Management." *American Economic Review* 68 (May): 290–294.

Schelling, Thomas C. (1980). "The Intimate Contest for Self-Command." *Public Interest* 60 (Summer): 94–118.

Schelling, Thomas C. (1984a). "Self-Command in Practice, in Policy and in a Theory of Rational Choice." *American Economic Review* 74 (May): 1–11.

Schelling, Thomas C. (1984b). *Choice and Consequence. Perspectives of an Errant Economist*. Cambridge, Mass.: Harvard University Press.

Schenk, Karl-Ernst (1983). "Institutional Choice und Ordnungstheorie." In: Boettcher, Erik, Herder-Dorneich, Philipp and Schenk, Karl-Ernst (eds). *Jahrbuch für Neue Politische Ökonomie* Vol. 2. Tübingen: Mohr (Siebeck), pp. 70–85.

Schenk, Karl-Ernst (1988). *New Institutional Dimensions of Economics*. Berlin: Springer.

Schmölders, Günter (1962). *Volkswirtschaftslehre und Psychologie*. Berlin: Reinbek.

Schmölders, Günter (1975). *Einführung in die Geld-und Finanzpsychologie*. Berlin: Reinbek.

Schmölders, Günter (1978). *Verhaltensforschung im Wirtschaftsleben*. Berlin: Reinbek.

Schneider, Friedrich and Frey, Bruno S. (1988). "Politico-Economic Models of Macroeconomic Policy: A Review of the Empirical Evidence." In: Willett,

Thomas D. (ed.). *The Political Economy of Money, Inflation and Unemployment*. Durham and London: Duke University Press, pp. 240-275.

Schneider, Friedrich and Pommerehne, Werner W. (1981). "Free Riding and Collective Action: An Experiment in Public Microeconomics." *Quarterly Journal of Economics* 96 (Nov.): 687-704.

Schoemaker, Paul J. (1980). *Experiments on Decisions Under Risk: The Expected Utility Hypothesis*. Boston, Mass.: Kluwer-Nijhoff.

Schoemaker, Paul J. (1982). "The Expected Utility Model: Its Variants, Purposes, Evidence and Limitations." *Journal of Economic Literature* 20 (June): 529-563.

Schotter, Andrew (1981). *The Economic Theory of Social Institutions*. Cambridge: Cambridge University Press.

Schotter, Andrew and Braunstein Yale M. (1981). "Economic Search: An Experimental Study." *Economic Inquiry* 19: 1-25.

Schultz, Theodore W. (1974). *Economics of the Family*. London and Chicago.

Schumpeter, Joseph A. (1942). *Capitalism, Socialism and Democracy*. New York: Harper, 1st ed.

Schwartz, Hugh H. (1987). "Perception, Judgement, and Motivation in Manufacturing Enterprises." *Journal of Economic Behavior and Organization* 8: 543-565.

Scitovsky, Tibor (1976). *The Joyless Economy: An Inquiry into Human Satisfaction and Consumer Dissatisfaction*. Oxford: Oxford University Press.

Scitovsky, Tibor (1981). "The Desire for Excitement in Modern Society." *Kyklos* 34: 3-13.

Seagrave, S. (1985). *The Soong Dynasty*. London: Sidgwick and Jackson.

Segal, Uzi (1988). "Does the Preference Reversal Phenomenon Necessarily Contradict the Independence Axiom?" *American Economic Review* 78: 233-236.

Selten, Reinhard and Tietz, Reinhard (1980). "Zum Selbstverständnis der experimentellen Wirtschaftsforschung im Umkreis von Heinz Sauermann." *Journal of Institutional and Theoretical Economics* 136: 12-27.

Sen, Amartya K. (1970). *Collective Choice and Social Welfare*. Edinburgh and London: Oliver & Boyd.

Sen, Amartya K. (1974). "Choice, Orderings and Morality." In: Körner, S. (ed.). *Practical Reason*. Oxford: Oxford University Press, pp. 54-67. Reprinted in: Sen, Amartya K. *Choice, Welfare and Measurement*. Oxford: Blackwell, 1982, pp. 74-83.

Sen, Amartya K. (1977). "Rational Fools: A Critique of the Behavioural Foundations of Economic Theory." *Philosophy and Public Affairs* (Summer): 317-344.

Sen, Amartya K. (1981). "Ingredients of Famine Analysis: Availability and Entitlements." *Quarterly Journal of Economics* 95: 433-464.

Sen, Amartya K. (1982). *Choice, Welfare and Measurement*. Oxford: Blackwell.

Sen, Amartya K. (1983). "Economics and the Family." *Asian Development Review* 1: 14-26.

Sen, Amartya K. (1985). "Goals, Commitment and Identity." *Journal of Law, Economics and Organization* 1 (Autumn): 341–355.

Sen, Amartya K. (1987). *On Ethics and Economics*. Oxford: Blackwell.

Sen, Amartya K. (1988). "Rational Behaviour." *The New Palgrave* 4: 68–76.

Sen, Amartya K. and Williams, Bernard (eds). (1982). *Utilitarianism and Beyond*. Cambridge: Cambridge University Press.

Shapira, Zur (1986). "On the Implications of Behavioral Decision Making Theory to Economics." In: MacFadyen, Alan J. and MacFadyen, Heather W. (eds). *Economic Psychology: Intersections in Theory and Application*. North Holland: Elsevier, pp. 621–644.

Shiller, Robert J. (1981). "Do Stock Prices Move too Much to be Justified by Subsequent Changes in Dividends?" *American Economic Review* 71 (June): 421–436.

Shiller, Robert J. (1984). "Stock Prices and Social Dynamics." *Brookings Papers on Economic Activity*: 457–498.

Shiller, Robert J. (1987a). "The Volatility of Stock Market Prices." *Science* 235: 33–37.

Shiller, Robert J. (1987b). "Comments on Miller and on Kleidon." In: Hogarth, Robin M. and Reder, Melvin W. (eds). *Rational Choice*. Chicago: University of Chicago Press, pp. 317–321.

Shirk, S. (1981). "Recent Chinese Labour Policies and the Transformation of Industrial Organization in China." *China Quarterly* 88: 575–593.

Shively, W. Philips (1972). "Party Identification, Party Choice, and Voting Stability: The Weimar Case." *American Political Science Review* 66: 1203–1224.

Simon, Herbert A. (1955). "A Behavioural Model of Rational Choice." *Quarterly Journal of Economics* 69: 99–118.

Simon, Herbert A. (1957). *Models of Man*. New York: Wiley.

Simon, Herbert A. (1978). "Rationality as a Process and Product of Thought." *American Economic Review* 68 (May): 1–16.

Simon, Herbert A. (1982). *Models of Bounded Rationality*. Cambridge, Mass.: MIT Press.

Simon, Herbert A. (1983). *Reason in Human Affairs*, Oxford, Blackwell.

Simon, Herbert A. (1986). "Alternative Visions of Rationality." In: Arkes, Hal R. and Hammond, Kenneth R. (eds). *Judgement and Decision-Making: An Interdisciplinary Reader*. Cambridge: Cambridge University Press, pp. 97–113.

Slovic, Paul (1986). "Psychological Study of Human Judgement." In: Arkes, Hal R. and Hammond, Kenneth R. (eds). *Judgement and Decision-Making: An Interdisciplinary Reader*. Cambridge: Cambridge University Press, pp. 173–193.

Slovic, Paul, Fischhoff, Baruch and Lichtenstein, Sarah (1977). "Behavioral Decision Theory." *Annual Review of Psychology* 28: 1–39.

Smith, Adam (1776). *An Inquiry into the Nature and Causes of the Wealth of Nations*. Reprinted 1981, London: Deut & Sane Ltd.

Smith, Vernon L. (1976). "Experimental Economics: Induced Value Theory."

American Economic Review 66 (May): 274–279.

Smith, Vernon L. (1989). "Theory, Experiment and Economics." *Journal of Economic Perspectives* 3 (Winter): 151–170.

Stacey, J. (1983). *Patriarchy and Socialist Revolution in China*. Berkeley and Los Angeles: University of California Press.

Stein, John P. (1977). "The Monetary Appreciation of Paintings." *Journal of Political Economy* 85: 1021–1035.

Stigler, George J. (1963). "The Intellectual and the Market Place." *Institute of Economic Affairs*, Occasional Paper 1. London.

Stigler, George J. (1984). "Economics—The Imperial Science?" *Scandinavian Journal of Economics* 86: 301–313.

Stigler, George J. and Becker, Gary S. (1977). "De Gustibus Non Est Disputandum." *American Economic Review* 67 (March): 76–90.

Stohl, Michael (ed.). (1979). *The Politics of Terrorism*. New York: Dekker.

Strickland, Lloyd, Lewicki, Roy W. and Katz, Arnold M. (1966). "Temporal Orientation and Perceived Control as Determinants of Risk Taking." *Journal of Experimental Social Psychology* 2: 143–151.

Stroebe, Wolfgang (1978). "Das Experiment in der Sozialpsychologie." In: Wolfgang Stroebe (ed.). *Sozialpsychologie 1*. Darmstadt: Wissenschaftliche Buchgesellschaft, pp. 3–49.

Stroebe, Wolfgang and Frey, Bruno S. (1980). "In Defense of Economic Man: Towards an Integration of Economics and Psychology." *Schweizerische Zeitschrift für Volkswirtschaft und Statistik* 116 (June): 119–148.

Stroebe, Wolfgang and Meyer, Willi (eds). (1982). "Social Psychology and Economics." *Special edition of the British Journal of Social Psychology* 21: 121–137.

Svenson, O. (1978). "Risks of Road Transportation in a Psychological Perspective." *Accident Analysis and Prevention* 10: 267–280.

Swedberg, Richard (1985). "The Analysis of Economics in Sociology: Its History and Recent Developments." *Mimeo*. Uppsala: Uppsala Universitet, Sociologiska Institutionen.

Swedberg, Richard (1986). "Economic Sociology and the Paradigm Crisis: From the United States to Sweden." *Acta Sociologica* 2: 91–112.

Swedberg, Richard (1990). *Economics and Sociology*. Princeton: Princeton University Press.

Swedberg, Richard, Himmelstrand, Ulf and Brulin, Göran (1985). "The Paradigm of Economic Sociology: Premises and Promises." *Mimeo*. Uppsala: Uppsala Universitet, Sociologiska Institutionen.

Tai Yen-hui (1959). *Zhouggo shenfen shi* (History of Status Law in China). Ministery of Law (ed.), Taipei.

Tarde, Gabriel (1902). *Psychologie économique*. Paris: Alcan.

Temin, Peter (ed.). (1973). *New Economic History*. Selected Readings. Harmondsworth: Penguin.

Thaler, Richard H. (1980). "Toward a Positive Theory of Consumer Choice." *Journal of Economic Behavior and Organization* 1 (March): 39–60.

Thaler, Richard H. (1985). "Mental Accounting and Consumer Choice." *Marketing Science* 4 (Summer): 199–214.

Thaler, Richard H. (1987a). "The Psychology and Economics Conference Handbook: Comments on Simon, on Einhorn and Hogarth, and on Tversky and Kahneman." In: Hogarth, Robin M. and Reder, Melvin W. (eds). *Rational Choice*. Chicago: University of Chicago Press, pp. 95–100.

Thaler, Richard H. (1987b). "The January Effect." *Journal of Economic Perspectives* 1 (Summer): 197–201.

Thaler, Richard H. (1987c). "Seasonal Movements in Security Prices II: Weekend, Holiday, Turn of the Month and Intraday Effects." *Journal of Economic Perspectives* 1 (Autumn): 167–177.

Thaler, Richard H. (1987d). "The Psychology of Choice and the Assumption of Economics." In: Roth, Alvin E. (ed.). *Laboratory Experimentation in Economics*. Cambridge: Cambridge University Press, pp. 99–130.

Thaler, Richard H. and Shefrin, H.M. (1981). "An Economic Theory of Self-Control." *Journal of Political Economy* 89 (April): 392–406.

Thaler, Richard H. and Ziemba, William T. (1988). "Parimutual Betting Markets: Racetracks and Lotteries." *Journal of Economic Perspectives* 2 (2): 161–174.

Thomas, William I. and Znaniecki, F. (1918). *The Polish Peasant in Europe and America*. Boston: Alfred A. Knopf.

Throsby, C. David and Withers, Glenn A. (1979). *The Economics of the Performing Arts*. London and Melbourne: Arnold.

Thurstone, L.L. (1928). "Attitudes Can Be Measured." *American Journal of Sociology* 33: 529–554.

Tietz, Reinhard (1974). "Experimente in den Wirtschaftswissenschaften." In: *Handwörterbuch der Betriebswirtschaft*. Stuttgart, pp. 289–307.

Tollison, Robert D. (1982). "Rent Seeking: A Survey." *Kyklos* 35:575–602.

Topley, M. (1975). "Marriage Resistance in Rural Kwangtung." In: Wolf, M. and Witke, R. (eds). *Women in Chinese Society*. Stanford: Stanford University Press, pp. 66–88.

Triandis, H.C. (1967). *Toward an Analysis of the Component of Interpersonal Attitudes. Attitude, Ego-Envolvement, and Change*. New York: Academic Press.

Tullock, Gordon (1965). *The Politics of Bureaucracy*. Washington, D.C.: Public Affairs Press.

Tullock, Gordon (1967). *Towards a Mathematics of Politics*. Ann Arbor: University of Michigan Press.

Tullock, Gordon (1991). "Casual Recollections of an Editor." *Public Choice* 71: 129–139.

Tversky, Amos and Kahneman, Daniel (1971). "The Belief in the 'Law of Small Numbers'". *Psychological Bulletin* 76: 105–110.

Tversky, Amos and Kahneman, Daniel (1974). "Judgement Under Uncertainty: Heuristics and Biases." *Science* 185: 1124–1131.

Tversky, Amos and Kahneman, Daniel (1981). "The Framing of Decisions and the Psychology of Choice." *Science* 211: 453–458.

Tversky, Amos and Kahneman, Daniel (1987). "Rational Choice and the Framing of Decisions." In: Hogarth, Robin M. and Reder, Melvin W. (eds). *Rational Choice.* Chicago: University of Chicago Press, pp. 67–94.

Ullmann-Margalit, Edna (1977). *The Emergence of Norms.* New York: Oxford University Press.

Vagts, Alfred (1938). *A History of Militarism.* London: Allen & Unwin.

Van Praag, Bernhard M.S. (1968). *Individual Welfare Functions and Consumer Behavior.* Amsterdam: North Holland.

Van Raaij, W. Fred (1985). "Attribution of Causality to Economic Actions and Events." *Kyklos* 38: 3–19.

Van Raaij, W. Fred, van Veldhoven, Gerry M. and Wärneryd, Karl Erik (eds). (1988). *Handbook of Economic Psychology.* Dordrecht: Kluwer.

Vanberg, Viktor (1988). "Rules and Choices in Economics and Sociology." In: Boettcher, Erik, Herder-Dorneich, Philipp and Schenk, Karl-Ernst (eds). *Jahrbuch für Neue Politische Ökonomie.* Tübingen: Mohr (Siebeck), pp. 146–167.

Veitch, R. and Griffith, William (1976). "Good News—Bad News: Affective and Interpersonal Effects." *Journal of Applied Social Psychology* 6: 69–75.

Voegtlin, W.L. (1940). "The Treatment of Alcoholism by Establishing a Conditioned Reflex." *American Journal of Medical Science* 199:802–810.

Von Neumann, John and Morgenstern, Oskar (1947). *Theory of Games and Economic Behavior.* Princeton: Princeton University Press, 2nd ed.

Vroom, Victor H. (1962). "Ego-Involvement, Job Satisfaction, and Job Performance." *Personnel Psychology* 15: 159–177.

Vroom, Victor H. (1964). *Work and Motivation.* New York: Wiley.

Walker, Thomas A.A. (1899). *A History of the Law of Nations.* Cambridge: Cambridge University Press.

Walzer, Michael (1969). "Prisoners of War: Does the Fight Continue after the Battle?" *American Political Science Review* 63: 777–786.

Watson, Francis M. (1976). *Political Terrorism. The Threat and the Response.* Washington and New York: Robert B. Luce.

Weber, Max (1920–1921). "Die protestantische Ethik und der Geist des Kapitalismus." In: Max Weber. *Gesammelte Aufsätze zur Religionssoziologie.* Tübingen: Mohr (Siebeck).

Weck-Hannemann, Hannelore (1983). *Schattenwirtschaft: Eine Möglichkeit zur Einschränkung der Öffentlichen Verwaltung? Eine Ökonomische Analyse.* Bern and Frankfurt: Lang.

Weck-Hannemann, Hannelore, Pommerehne, Werner W. and Frey, Bruno S. (1984). *Schattenwirtschaft.* Munich: Vahlen.

Weinstein, Neil D. (1979). "Seeking Reassuring or Threatening Information about Environmental Cancer." *Journal of Behavioral Medicine* 16: 220–224.

Weinstein, Neil D. (1980). "Unrealistic Optimism About Future Life Events." *Journal of Personality and Social Psychology* 39: 806–820.

Weizsäcker von, Carl-Christian (1971). "Notes on Endogenous Changes of

Tastes." *Journal of Economic Theory* 3 (Dec.): 345–372.

Weizsäcker von, Carl-Christian (1976). "Die Welt aus Sicht des Ökonomen." In: Körner, Heiko et al. (eds). *Wirtschaftspolitik—Wissenschaft und politische Aufgabe*. Berne: Haupt, pp. 67–83.

Weizsäcker von, Carl-Christian (1986). Zeit und Geld, Eine Skizze. *Mimeo.* Berne: University of Berne, Institute for Applied Micro-Economics.

Wenig, Alois (1985). "Überbevölkerung eine Kriegsursache? Einige Anmerkungen zur Bevölkerungslehre von Thomas Robert Malthus." *Kyklos* 38: 365–391.

Werner, Georges (1928). "Les prisonniers de guerre." *Recueil des cours de l'academie de droit international* 21: 5–107.

Wernette, Dee R. (1976). "Explaining the Nazi Vote: The Findings and the Limits of Ecological Analysis." Working Paper No. 34. Ann Arbor: University of Michigan, Center for Research on Social Organizations.

Wicker, Allan W. (1969). "Attitudes Versus Actions: The Relationship of Verbal and Overt Behavioral Responses to Attitude Objects." *Journal of Social Issues* 25: 41–78.

Wilkinson, Paul (1974). *Political Terrorism*. London: Macmillan.

Wilkinson, Paul (1977). *Terrorism and the Liberal State*. New York: Macmillan.

Wilkinson, Paul (1986). "Trends in International Terrorism and the American Response." In: Royal Institute of International Affairs (ed.). *Terrorism and International Order*. London: Routledge and Kegan Paul.

Willemin, Georges and Heacock, Roger (1984). *The International Committee of the Red Cross*. Boston: Nijhoff.

Williamson, Oliver E. (1975). *Markets and Hierarchies: Analysis and Antitrust Implications*. New York: Free Press.

Williamson, Oliver E. (1979). "Transaction Cost Economics. The Governance of Contractual Relations." *Journal of Law and Economics* 22: 233–261.

Williamson, Oliver E. (1980). "The Organization of Work: A Comparative Institutional Assessment." *Journal of Economic Behavior and Organization* 1 (March): 5–38.

Williamson, Oliver E. (1985). *The Economic Institutions of Capitalism. Firms, Markets, Relational Contracting*. New York: Free Press.

Williamson, Oliver E. (1986). *Economic Organization. Firms, Markets and Policy Control*. Brighton: Wheatsheaf.

Williamson, Oliver E. (1990). "A Comparison of Alternative Approaches to Economic Organization." *Journal of Institutional and Theoretical Economics* 146 (March): 61–71.

Williamson, Oliver E. (1992). "Operationalizing the New Institutional Economics. The Transaction Cost Economic Perspective." *Journal of Institutional and Theoretical Economics* (forthcoming).

Winston, Gordon C. (1980). "Addiction and Backsliding: A Theory of Compulsive Consumption." *Journal of Economic Behavior and Organization* 1 (Dec.): 295–324.

Winter, Sidney G. (1971). "Satisficing, Selection and the Innovating Remnant."

Quarterly Journal of Economics 85 (May): 237–282.

Witt, Ulrich (1985). "Economic Behavior and Biological Evolution—Some Remarks on the Sociological Debate." *Journal of Institutional and Theoretical Economics* 141: 365–389.

Witt, Ulrich (1987). *Individualistische Grundlagen der evolutorischen Ökonomik.* Tübingen: Mohr (Siebeck).

Wolf, Margery (1968). *The House of Lim.* Englewood Cliffs: N.J.: Prentice-Hall.

Wolf, Margery (1972). *Women and Family Life in Rural Taiwan.* Stanford: Stanford: Stanford University Press.

Wolf, Margery (1975). "Women and Suicide in China." In: Wolf, M. and Witke, R. (eds). *Women in Chinese Society.* Stanford: Stanford University Press, pp. 111–142.

Yang, C.K. (1959). *The Family and the Village.* Cambridge, Mass.: MIT Press.

Zeckhauser, Richard (1987). "Comments: Behavioral versus Rational Economics: What You See Is What You Conquer." In: Hogarth, Robin M. and Reder, Melvin (eds). *Rational Choice.* Chicago: University of Chicago Press, pp. 251–265.

Zunich, M.A. (1961). "A Study of Relationship Between Child-Rearing Attitudes and Maternal Behavior." *Journal of Experimental Education* 30: 231–241.

Zweifel, Peter (1982). *Ein Ökonomisches Modell des Arztverhaltens.* Berlin: Springer.

AUTHOR INDEX

245

SUBJECT INDEX

251